40 Reasons to Trust the Bible

Martin Johnson,
Jamie Austin, and
Kate Wiltshire

Onwards and Upwards Publishers

3 Radfords Turf, Cranbrook, Exeter,
EX5 7DX, United Kingdom.

www.onwardsandupwards.org

This first edition published in the United Kingdom by Onwards and Upwards Publishers (2017).

ISBN: 978-1-78815-673-8
Typeface: Sabon LT
Graphic design: LM Graphic Design

Printed in the United Kingdom.

About the Authors

Martin Johnson retired as the Director of the Thalidomide Trust in 2014. He has gained degrees in Divinity (BD), Management (PhD), and Behavioural Science (MSc). He has published several research and professional papers in Management, Medical, and Psychology journals, ranging from the founding and development of the Modern Hospice Movement to advanced theories of organisation, and managing rare diseases. He has lectured at Kings College London and Warwick Business School on management theory, and at the Royal Society of Medicine.

He served twenty-one years in the Royal Air Force, first as a pilot on Vulcan nuclear strike and Canberra Electronic Warfare aircraft, and later in administrative roles and as an Intelligence specialist.

During recent years he has been conducting historical research into the origins of the drug Thalidomide, cause of the world's worst medical and pharmaceutical disaster, and the background of the company which made it. This will be published as a book in 2018, *The Thalidomide Catastrophe: How it happened, who was responsible and why the search for justice continues after more than six decades.* Martin has taught biblical subjects in a variety of Christian settings for the past thirty years.

Contact: *martin.w.johnson@ntlworld.com*

Jamie Austin is a Chartered Geologist with over nineteen years' experience in geotechnical and geo-environmental consultancy. He has a BSc in Geology from Royal Holloway, London and a Masters in Mining Geology from Camborne School of Mines for which he spent three months in central Zimbabwe mapping and prospecting banded ironstone deposits for gold.

Since graduating he has worked as a geoenvironmental and geotechnical engineer with experience ranging predominantly across the UK and Ireland, but he has also undertaken work in Sierra Leone, Iran, Egypt, Mexico, France and the United Arab Emirates.

Kate Wiltshire is a Veterinary Surgeon (MRCVS) who qualified at the Royal Veterinary College in 1996 with B VetMed. Since that time, she has worked in small animal practice, treating dogs, cats and what are known in the trade as 'small furries' (rabbits, guinea pigs, other rodents and even the occasional hedgehog and sugar glider).

As a professional who has treated a large number of very different types of animal, Kate is convinced that the complex interplay of biochemical, physiological, anatomical and neurological forces that enable life from conception to adulthood and ultimately death could not possibly have arisen by chance.

Contents

THE TEXT OF THE BIBLE

THE BIBLE AND PROPHECY

Introduction

The Bible is the most remarkable book in the world, there is nothing else like it. It can be found in virtually every country and every written language, and it attracts devotion and controversy in almost equal measure.

The aim of this book is firstly to give confidence to those readers seeking to grow their faith in God, by showing that the word of God in the pages of the Bible is indeed trustworthy.

This book will show that the Bible is reliable in respect of its factual claims, and although we have selected only forty themes or teachings supported by compelling evidence, we could easily have chosen many more.

Matters of fact

This book will show that the Bible speaks factual truths in the fields of history, science, and fulfilled prophecy, and that it is testable as a document of integrity. The evidence shows that it is not composed of myths and folklore handed down by word of mouth, but has been kept as a set of written records from the beginning.

Factual truths will be demonstrated using normal 'rules of evidence' as would satisfy a court of law. We will provide an extensive range of evidence, and let the reader test our claims for themselves. In the history chapters (1-10), we have created a few fictional characters, in order that the context of the time can be presented in a more personal and direct way than is possible just by relating bare facts. Everything they bring out, however, is related to fact, as you will see. Chapters 11-20 deal with the relationship between the Bible and Science; while chapters 21-30 deal with textual matters concerning the Bible as a written document, and chapters 31-40 cover examples of biblical prophecies which have been fulfilled over time.

Written records

The Bible is a collection of 66 main documents, recording events from the beginning of time until about 100 AD. It also deals with the history of a family who became the nation of Israel for a period of more than two thousand years, up to the middle of the 1st century AD, and of the many peoples, nations and empires they engaged with during that time. It is full of the names of places many of which can now be identified, and of kings whose records can be independently checked from written documents. This in itself is amazing, as can be seen from a comparison with British history.

The British people are generally believed to have a long history, but compared to the Bible, British history is almost non-existent. The legends of the founding of Britain by Brutus (great grandson of Aeneas king of Troy, ca. 1,000 BC) are not taught in schools, and are widely disregarded by historians, because of the lack of supporting evidence. No one knows who built Stonehenge about 4,000 years ago, which was in use around the time of Abraham, why they built it, or how it was used. There is as yet no hard evidence for the existence of the famous King Arthur, who is believed to have died about 1,500 years ago, 500 years after the time of Jesus. There are many theories about who King Arthur was and where the true site of his 'castle' of Camelot may be, but they remain theories for lack of evidence. Almost everyone in the English-speaking world knows of the legend of Robin Hood, but the best that can be said is that such a person probably existed, possibly in the 14th century AD, only 700 years ago.

The Bible, in contrast, tells detailed stories of peoples and kingdoms and empires which were already ancient at the time the Romans came to Britain, 2,000 years ago. And these stories are as fresh and relevant today as they were when they first happened.

Archaeological research has so far only uncovered a fraction of the possible evidence available. In the Middle East, where many of the Bible stories are set, there are more 'tells' (ancient mounds which were once towns and cities) yet to be explored and identified than have so far been excavated by the archaeologists. The 19th and 20th centuries saw the discovery of several enormous 'libraries' of written documents (mainly clay tablets and papyrus fragments) from the period around 100 AD to around 2000 BC, large numbers of which have yet to be translated. While much of this material is in known languages that can be read and translated, there are still many examples of ancient writing which are yet to be deciphered, even from the lands and times of the Bible. These include the Etruscan language from Italy, the linear A script from Crete, the Meroitic language from the Sudan, and the Proto-Elamite script from Iran.

The fact that so much written evidence has come to light in scripts that can be deciphered and languages that can be interpreted means that windows on the distant past are open, offering fascinating glimpses of these far-off worlds. These are then reinforced by the evidence from the ground, buildings, pottery, tools, occasional human remains and, very rarely, examples of foodstuffs and other items from day-to-day life.

Dating archaeological finds and sites can be very difficult, especially if no documents are found. Archaeologists rely on the styles of architecture, the types of pottery found, and more recently such scientific aids as carbon and tree-ring dating. Universal agreement among historians and archaeologists about the dates of events earlier than about 800 BC, such as the reigns of the Pharaohs of Ancient Egypt, is hard to find. The possibility of a 'generally agreed' date changing by a hundred years or more in the light of new evidence is very high. There are several arguments being put forward at present for changing the dates of several Egyptian rulers by between one hundred and five hundred years. This involves eliminating a similar period from the history of ancient Greece and half a dozen other contemporary civilisations, in many cases eliminating problems created by earlier Egyptian dating schemes.

Chronologies

Throughout this book, therefore, dates cited for biblical events will be based on the timelines given in the Bible. As this itself is a complex matter, we will use the chronology demonstrated by Dr Floyd Nolen

Jones in his book *The Chronology of the Old Testament*[1]. This sets the arrival of Abraham in Canaan at 1921 BC, the Exodus of the Israelites from Egypt in 1491 BC, the Destruction of Jerusalem by the Babylonians in 586 BC and the Crucifixion of Jesus in 30 AD.

We will see several occasions where the actual events on the ground match the Bible record with great precision, meaning that where historians and archaeologists dispute them, it is their dating assumptions that are at fault, rather than the physical evidence plain for all to see.

History matters!

The impact of ancient history on the present day should not be underestimated. In 1985, the late Iraqi dictator Saddam Hussein began a project to restore the ruins of the city of Babylon. This city first features in the Bible in Genesis 11:4-9 as Babel. Saddam Hussein said he was the reincarnation of Nebuchadnezzar, the emperor who ruled there 2,600 years ago. Part of his plan in the war he triggered in 1990 was to destroy Israel and rain missiles on the city of Jerusalem, which first features in the Bible as "Salem" in Genesis 14:18. Nebuchadnezzar was the ruler who destroyed Jerusalem in 586 BC, and with it the first temple built by King Solomon.

Jerusalem was home to the next temple, built after the end of the Jewish people's exile in Babylon, and is also the place where Jesus was crucified and resurrected from the dead. Jerusalem and Babylon are two of a very small number of cities in the whole world which have remained identifiable for more than 4,000 years.

The Bible tracks the story of these two cities, and contains many prophecies about their future right through to the final destruction of "Mystery Babylon" in Revelation 18, and the arrival of "New

---

[1] *The Chronology of the Old Testament;* Floyd Nolen Jones; Master Books, Green Forest, AR USA (2015 printing). Of the many works on Bible chronology this one sets out to establish dates using the Bible as its primary source, rather than beginning with various archaeological finds. Floyd Nolen Jones demonstrates that this method ultimately makes it possible to harmonise the Bible with the key archaeological data. This book has the most compendious set of information so far available in one volume.

Jerusalem" in Revelation 21. Throughout the Bible these two cities above all symbolise man's possible relationships with God. In Genesis 11, Babel (Babylon) was the place where man's rebellion against God came into the open, while Salem (Jerusalem) in Genesis 14 was where Abraham went to worship God. In Revelation, Mystery Babylon symbolises lust for fleshly pleasure and greed for wealth and worldly power which separates mankind from God, while the New Jerusalem is the place of saved mankind's eternal communion with the God of love.

We have in the story of these two cities examples of how the Bible interlaces real places and events with inspired truths and spiritual realities which cannot be proved in any earthly court of law. The history of God's dealings with these places and their people, however, gives us confidence to put our trust in the spiritual truths the Bible brings.

Prediction is difficult...

The final ten chapters supply details of events foretold in the Bible long before they happened, and which have happened in such a way as to show that the writers of the Bible were being given accurate information of what would happen. This is the ultimate test of the written record that God claims for Himself in the Bible:

> *Let them bring forth and show us what will happen;*
> *Let them show the former things, what they were,*
> *That we may consider them*
> *And know the latter end of them;*
> *Or declare to us things to come.*
> *Show the things that are to come hereafter,*
> *That we may know that you are gods...*
>
> *Isaiah 41:22-23a (NKJV)*

This, then, is the best possible test for the Bible in its own terms. If prophecies have been fulfilled then you know that God's inspiration is the only logical explanation, and the challenge in the Isaiah passage is to those worshipping the false gods of that day. Today we live in a world where people are regularly attempting to predict the future course of such things as elections, economies or technology, and routinely getting it wrong even over very short time periods. The old Danish saying which goes, "It is difficult to make predictions, especially about the future,"[2] gets validated in our experience all the time.

The Bible, as we will show, makes predictions of very long-range events in human history which time and again happen exactly as foretold. This means we should take very seriously the prophecies of events that have not yet happened – but that is a subject outside the scope of this book!

Reference links

At the end of each chapter is a set of *Reference links,* where we have tried to find easily accessed sources of information covering the subject concerned. We hope these links will be functioning, should you want to look them up. If not, you should use a search engine to try and find the website or document concerned, as links sometimes do not get updated when websites are upgraded. Our aim is to help you set out on your own journey of discovery in the vast world of Bible knowledge.

---

[2] "Det er svært at spå – især om fremtiden."
See *listserv.linguistlist.org/pipermail/ads-l/2005-February/045786.html*

CHAPTER ONE

Sodom and Gomorrah Were Destroyed in a Catastrophe

And Abraham went early in the morning to the place where he had stood before the LORD. Then he looked toward Sodom and Gomorrah and toward all the land of the plain; and he saw, and behold, the smoke of the land which went up like the smoke of a furnace.

Genesis 19:27-28 (NKJV)

It was an early summer morning, nearly 4,000 years ago. Abraham was standing on the hills overlooking the Jordan valley. As the sun came up he could see the mist rising over the Salt Sea to his left, and to his right he could see the dawn breaking over the cities of Sodom and Gomorrah some thirty kilometres away. He was dreading what he was about to see. The day before he had had a disturbing visit from three strangers who had shown him they were messengers from God, angels in the form of men. One had spoken to him as if it were God himself speaking, and had told him that destruction was to fall on Sodom and Gomorrah. Abraham had then watched as the other two made their way across the valley during the late afternoon towards Sodom.

Abraham felt compassion for Sodom. It was a mighty city, but due to an event some twenty years earlier, its king was in Abraham's debt. An army had come from the East, led by the rulers of Sumer and Elam (territories we today call Iraq and Iran), together with allies from the northern lands. Intent on re-establishing their dominance over the

Amorite peoples of Canaan (today's Israel and Jordan), they had burned Sodom, Gomorrah, and several other towns and cities. In a ferocious battle, their armies had defeated Sodom and Gomorrah and their allies. They had taken all the loot they could carry, and captured and enslaved many of the people of the city, including Abraham's nephew Lot and his family.

Abraham had mustered his private army, far smaller than the armies of the kings who had caused the destruction. Young men of the towns near his camp had volunteered to join him. He had led them about 180 kilometres northwards following the easterners as they withdrew, and attacked them at night in a Commando-style raid. They had routed the enemy force, driven it another fifty kilometres back towards the land they had come from, recovered all the loot they had taken and freed their captives.

In the twenty years that followed, the armies of Sumer and Elam and their vassal lords had not returned, and the land had been at peace. The main trade of the cities was extracting petroleum products such as bitumen and asphalt, and selling them as far away as the great cities in Syria and Egypt. The fruitful land around the cities had helped them recover their prosperity, and they had rebuilt the cities with improved defences in the years in between. The traders travelling down the route at the east side of the Salt Sea enjoyed sharing in the prosperity the cities brought. The trouble was that prosperity had gone hand in hand with every kind of depravity. Later, Abraham was to discover that the messengers of God who stayed with his nephew in the city had been attacked by a gang of men who wanted to drag them out of the house and rape them.

As the sun started its slow rise above the mountains beyond Sodom, Abraham could see thick smoke and flames leaping up out of the land to a great height. It looked as if the land had become a blazing furnace. He could feel repeated tremors beneath his feet as the land was shuddering. Over in one of the cities, a big defensive tower collapsed, crushing two men to death. In another place, the rain of fire falling on the roofs of the buildings had caused them to collapse before the occupants could escape. People stopped only to pick up what they could, and ran.

The bodies of the people crushed by the falling buildings would be buried under thick layers of ash, not to see the light of day for another four millennia. Had this been an ordinary earthquake, then those who made it out of the buildings and away from the walls and towers would have been safe. This was not to be. The earthquake had forced one or more bubbles of molten magma close to the surface of the ground, and into contact with deposits of sulphur-rich crude oil and layers of rock salt. The immense pressures caused by the subterranean movement meant that these materials were being ejected hundreds and even thousands of feet into the air. The sky was raining burning oil and sulphur. Large pyroclastic blobs of molten rock salt were being forced up from splits in the ground. Those who ran towards the sea were at risk of the ground liquefying under their feet and sucking them in. Landslides were falling down the mountains, and the surface of the ground was moving up and down by thirty metres or more. The smoke and the rain of ash was choking and suffocating people.

Abraham only saw the cataclysm from far off. Lot, who had been helped to flee the city before the first tremor hit, narrowly escaped death. His wife, transfixed by the destruction taking place, did not move quickly enough, and was engulfed by a large pyroclastic fall of molten rock salt. She was suffocated and incinerated almost instantaneously. The tens of thousands who lived in Sodom, Gomorrah, and several other towns and villages nearby were destroyed. Burning sulphur rained down for miles around. Trees and crops were ruined by the smoke and fire. Nothing lived. When the smoke cleared, in the following days Abraham could see smouldering ruins where there had once been towns and cities. The Salt Sea had changed its shape, engulfing some of the cities where people had once lived. The fertile ground with its irrigation channels had gone – burned beyond recognition, swamped with salt water rising through the soil, fissured by cracks from the earthquake. All over the area were cooling masses of rock salt, like pillars.

What are the facts?

This story of Abraham and Lot and the fall of Sodom and Gomorrah comes from Genesis chapters 18-19. There are many aspects of the life of Abraham that can be supported by archaeology, but the catastrophe of Sodom and Gomorrah gives a very good example of what can now be confirmed and what cannot. To identify a specific town site as one in the Bible, you would normally need some document (clay tablet, inscription carved in stone, or papyrus document preserved in a very dry environment). For the cities of the plain around the Dead Sea (always known in ancient times as the "Salt Sea") this has not yet been achieved. We can, however, piece together a lot of the story of the disaster that struck this area about 4,000 years ago.

The fall of Sodom and Gomorrah (Gen.19)

The names of Sodom and Gomorrah together with the other three "cities of the plain" mentioned in this passage (Admah, Zeboiim and Zoar) have all been found in the Ebla tablets, written before the time of Abraham, six or seven hundred years before Moses, so there is no question now of the Bible's accuracy in identifying these towns. Their locations are more problematic.

Several sites along the East side of the valley containing the Dead Sea have been excavated since 1973. These include places now named Bab edh-Dhra, Numeira, and es-Safi at the southern end of the Dead Sea, and Tall el-Hammam to the north.

At Bab edh-Dhra and Numeira, the remains of two towns have been found, both of which suffered destruction by burning and earthquake sometime around 2000 BC.

Both towns had suffered an earlier destruction no more than a few decades prior to the final destruction. Building following the first destruction shows improvements to the defences of each town. This implies a fear of further attacks, and is a strong indication that the destruction seen on the site was from an enemy attack rather than a more natural cause.

The final destruction happened in the late spring or early summer, as shown by a large quantity of whole carbonised grapes and watermelon seeds at Numeira. (Deuteronomy 32:33 speaks of the grapes of Sodom!)

Paleo-botanical studies have shown that crops grown at these two sites included barley, wheat, grapes, figs, lentils, flax, chickpeas, peas, broad beans, dates and olives. This means irrigation systems were in use, and there was a plentiful (fresh) water supply, presumably from rivers flowing down from the mountains to the east. Each of the southern sites sit at the point where a river once flowed into the plain. This level of agriculture has not been evidenced in this area at any subsequent date.

A cemetery has been found at Bab edh-Dhra containing an estimated 20,000 tombs. An even more enormous Early Bronze Age cemetery has been found at Feifa, south of Numeira and es-Safi. The population of the area in that era clearly numbered many tens of thousands, far greater than in any subsequent age.

Several geological investigations during the 20th century showed that the area is very unstable, with several major geological faults, including one along the east side of the valley. Bitumen and petroleum have been found in the area, as well as natural gas and sulphur. Fumaroles may be found today in the area, indicating the presence of one or more magma pockets close to the surface. Extensive salt formations have been found in thick layers below the ground in this area. Areas where the ground has embedded balls of sulphur have been found on the west side of the Jordan valley, south of the Dead Sea. This indicates a fall of burning sulphur.

At Numeira, the earthquake which took place at the time of the final destruction of the city caused an uplift giving a 50-metre differential between the town site and the wadi on the north side. At Bab edh-Dhra a similar shift has been measured at 28 metres.

This shows that there were enormous pressures underneath the ground at the time of the earthquake. If this is coupled with magma pockets close to the surface, then the possibility of the magma melting some of the layers above them (including rock salt) is high. Whether these pyroclastic flows just squirted up through splits in the ground and were also ejected with enough force to go up in the air and fall back to earth (while still molten) is not known at present.

Figure 1. Map of the Dead Sea showing possible locations of Sodom and Gomorrah. Courtesy: Origins, OSU.

"But Lot's wife looked back, and she became a pillar of salt." (Genesis 19:26, NIV)

Examples of people being killed by being engulfed in pyroclastic materials have been found at Pompeii, where Vesuvius erupted in 73 AD. The difference in the Jordan valley is the existence of layers of rock salt rather than the materials found at Pompeii. There are many pillars of salt in the area at the South of the Dead Sea.

Excavations continue at Tall el-Hammam to the north of the Dead Sea, and while destruction has been reported, including evidence of great heat on pottery fragments, further information is not yet available. Archaeologists are currently making claims that Bab edh-Dhra and Tall el-Hamman are to be identified as Sodom and Gomorrah, but there is controversy about which site is which city, while they could easily be among the other three of the five "cities of the plain", and about what dates are appropriate (both for Abraham and the sites in question). The evidence shows a number of cities, towns or villages destroyed along the east side of the Jordan valley, above the major geological fault system, most of which were never rebuilt. There is strong suspicion that there may be more remains of towns under the southwestern end of the Dead Sea. It is possible, therefore, that the remains of Sodom and Gomorrah are hidden under the southern waters of the Dead Sea, while Bab edh-Dhra and Numeira would then be Admah and Zeboiim respectively.

The release in pressure caused by outflow of oil within the permeable bedrock (bitumen, asphalt etc.) could result in a collapse of the ground above those strata, which could easily cause the ground level to sink beneath the level of the adjacent sea. The level and shape of the Dead Sea has changed considerably during the past 4,000 years.

Conclusion

The account of the destruction of Sodom and Gomorrah (and the neighbouring cities) is supported by the evidence of catastrophic destruction at Bab edh-Dhra Numeira, and Tall el-Hamman. The passages, particularly in Genesis 19 verses 24, 26 and 28, appear to be eyewitness accounts from at least two locations (from a distance and in the immediate vicinity of the disaster) which we can now make sense of, following several geological surveys and other studies of the area in the 20th century.

Comment

In the second half of the 19th century, many scholars took a position of extreme scepticism towards the historical narratives in the early books of the Bible. They regarded such stories as the fall of Sodom and Gomorrah as myth or fable, written around 1,500 years after the events. This was on the basis that we should only accept as true in these narratives what can be proved beyond doubt from archaeological records. We will see this attitude again and again, and what it overlooks is that it is the Bible text itself which is the primary and best evidence of the historical events. What the many excavations in this area have shown us is a wide range of archaeological evidence which corroborates the Bible account of a disaster which wiped out prosperous cities in an area that had up until then been very fertile and productive. The attempts to argue that the timing is wrong by say 2-300 years, as some archaeologists have done, arises from spurious precision in their attempts to date the 'Early Bronze Age', coupled with assumptions about biblical chronology not drawn from the Bible itself.[3]

What we have shown here is that, in the chapters of Genesis that deal with the story and relationships between Abraham and Lot, the natural catastrophe at the end of the narrative is supported by both archaeological and geophysical evidence. The most important sections of the story lie in between, and archaeology and science together can take us no further into these areas in our quest for truth.

In the Hebrew Apocrypha (ancient books without the status of scripture), the following passage from The Wisdom of Solomon displays

---

[3] *www.biblicalstudies.org.uk/epn_3_bimson.html*
John Bimson gives a comprehensive overview of the arguments about the relationship between the findings at Bab-edh-Dhra and nearby sites to the time of Abraham. These hinge on assumptions about the end of the Early Bronze Age, which David Rohl shows could easily be several centuries "adrift", in *The Lost Testament, from Eden to Exile: the five-thousand-year history of the people of the Bible;* David Rohl; Frome, Butler & Tanner (2002).

knowledge about the conditions after the fall of Sodom subsequent to that contained in Genesis:

> *She (wisdom) saved a good man from the destruction of the godless, and he escaped the fire that came down on the Five Cities, cities whose wickedness is still attested by a smoking waste, by plants whose fruit can never ripen, and a pillar of salt standing there as a memorial of an unbelieving soul.*
>
> *Wisdom of Solomon 10:6-7 (NEB)*

Smoking ground and poisoned plants, just as recent archaeology and geology confirm!

In the *Reference links* section below, there is a range of sources given for evidence. Readers will see that there are controversies about the dating of sites and the identification of the cities. What is not in doubt is the original existence of these long-destroyed cities and the occurrence of the events themselves.

Reference links

John Bimson on dating the Patriarchs: *www.biblicalstudies.org.uk/epn_3_bimson.html*

The Institute for Creation Research (ICR) have a good article on the Ebla tablets, at: *www.icr.org/article/ebla-its-impact-bible-records*

Associates for Biblical Research, on the archaeology of Sodom and Gomorrah: *www.biblearchaeology.org/post/2008/04/16/The-Discovery-of-the-Sin-Cities-of-Sodom-and-Gomorrah.aspx#Article*

Useful details and images on the Bab edh-Dhra site, at: *www.bibleplaces.com/babedhdhra*

Rethinking the Location of Zoar: An Exercise in Biblical Geography; Steven Collins; Biblical Research Bulletin, Trinity Southwest University, Albuquerque (2006), at: *nebula.wsimg.com/a837ced04d6b98abcb16436e9b6aca82?AccessKeyId=0DC57D8CA671AC05ECA4&disposition=0&alloworigin=1*

David Rohl's blog gives background information on his work, and details of his many publications: *davidrohl.blogspot.co.uk*

Support from the New Scientist for the geological instability in the Jordan Valley, at: *www.newscientist.com/article/mg13117765.700-and-the-walls-came-tumbling-down-old-testament-writings-ofdoom-and-destruction-are-now-providing-researchers-with-a-record-ofearthquakes-spanning-4000-years-.html*

On the Reliability of the Old Testament; K A Kitchen; Eerdmans, Grand Rapids (2006); details at: *www.logos.com/product/49491/on-the-reliability-of-the-old-testament*

CHAPTER TWO

Joseph Really Was in Egypt (According to the Egyptians)

And Pharaoh said to Joseph, "See, I have set you over all the land of Egypt." Then Pharaoh took his signet ring off his hand and put it on Joseph's hand...

Genesis 41:41-42 (NKJV)

Egypt, about 1640 BC

Joseph sat in the garden of his palace. The house servants stood at a respectful distance waiting in case their venerable master needed any refreshment. He looked over the beautiful colours of the flowers around, and beyond that to the homes of his children and brothers and their rapidly growing families. What a far cry it was from the hills of Canaan and the struggle to find good grazing for their flocks. He reflected that there had been four times when he had been appointed to be in charge of all around him.

What was the point in time when he had really put his trust in the Lord, he wondered? It was not as a youngster of seventeen years, when he had been set over his brothers by his father. His extravagant coat, the badge of the overseer, had provoked them to resentment, and his own attitude towards them had made things worse. Twenty silver shekels they had sold him for – look at all the wealth in the family now! In Potiphar's household, it had seemed easy to take authority, but again his youthful inexperience had blinded him to the risk he was in from his mistress until it was too late. The other servants had been only too glad to join in her protests about him and see him thrown out of the household.

No, it was the years in that prison – learning to cope in the foul conditions, and with some of the hardened criminals he found in there. That was the third time he had been raised into authority, but the first time he had understood that his first obedience was to the Lord, no matter what. This time, he was instead raised up in front of the wealthiest ruler in the world. Thirteen years after his brothers had abandoned him in a pit, he was set in charge of the entire nation of Egypt. There were seven years of preparation and then seven years of famine, during which he had brought complete control of the whole land and its wealth under Pharaoh all the way from the borders of Ethiopia to the shore of the Mediterranean Sea. And he had put in place the great projects to ensure that the Nile floods would be used to create a huge reservoir to help the nation cope with future droughts and floods.

And now he looked just over to one side of his palace, at the tomb that Pharaoh had insisted on building for him; Joseph had said that his body was not to stay in this land for ever, and the time would come for all his people to leave, but they took little notice. The king wished to see he would be properly honoured in death, and since his one hundredth birthday was already a few years past, he knew that time was not far off.

What are the facts?

The story of Joseph's time in Egypt is in Genesis chapters 39-50. The biblical timeline runs from his arrival in Egypt as a boy of seventeen in 1728 BC to his death in 1635 BC. Several archaeologists and Egyptologists affirm that the story of Joseph is fully consistent with Egypt in the time of the 12th Dynasty (during the 'Middle Kingdom'). After this era, Egypt was ruled for a long period by non-Egyptian kings, known as the 'Hyksos'.

It is important to note that all the key aspects of Joseph's life in Egypt match a period when Egyptian rulers were on the throne.

- 'Potiphar' is an Egyptian name meaning 'devoted to Ra', the chief Egyptian God worshipped in the 12th Dynasty. This is not a name that would have been used by a top official under the Hyksos dynasties (dynasties 14-18, covering a period of more than 400 years afterwards).
- The role Joseph was given in Potiphar's household was a common one for foreign slaves during this time.
- The price the Midianite traders paid for Joseph, twenty silver shekels, was the appropriate (and average) price during this time. Before 2000 BC prices were around ten shekels; after this period, they rose sharply.
- Dreams were taken very seriously in Egypt at this time.
- The title 'Chief of Bakers' has been found, and is for a high official of the court.
- The cow(s) of Pharaoh's dreams represents Isis-Hathor, goddess of fertility.
- Pharaoh assigning Joseph rulership over "all Egypt" indicates that this was during a period when there was a united rule; often, there were separate rulers over northern and southern Egypt. United rule was in force during the 12th Dynasty.

There are many other details that can be set out. What has not been identified is a conclusive correlation with Joseph and any specific Pharaohs, although there are several clues pointing to Sesostris 1. Some archaeologists have identified a vizier of Sesostris 1 named Mentuhotep as a possible candidate for Joseph, a man given extraordinary power and authority under this Pharaoh. David Rohl, on the other hand, presents a lot of evidence to link Joseph to Amenemhat III, and argues that he is another 12th Dynasty vizier, Ankhu. But this debate (which Pharaoh, which Vizier) is minor, and ultimately capable of being resolved once more information is unearthed.

David Rohl believes that Manfred Bietak has identified the location of Joseph's palace in Avaris, that the tomb prepared for him is there, and that a statue found in pieces in this tomb is probably a representation of Joseph himself. He believes that this site also contains the tombs of Joseph's eleven brothers.

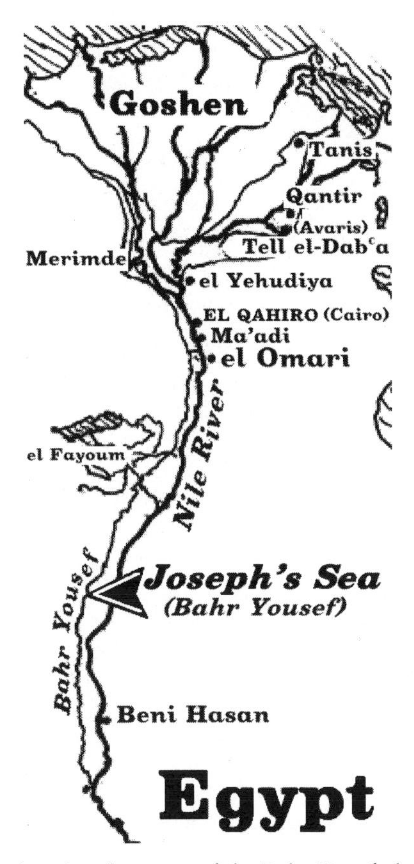

Figure 2. Map showing the route of the Bahr Yusuf alongside the Nile.

An ancient waterway, known as Bahr Yusuf (the Canal of Joseph, also spelt Bahr Yousef) runs for hundreds of kilometres through Egypt. David Rohl shows how this served as a flood relief channel,[4] and thereby helped prevent famines caused by excessive Nile flooding, such as happened in up to twelve years of Amenemhat's reign. This canal helped to balance and regulate the flow of the Nile, and it once helped irrigate vast areas, as well as feeding Egypt's third largest lake, Birket Qarun. This was a project that could also compensate if the Nile failed to flood as needed, by storing water from previous years. The Egyptian tradition is that this work was carried out by Joseph, and most of the

---

[4] *A Test of Time, volume 1, The Bible – From Myth to History;* David Rohl; Century Ltd., London (1995); pp. 346-347.

work dates to 12th Dynasty Pharaohs. David Rohl shows that Amenemhat III was a Pharaoh who identified himself with aspects of this project.

Some recent archaeologists have argued that the chronology of the 12th Dynasty belongs between the late 18th and the middle 16th centuries BC. This would put the role of Joseph, and the seven years of famine, somewhere around 1700 BC.

There are Egyptian records from a regional governor of this era (Khnumhotep, Nomarch under Pharaoh Sesostris 1), showing the gathering of grain into royal storehouses, and also his son Ameni, for a time co-nomarch with his father) reporting soon afterwards distributing grain in years of famine. The tomb paintings show that people came from Africa and Canaan to buy grain during this time (therefore the famine was part of a much more widespread catastrophe). The Bible record shows Jacob sending his sons to Egypt for grain, therefore this was not a local Egyptian famine from the biblical perspective, either.

Interestingly, at around this same period, tree ring records show seven years of cold weather (lack of sunlight) in northern Europe, which would have produced a severe famine there, while Chinese records speak of a seven-year drought and famine in China at the same time. These latter records have been linked to the explosion of the super-volcano of Santorini in the Mediterranean, which is now being argued to have erupted in the second half of the 17th century BC (carbon dating at Santorini, ice-core traces from Greenland). Santorini is now believed to have ejected sixty cubic kilometres of magma, making it quite capable of producing a dust cloud which could have circled the earth for several years.

Comment

Many scholars have tried to argue that the story of Joseph is a complete myth. The progressive discovery of records in Egypt has, instead, shown that it is a very plausible story, and typical of the age. The arguments for placing the 12th Dynasty of Egypt at a date too early for Joseph are now looking unsustainable; adjusting the timeline of ancient Egypt to the later period harmonises the Bible record closely with archaeological findings. And who else could the Bahr Yusuf (Canal of Joseph) possibly have been named after?

One interesting development is the possible alignment of the eruption of the Santorini supervolcano in the Mediterranean with a seven-year famine covering Europe, China, the Middle East and Egypt. Famines that last a full seven years are extremely rare in world history, and here we have a connection between geology, archaeology and the Bible, which all describe such a catastrophe from differing perspectives. Aligning Joseph with the 12th Dynasty, in the 'Middle Kingdom era', and particularly Sesostris 1, not only harmonises the biblical chronology with the actual conditions in Egypt as supported by very many archaeological finds, it also supplies a very powerful explanation as to how this particular Pharaoh became one of the wealthiest Egypt ever saw, in the latter part of his reign.

Reference links

David Rohl's blog gives background information on his work, and details of his many publications: *davidrohl.blogspot.co.uk*

On the Reliability of the Old Testament; K A Kitchen; Eerdmans, Grand Rapids (2006); details at: *www.logos.com/product/49491/on-the-reliability-of-the-old-testament*

Unwrapping the Pharaohs; John Ashton & David Down (2006); details at: *answersingenesis.org/answers/books/unwrapping-pharaohs*

Wikipedia has a summary of the book *Exodus to Arthur: Catastrophic Encounters with Comets;* Mike Baillie; Batsford, London (1999), at: *en.wikipedia.org/wiki/Mike_Baillie*

CHAPTER THREE

Hebrew Slaves Really Made Bricks of Mud, Their Baby Boys Were Killed

You in Your mercy have led forth
The people whom You have redeemed;
You have guided them in Your strength
To Your holy habitation.

Exodus 15:13 (NKJV)

A Hebrew mother, Northern Sinai, 1470 BC

"Children, it was a terrible time." The family listened to their mother as she recalled what had happened in the land of Mizraim (Egypt) before they were born. "My mother had two sons, before she had me, and they were both killed in front of her, drowned in the river by the people the rulers sent. They were only babies; what harm could they have done? My father still wept years later when he told me how he had dug holes in the middle of our home to bury their tiny bodies. Some had been forced to throw their little boy babies to the crocodiles in the river for them to be eaten alive – a sacrifice to Sobek (the crocodile god), the Mizraim rulers said. Father also said how hard it had been to make mud bricks day after day, an endless toil for the endless buildings which the Pharaohs wanted to make.

"And then came that final year there. It was so strange, just a short distance away we heard of such terrible things happening to the people and rulers of Mizraim. At the end, we helped to dig pits for the burial of several of them. And there was no ceremony or preparation of the dead according to their customs. There were simply too many dead bodies – some even had just fallen in the streets, and it was a case of getting them buried before they putrefied. These were the very people who had laughed at us and mocked us because we were their slaves. And they thrust gold and jewellery on us just to get us out of their sight – they who once refused to spare us the peelings from their fruit!

"I remember my parents as they first spoke of this prince, Moses – many had thought him to be one of the Mizraim themselves, but we learned he was born Hebrew, like us. We could not understand how someone who had been so great in the courts of Pharaoh, and a mighty warrior leading the army in battle against the Ethiopians, could really be one of us.

"And yet we know, he was raised up by God to be our leader too. He would take us out of that land before the last destructions brought the anarchy of the Amalekites and the Libyans, people even more cruel and murderous than the Mizraim. And now we are here, in this empty land. I know the food is dull and monotonous, but we are no longer oppressed, there is no-one who will snatch my beloved boys from me, or send my daughters to be palace slaves, and Moses is telling us to trust God, for a new land and a great future await us. I remember the night we walked through the middle of the sea, yet on dry land. I remember, too, the pillar of smoke we followed by day, and the fire by night. Most of all, though, I saw the great Moses himself when he came down from the mountain; his face truly shone with light. They say it still shines today, but he veils himself so we cannot see. I tell you, my children, you must follow this man in all he says."

What are the facts?

The story told by our fictional woman is typical of that experienced by many thousands of Hebrew mothers in that period, and the events described have been attested by Josephus, the Jewish general and historian, using records in addition to the Bible.

The story of the departure of the Israelites from Egypt is in Exodus chapters 1-15. The biblical timeline for this period runs from the Exodus in 1491 BC to the arrival in Canaan in 1451 BC. The facts we can check relate to the evidence for a large population of non-Egyptian people living in the Nile Delta, at a time when mud-brick manufacture was at a very high level. Then, there is evidence needed to show that these people were oppressed (specifically, the boy babies were being killed), and that they left suddenly. The time of their departure should match a time of disasters corresponding to the plagues recorded in Exodus.

The final rulers of Egypt's 13th Dynasty became cruel and oppressive. They also were less wealthy, as can be seen from the pyramids they built; instead of using stone throughout as their predecessors had, they cut costs by using mud brick, with a skin of stone on many buildings. Sesostris 3 and his son Amenemhat III, almost the last rulers of this dynasty, built two cities, identified as the "Pithom and Raamses"[5] mentioned in the Bible, using mud brick almost exclusively for their building materials. There were large numbers of people living in the Nile Delta area at this time who originated from Palestine or Syria, just as the Israelites did, and this corresponds exactly with the territory of "Goshen"[6] mentioned in the Bible. They have been identified as probably being the Israelite slaves, and the sudden disappearance of vast numbers of these people as evidenced by the Egyptian archaeological record supports the Exodus narrative in a most compelling way. The whole population of this area just 'upped and left' one day, leaving many belongings behind.

In later times, there was no more evidence of these people living in Egypt. Even though they all seem to have left, yet they had been most of the population of the eastern Nile delta. The great Egyptologist, Flinders Petrie, reported that many houses occupied by these people contained small coffins, with the bodies of babies up to three months old, up to three in a box. These finds are unique to these peoples and this time.

In addition, analysis of the graves of these people at Avaris has shown that there were many more women than men in the population, and some contemporary Egyptian lists of household slaves reflect the same situation, exactly as would be expected if the slave population was

---

[5] Exodus 1:11(NKJV)

[6] Genesis 47:6

being compelled to kill off their boy babies. One list of slaves (the Brooklyn Papyrus[7]) shows that many of the names are clearly Hebrew. Given that it was the custom to give slaves Egyptian names, this fact alone is very compelling. The Brooklyn Papyrus is strong documentary evidence of Hebrew people living as slaves in Egypt.

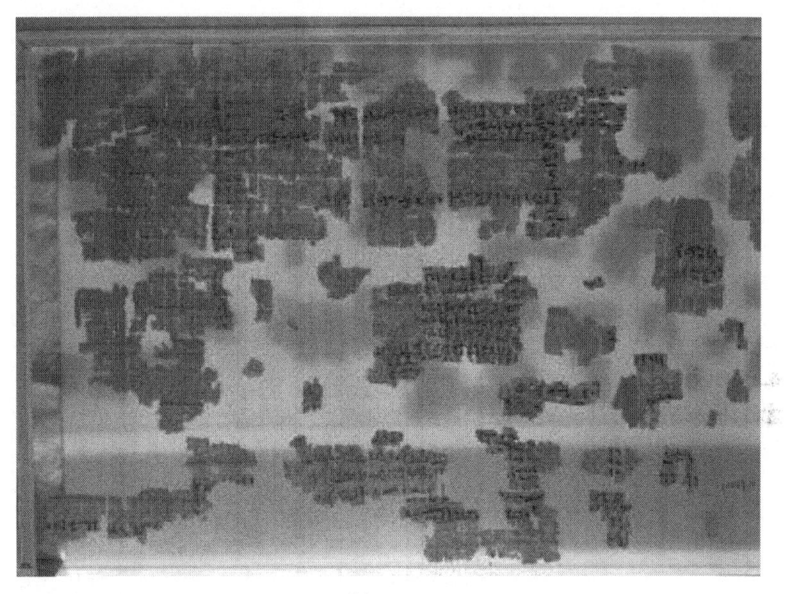

Brooklyn Papyrus.
Courtesy: Brooklyn Museum, New York.

In this same area, Manfred Bietak has uncovered many shallow burial pits into which the victims of some disaster or plague have been thrown, without any of the normal burial arrangements; these also date from about the end of the 13th Dynasty. A papyrus, held at the museum in Leiden in the Netherlands, and dated to around the 3rd century BC, is believed to be a copy of one written about the end of the 13th Dynasty by a priest named Ipuwer. It seems to describe at least five of the ten plagues of Exodus, but from an Egyptian perspective, including the Nile turning to blood, a fiery storm of hailstones (possible

[7] Papyrus Brooklyn 35.1446.
www.brooklynmuseum.org/opencollection/objects/3369

meteorite shower), the thick darkness, the disease of the cattle and the death of "firstborn"[8].

Very strikingly, several of the ten plagues match the area of 'authority' of one of the chief gods of the Egyptians. Each successive plague showed that the god concerned was useless (or non-existent) compared to the God of the Hebrews.

Comment

We cannot prove specifically that a large group of Israelites left Egypt through the Red Sea, after a series of plagues in Egypt. However, the circumstantial evidence that a major catastrophe struck Egypt after the end of the 13th Dynasty is very considerable. The details of the oppression before the Exodus tie in closely with the archaeological evidence, and the fact that there was a large population of 'Asiatics' (people from the general area of Palestine) at that time who within a short space of time had gone is very striking. And there is evidence showing that there were Hebrew-named slaves there too. And these people left the buried remains of many babies, in the heart of their homes. The main issue to confront is the controversy over chronology, which has affected all the comparisons between the Bible narrative and the history of ancient Egypt. The truth is that trying to determine an accurate chronology of ancient Egypt without using the Bible as a datum is like 'trying to nail jelly to a wall'! As we shall see in the next chapters, the Bible narrative continues to show an accuracy which archaeology has often ended up vindicating.

Reference links

Riddle of the Exodus Springdale; James D Long; AK, Lightcatcher Books (2006); reviewed at: *https://vernerable.files.wordpress.com/2015/08/bookreview-long.pdf*

David Rohl's blog gives background information on his work, and details of his many publications: *davidrohl.blogspot.co.uk*

On the Reliability of the Old Testament; K A Kitchen; Eerdmans, Grand Rapids (2006); details at: *www.logos.com/product/49491/on-the-reliability-of-the-old-testament*

Unwrapping the Pharaohs; John Ashton & David Down (2006); details at: *answersingenesis.org/answers/books/unwrapping-pharaohs*

---

[8] Exodus 11:15

CHAPTER FOUR

The Fall of Jericho Really Happened

So the people shouted when the priests blew the trumpets. And it happened when the people heard the sound of the trumpet, and the people shouted with a great shout, that the wall fell down flat. Then the people went up into the city, every man straight before him, and they took the city.

Joshua 6:20 (NKJV)

A Hebrew soldier, about 1420 BC

"I won't deny Jericho looked awesome. You can't say we were afraid of battle – me and my comrades were seasoned warriors by then, in our group. We had fought the Canaanites of Arad and destroyed their cities. The Amorites under Sihon had fallen before us, and their cities, too, we had destroyed. Then there was mighty King Og and his army from Bashan. I was near enough to see him – towering head and shoulders above any other man on the battlefield, but his size didn't save him that day! Made him a better target for spears and arrows, if anything. Finally, there were the Midianites, including that prophet-chieftain Balaam whom the Moabites had tried sending out to curse us. We knew there were none who could face us in open battle and win.

"I can't say that I mightn't have felt more comfortable if a few more of my old mates were still with us – those that fell to the plague. The priests said that was their own fault for going with the Moabite girls. I can't deny they were very good to look at, real stunners some of them, and they seemed very keen on hardened warriors like us. But the truth was, this Jericho place was different. Everything was different now. First, we didn't have Moses as our leader any more, and every warrior will tell you it's no little thing to go to battle without the man God had sent to see us through such times as we had been through. It was obvious that Joshua had got God with him, though. I mean, just seeing the Jordan dry up under our feet that day... Was that the priests with the Ark? Or what? But then, there we were, the greatest army in the land, and he calls us all to be circumcised!

"Well, I could hardly walk with the pain for days; they could have sent the children out to fight us then and we'd have struggled! But by the time we went for Jericho we were fine. The trouble was, they weren't going to come out and fight, and you should have seen their city. We'd seen nothing like it. The walls towered up to the sky, but worse than that, we couldn't even get to the bottom to set ladders up, because of the slope they had built. It was too steep and smooth for a man to scramble up. Then around that was a deep ditch, to further hinder any attack. And if you tried to attack the wall? Arrows, spears, rocks raining down on our heads and us not able to fire back. Mind you, the people in the city did seem to be cowering behind the walls, rather than spoiling for a fight. Some said they'd had a plague inside the city. I wonder if the Moabite girls had anything to do with that?

"So, every day for six days Joshua had made us turn out and march around the walls – nothing more. I thought he was trying to call them out to fight, but they weren't having any of that. It was that seventh day: 'When the priests blow a long call on the shofars (ram's horn trumpets), all you men, yell at the top of your lungs," he said. So we did, and that was when it happened. The shofar call hadn't finished and we felt the ground shaking like jelly underneath us.

"The officers told us to stand fast, and then we saw it – those great walls all crumbling to dust, and cascading down over the lower slopes. The dust had hardly started to settle, and he yelled, 'Charge!' so we did. Right up and over that ditch, now filled with rubble which was also covering those slopes, so climbing them was easy. It was a massacre; there was hardly anyone in the city with any fight left. 'No looting or you die,' said our officers, 'and when you're done, set fires so that everything burns.' I had never seen such a burning. The smoke went up for a couple of weeks, and there was nothing left but ash. I tell you, we would have followed Joshua anywhere after that, and many of us did. The battles went on until I was too old to fight anymore, and my sons became farmers rather than fighters. The herds of our household became bigger and bigger, until they are as you see them now. But I wouldn't have missed being a warrior in those days for anything."

What are the facts?

The fall of Jericho is in Joshua chapter 6, and the preparatory times in Joshua chapters 1 to 5. The battles immediately before the arrival at the Jordan below Jericho are in Numbers chapters 21 and 31, and Deuteronomy chapters 2 and 3. The story of the prophet Balaam is in Numbers chapters 22 to 24, while the encounter with the Moabite women and the outbreak of plague is in Numbers chapter 25. Most of these events took place during the year before the Israelites arrived at Jericho in 1451 BC. The story told by our fictional man is typical of the experience of many thousands of Israelite soldiers, as they lived through seven more years of warfare before being able to settle down.

To evidence this story, we need to find a large city with substantial fortifications which collapsed. Specifically, the walls must have collapsed outwards. The evidence of devastation should then include a destruction by burning and, to complete the story, the site should then show a long period before reoccupation.

There are the remains of a just such a great city, under a mound named Tell es-Sultan, covering about four hectares, which has been identified as the ancient city of Jericho. The city that was there was destroyed by a combination of earthquake and fire. It once had double defence walls, and the outer wall had a glacis slope all round at its foot. A layer of ash and burned debris has been found in places up to a metre thick. A later Jericho was built, a small distance away from the original city mound.

Figure 4. Tell es-Sultan with modern Jericho to left of picture.
Courtesy: teachmiddleeast.lib.uchicago.edu/foundations.

This took place during the Middle Bronze Age, a period when most recent archaeologists would now set the time of Joshua (Bible dating of the event sets it at about 1450 BC). In the city, some graves have been found with multiple hasty burials of people who had not died from injuries (e.g. battle wounds), suggesting plague. Some graves contained grave goods including food, and the state of preservation of bodies and foodstuffs in some of these graves is so good that the best explanation offered is that the tombs were filled with methane and carbon dioxide, such as is typically released during an earthquake.

It has been reported a few times in history that the Jordan has temporarily dried up at this point. The most recent occasion was in 1927, when an earthquake collapsed a soft cliff into the river a little way upstream, blocking it for twenty-one hours until the lake forming behind the earth dam created by the cliff fall broke through and washed the dam away.

- Not all the walls of Jericho fell – and the Bible record says that the section adjoining the house of Rahab the prostitute was

preserved, keeping her safe. A section of wall containing houses has been found that did not collapse.
- In 1967, at Deir Alla in Jordan, an ancient inscription was found naming Balaam son of Peor as a prophet operating in the same territory as the Bible narrative indicates.
- The geological record of this part of the Jordan valley is one of considerable instability, with earthquakes a frequent occurrence during recorded history.

Comment

The archaeological evidence at Tell es-Sultan is overwhelmingly supportive of the Bible account of the fall of Jericho. It should come as no surprise that many writers have advanced reasons why they think the fall of Jericho shown at this site is at the wrong time for Joshua. These arguments have been comprehensively demolished by the work of John Bimson and others. Once the Exodus is established at the biblical date of 1491 BC, then the fall of Jericho took place in about 1450 BC. The evidence at the site supports a destruction of the city at this era.

The pattern of destruction found at the sites of the other cities recorded as destroyed by Joshua in the Bible also matches the Bible account precisely. The recent evidence of the Jordan river drying up for nearly a day, and the independent evidence for a contemporary prophet named Balaam who was at one time very important in the correct area, is just 'icing on the cake'!

And, almost as an afterthought, Jericho is where we meet the figure of Rahab, a prostitute according to the book of Joshua, yet the person who provided the vital intelligence needed by Joshua and his army, and who sheltered the Israeli spies at great risk to herself and her family. She went on to become the great-great-grandmother of King David. Despite the embarrassment of later apologists, there is no doubt that Rahab's trade was prostitution, and yet the Bible records her being given great honour by God for her faithfulness. Matthew chapter 1 lists her as the second of three women specially honoured in the Temple records that Matthew copied from. These were Tamar, Rahab and Bathsheba, all of whom behaved in ways the society of the time strongly disapproved of yet were honoured by God! This reference alone is strong support for the authenticity of this story, as it is unimaginable that later kings would want to include a prostitute in their lineage.

Reference links

Redating the Exodus and Conquest; John J Bimson; The Almond Press, Sheffield (1981). John Bimson on dating the Patriarchs:
www.biblicalstudies.org.uk/epn_3_bimson.html

David Rohl's blog gives background information on his work, and details of his many publications: *davidrohl.blogspot.co.uk*

Unwrapping the Pharaohs; John Ashton & David Down; Master Books, Green Forest AR (2006).

Is there any evidence to prove the existence of the prophet, Balaam? Bryant G Wood (1995). Evidence about Balaam at: *www.christiananswers.net/q-abr/abr-a014.html*

Who was Rahab? See: *www.biblegateway.com/resources/all-women-bible/Rahab*

The New Scientist on the earthquakes which brought down Jericho, at:
www.newscientist.com/article/mg13117765.700-and-the-walls-came-tumbling-down-old-testament-writings-ofdoom-and-destruction-are-now-providing-researchers-with-a-record-ofearthquakes-spanning-4000-years-.html

CHAPTER FIVE

Solomon Really Married Pharaoh's Daughter

Now Solomon made a treaty with Pharaoh king of Egypt, and married Pharaoh's daughter. Then he brought her to the City of David until he had finished building his own house and the house of the LORD, and the wall all around Jerusalem.

1 Kings 3:1 (NKJV)

An Egyptian maid in the Court of the Daughter of Pharaoh, Solomon's Queen

"The day the men of the Vizier came and told me I was to accompany the princess, and to be her personal servant, I felt filled with joy. My whole family would be so proud that we had such a great honour, more than any of our honoured ancestors. You see, we knew that the princess was to marry the king of the Israelites, Solomon, son of the great warrior King David. So I would be serving a queen of Israel!

"I was surprised to see how small was the city where my princess was to be a queen, but it seemed no time at all before great buildings went up all around. There was the new palace, where we lived for some time, and then the Temple (not as fine, to be sure, as some of our temples in Egypt). And my princess was such a beautiful bride, and the king was so much in love with her back then.

"I learned that one of his forebears, a great leader called Abraham, was said to have married a princess of Egypt, and her son had also gone on to be a mighty king, whose descendants also ruled wonderful kingdoms in the east. Sadly, that story ended with Abraham's first wife making sure it was her own son who became heir, and I can see that this will happen again.

"Naamah, the chief Queen, has allowed no sons of any of the other queens (and now there are so very many other queens for Solomon) to gain the favour of their father. Not that this matters to my queen, for she has had no sons by Solomon so far, and now she sees so little of him, it is not likely there will be any. Why has my mistress not borne sons to Solomon? Perhaps it is because she is the daughter of Pharaoh, who is a god and the descendant of gods, while the Israelite kings worship a god who is invisible. I do not understand these things; I wonder sometimes if I will be allowed to accompany my mistress on her journey to the next life, among the gods who are her ancestors, in the way of our people. I do not know anyone here who can tell me the answer to this.

"Once, they were so much in love, and he was such an ardent lover to her. He even wrote a wonderful song for their marriage, using ways of writing he said called on the great traditions of our own country. It was funny to me that in the song he called her "shepherdess", for in our country these are people to be despised, common keepers of the flocks. But he told my queen that a great pharaoh who had raised one of the ancestors of the Israelite people to be Vizier over all Egypt had liked to be known as the shepherd of his people. Imagine that! Solomon is so wise, and knows so much. It is said that the great ancestor Abraham actually taught the Pharaoh Khufu about mathematics and astronomy, which is why Khufu built the greatest pyramid ever.

"But even though Queen Naamah rules the household, and keeps the many new queens and concubines in subjection to her will, the love Solomon had for my queen was great. He built for her a lovely palace, on the mountain overlooking his own palace, outside the city but on the highway to Egypt. He brought in skilled masons and craftsmen from Egypt, so the palace could be a true reminder of home. He also honoured her in the decorations he commanded for other palaces, such as the great one at Megiddo.

"My mistress sometimes pines for the great river and the green of the land, the flowers and fruits that were all around us. And, loyal and hardworking as the local girls are, they are not skilled in the ways of make-up and hair. This means more work for the few in the palace still trained in the proper Egyptian ways. But, the king showers his wealth on us, and my mistress also has the revenues of Gezer; I do not believe even Queen Naamah commands so much wealth as my mistress does, but her jealousy cannot touch us now that we have a palace of our own. My mistress' father and the king remain very close; there is so much trade all the time coming from Egypt – not just the chariots and horses! Did ever a king make such wealth from war without going to war, as Solomon does?"

What are the facts?

The Egyptian princess who married Solomon will undoubtedly have taken her own household servants with her, especially maids and cooks, so this is the background for our fictional maid.

The story of Solomon marrying Pharaoh's daughter is found 1 Kings 3:1; 7:8; 9:24; 11:1; and 2 Chronicles 8:11.

> *Then he made a hall for the throne, the Hall of Judgment, where he might judge; and it was panelled with cedar from floor to ceiling. And the house where he dwelt had another court of like workmanship. Solomon also made a house like this hall for Pharaoh's daughter, whom he had taken as wife.*
>
> *1 Kings 7:7-8 (NKJV)*

> *(Pharaoh king of Egypt had gone up and taken Gezer and burned it with fire, had killed the Canaanites who lived in the city, and had given it as a dowry to his daughter, Solomon's wife.) And Solomon built Gezer, Lower Beth-Horon...*
>
> *1 Kings 9:16-17 (NKJV)*

What is the evidence of Egyptian trade and marriage connections with a king of Israel at the time of Solomon?

David Rohl describes the finding of a range of Egyptian architectural remains beneath the church of St Etienne in Jerusalem.

This site fits the biblical location of the palace Solomon built for Pharaoh's daughter. The famous Megiddo ivory, probably a panel from a chair (throne) has strong indications of Egyptian links, and Rohl suggests that this commemorates Solomon and Pharaoh's daughter together. There is other evidence of Egyptian craftsmanship in the remains found in the Late Bronze Age city at Megiddo, again the appropriate time for Solomon (on the chronology proposed by Rohl).

Figure 5. Megiddo Ivory: Egyptian winged sun-disk above chariot, Egyptian queen offering lotus flower to Canaanite king on Sphinx throne. Courtesy: forums.catholic.com.

On Rohl's chronology, Horemheb (last Pharaoh of the 18th dynasty) would be the Pharaoh who captured Gezer and gave his daughter to Solomon. Excavations at the site show it was destroyed and rebuilt immediately afterwards, presumably during a military campaign to the north of Egypt, which Horemheb certainly did. An interesting alternative possibility is that it could have been an earlier 18th Dynasty king, Thutmosis 1. There is good evidence that his army, too, campaigned as far as the Euphrates river (which could have happened during the alliance with Solomon which this marriage implies). Thutmosis 1 had two daughters, princesses Hatshepsut and Nefrubity. Hatshepsut later became the sole ruler of Egypt, a female Pharaoh, but there have been found no later references to her sister. This is what would be expected if Nefrubity had left Egypt and married Solomon.

The Song of Songs resembles several ancient Egyptian love poems. It has been traditionally believed that this is a song that Solomon wrote to honour Pharaoh's daughter. The Pharaoh Sesostris 1 (possible pharaoh who made Joseph his Vizier) chose to have himself represented as a shepherd on some statues.

Josephus, writing in the 1st century AD, records the traditions about Abraham taking the knowledge of mathematics and astronomy to Egypt, attributing them to Berosus. That Hagar (Abraham's second wife) was also a daughter of a Pharaoh is an ancient Jewish legend.

Comment

The time of Solomon is a 'golden age' of peace and plenty for the land of Israel and its people. Before Solomon, in the time of King Saul and David, there were battles with various neighbouring tribes and nations. After Solomon's time, Egypt became powerful once more, and successive Pharaohs sent their armies through Israel and the surrounding territory.

After the Egyptians came the time of the Assyrians and then the Babylonians. The latter part of David's reign and the reign of Solomon marked a relatively short period when there were no nearby 'superpowers' seeking to expand their empires. The story of Solomon, his Egyptian princess, and the later visit by the queen of Sheba, all fit into this narrow window of opportunity in history when it was possible for the Israelite kingdom to prosper and be at peace.

Reference links

David Rohl's blog gives background information on his work, and details of his many publications: *davidrohl.blogspot.co.uk*

Riddle of the Exodus; James D Long; Lightcatcher Books, Springdale AK (2006); reviewed at: *vernerable.files.wordpress.com/2015/08/bookreview-long.pdf*

The Antiquities of the Jews; Josephus (translated by William Whiston, 1867); available at: *sacred-texts.com/jud/josephus*

CHAPTER SIX

Herod Had Good Reason to Fear the Magi

Now after Jesus was born in Bethlehem of Judea in the days of Herod the king, magi from the east arrived in Jerusalem, saying, "Where is He who has been born King of the Jews? For we saw His star in the east and have come to worship Him." When Herod the king heard this, he was troubled, and all Jerusalem with him.

Matthew 2:1-3 (NASB)

An army barracks in Susa, capital city of Parthia

The tall man wearing a commander's robe called out to the officer just then leading his troop into the barracks: "Hey there, Hormisdas!"

The officer turned to his second-in-command, and dismissed his troop of one hundred heavily armoured Parthian cavalrymen. Then he went to greet his chief.

"I have good news for you: you are being promoted to command the first squadron of the king's escort," the commander said. "Someone high up in court must have spoken up for you!"

Hormisdas saluted, dismounted, and walked with his commander into their rooms. He said, "The Rab Mag must have kept the promise he made to me when we got back. Did I tell you about the escort duty I finished two weeks ago?"

"No," the commander replied. "Remember, I was away on a lion-hunt with the king. A great time we had; the king himself speared two lionesses from his horse on two consecutive days. He felt he was once more reliving his youth, as a true Parthian. I only know, Hormisdas, that you went on some special embassy to the west. It must have made a change from escorting the usual camel caravans eastwards on the trade route to China."

The servants brought wine, and they settled to talk. Hormisdas said, "That will make me the third in my family to have held that post. You know my grandfather was appointed to command the king's guard after they fought the Romans at Carrhae, that great victory. Then my father was a squadron commander when our present King of kings chased the Romans out of Parthia just over thirty years back.

"The Roman leader – Mark Anthony, wasn't it? – Well, he tried to say it was *his* victory, but ten thousand of his men fell to only eighty of ours, and that great army left with their tails between their legs! Being a soldier nowadays is tame stuff compared to then. I hoped that I might see a bit of action – against the Romans, or at least the Judeans – on this embassy, but nothing happened. We were escort for a party of the Magi, twelve there were altogether, with the Rab Mag himself in charge.

"You know all these rumours there have been for many years now, about a great king to be born who will bring peace to the world? Well, that is just whom the Magi went to find. We took the trade route as far as Palmyra, but then we headed on down into Judea, a journey of just over one month. The Magi would not tell us where we were going; they studied the stars every night, and there was a special great star – you must have seen it too – that was the sign in the heavens that began this journey.

"Did I tell you about how my father was part of the army that defeated the Judeans, after they had chased the Romans all the way back to Asia? He told me about how our King of kings had helped to set Herod on the throne of Judah, in Jerusalem. Herod was a real piece of work, I've been told. He switched his allegiance back again to the Romans after that – there's gratitude for you. Do you know how many of his own sons he has had murdered? Three, so far! Now I've seen him with my own eyes, I can well believe it. Of course, he's old now – and looks pretty sick, to me. Can't have much longer to go, I'd say. I hear since we left he's now moved his court to Jericho, where he's built himself another palace. For all he's a ruthless old fox, I was astonished by what I saw in Jerusalem. I've travelled from the shores of the Great Sea practically all the way to China, but I've never seen such splendid building work as he's done there in Jerusalem.

"Still, the old fox was taken by surprise when we arrived. We were only a small escort, given the group of Magi that went. One troop of heavy cavalry, two of light cavalry, three-hundred-horse in all. I felt so proud to be in command of them all. We sent out scouts all the time, but we never saw any other troops. There were a few bandits we surprised in the hills along the Jordan valley; the light cavalry dealt with them in no time. Of course, there were no Roman legions in the whole region, but even so, I thought there might be a possibility of the Judeans cutting up rough. They can be very fierce fighters, you know! But there were none of Herod's troops to be seen, only the household guard. Fat and old; we'd have cut them to shreds if they had dared to lift a sword!

Figure 6. Armoured Parthian warrior fighting a lion.
Courtesy: British Museum.

"I tell you, when we rode into town and into the palace, people were running for their homes and barricading their doors. When Herod realised it was Magi we brought with us, he looked petrified. Probably thought he was about to be deposed! The Rab Mag told him their mission. You should have seen his face; after all, he is the King of Judea, but they said they were looking for one who was born to be King of the Jews. Obviously, that could not be Herod or any of his sons that hadn't yet been murdered by their father, as they are all Idumeans and not Jews at all!

"Their priests of Jerusalem said we should go and look in Bethlehem; Herod asked the Magi to come back and tell him who they'd found. Funny, I thought, that's barely two hours' ride away on a slow camel – why not send some of his own troops along with us to report back? Of course, I think he was doing that to buy time and round up more of his army, in case things turned nasty. I noticed the city gates were closed and barred soon after we left, so we wouldn't be able to ride right back into the palace without warning (in case the Magi did appoint this new man to be King of Judah, I suppose).

"Well, we got to Bethlehem, and the Magi took us to a house on the outskirts of the little town. Poor people, not at all what I expected, and not a grown man after all but a baby! Anyway, the Magi did what they had come for, and told me we were leaving direct for Syria.

"We took the road down into the valley of the Salt Sea, and north up past Jericho, so we avoided Jerusalem on the way home. We stopped to do some business in Damascus. I heard news that Herod sent his troops into Bethlehem soon after we left, to kill all the boy babies. Didn't surprise me at all – that's exactly how I expected him to react. I doubt if the baby the Magi saw could have survived that, but the Rab Mag didn't seem troubled. He told me one night that this birth had been foretold by one of his greatest predecessors, the great Rab Mag Daniel, and that while the baby would surely die, it would not be until he had come into his kingdom. I remember the baby's father telling the Magi the boy's name was Yeshua."

What are the facts?

The Parthian Empire lay to the east of Judea. At the time of Jesus' birth, it stretched from Syria to China and south to India. The Magi first appear in the Bible in the time of Jeremiah (when Judah and Jerusalem fell to the Babylonians). They were a combination of priests, astronomers and government advisors in the Babylonian, Persian and Parthian empires. Daniel was appointed Chief of the Magi (Rab Mag) by Nebuchadnezzar, Emperor of Babylon. They were involved in the origin of the religion now known as Zoroastrian (or Parsee). There is no independent verification of the account in Matthew's Gospel, but it is highly probable that this is a report of a group of Magi following the teachings of Daniel.

The story above is a fiction based on a typical soldier's experience. The Parthian Empire was a very important part of the balance of power in the region around Judea when Jesus was born, and the Magi were very important people in the Parthian Empire. Members of the Parthian elite would not have travelled without a heavy military escort (possibly much bigger than in our story – one member of the ruling council had a personal escort of a thousand troops).

The story above tells the history of Parthia between 53 BC (the battle of Carrhae) and the birth of Jesus from the perspective of a Parthian soldier. The Romans in a number of battles had been unable to defeat the Parthian combination of heavy cavalry and light cavalry, and during this period the 'Silk Road', the great trade route from Europe to China, was developed and became established for centuries. The Parthian heavy cavalry wore chain mail armour from head to toe, and their horses were similarly equipped. Their horses were also bigger and stronger than anything available elsewhere. The heavy cavalrymen were armed with swords and spears, and with their armour and big armoured war horses were the most formidable warriors of their day. The light cavalry carried a powerful bow, and were famous for being able to turn in their saddle and shoot at targets right behind them. This is the famous 'Parthian shot'.

The Eastern tradition is that there were twelve Magi in the group that went to find Jesus ('Yeshua' in Hebrew). The idea that there were only three is a much later Western tradition, probably based on the fact there were three gifts. The presentation of gifts was correct protocol for greeting royalty; the gifts would not be big and lavish (that would imply the recipient was poor) but were selected to signify the attributes of kingship. The title 'Rab Mag' used in the story means 'Chief of Magi', and can be found in Jeremiah 39:3,13 and again in Daniel 5:11. It is usually translated "chief of magicians", which is misleading, because they did not do what we would nowadays call 'magic'!

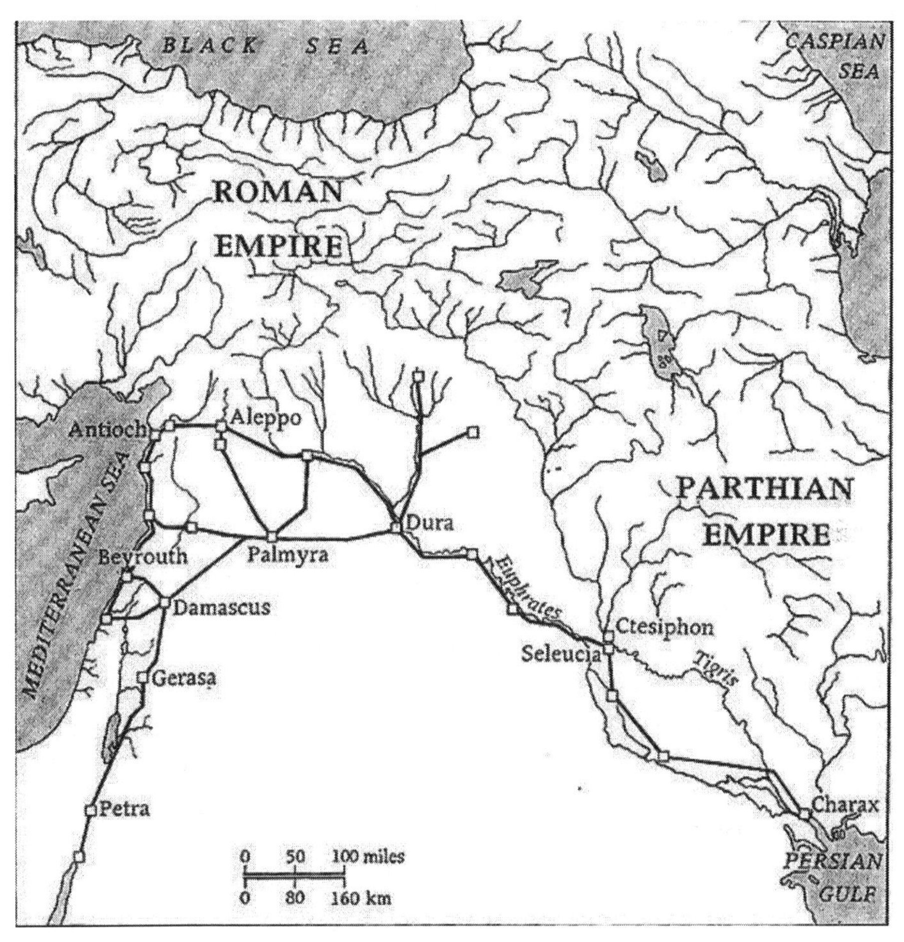

Figure 7. Map of trade routes between Parthia and the Mediterranean Region. (Susa is approx. 300km southeast of Ctesiphon.)

It is a reasonable assumption that this mission was of such importance that the Magi would have travelled with their chief. They were skilled in astronomy, which in those days included knowing the precise measurement of years and seasons. The prophecy in Daniel 9 of the "seventy weeks" would have been passed on to those Magi who were his successors in the Persian and later Parthian empires. Within the Parthian Empire they were involved in all the appointments of kings, and soon after this story they would be involved in helping select the replacement for the elderly ruler Phraates IV, "King of kings", the one who had chased the Romans under Mark Anthony out, conquered Judea and (after some intriguing against Herod) helped confirm Herod (the Great) as king of Judah by releasing a chief priest to serve in Jerusalem. Of all the rulers on the border region between the Roman Empire and the Parthian Empire, Herod had more reason than most to fear Parthian intervention in his kingdom, as he had indeed switched his allegiance from Parthia to Rome.

In Rome about forty years earlier, a "portent" was reported that "nature" was preparing to provide them with a king who would bring peace to the world. This so frightened the Roman Senate that they passed a decree forbidding the rearing of any male child for a year. This means that a "massacre of the innocents" was ordered in Rome while Herod was living there as a young man. Even though this order was cancelled, it can be seen to have given Herod a way to handle such things a generation before he ordered the same thing in Bethlehem.

Octavius, the adopted son of Julius Caesar, by 40 BC was declared to be this ruler. (He became Caesar Augustus – "The August One".) The expectation that a king would arise who would bring peace to the world was widespread in this era. A few years after the birth of Jesus, in 1 AD, the king of India, who knew of a prophecy about a coming world ruler, sent out emissaries to find out if the foretold royal child had actually been born.

A stone carving from Palmyra in Syria shows a Parthian cavalryman escorting a camel caravan. Parthian dominance over the lands from Syria to China and south to India was helped by the Roman civil war at the time of Julius Caesar. The Parthian Empire started to lose its power and territory from about the end of the 1st century AD.

For a king over a minor border territory at the edge of the Roman Empire, Herod the Great was very shrewd and successful. He was also bloodthirsty and ruthless even by the harsh standards of the age, and murdered several members of his own family whom he thought might threaten his position. When he knew he was sick and dying, he moved to his new palace at Jericho, and took with him several of the leading citizens of Jerusalem. He gave orders that they were to be executed when he died – just so that there would be grief in Jerusalem after his death! Yet the buildings he caused to be erected in Jerusalem and Judea were the finest that had ever been built there. The Temple was made spectacular, and the stonework was covered in parts with gold. The size of some of the remaining stones used in the foundations of the Temple still astonishes people today.

We do not know for certain in which year Jesus was born, but it has to have been before Herod the Great died in late 4 BC and the Magi must have visited before he made his final move to Jericho, shortly before he died. This move may have been motivated by the hope that Dead Sea waters might help heal his serious illnesses (which included rotting genitalia!) 4 BC is the most likely year, though many suggest 6 BC. Others argue for an even earlier date. Our present calendar starts from a date calculated in error by a monk named Dionysius in 525 AD, hence the year 'zero' was omitted (it goes from 1 BC to 1 AD without a year in between), and the date of Jesus' birth was miscalculated.

There is no agreement about what the stars were that the Magi could have seen and followed, but there are several possibilities (including Halley's comet, 12-11 BC). No identifiable stars or astronomic events can account for the description of a star that "went ahead of them until it stopped over the place where the child was" (Matthew 2:9).

Comment

The story of the birth of Jesus is rooted in a period of history when a lot of nations were apparently expecting a very special king. This may have been partly a result of the prophecy of Daniel being made more widely known than we might have expected, but then, the Magi were known to have travelled far afield.

The story of the Magi underlines the historical authenticity of the nativity, and especially the relationship between Herod the Great and the Parthian Empire. The idea that there were three kings is a late Western church tradition. There is a remote possibility that one of the Magi later became a king of Parthia; a prince named Gundophar ascended to the throne of Parthia in AD 1. Tradition says that he was one of the Magi who visited Jesus, but this does not appear to have been known in the West at the time.

These Magi in Matthew's Gospel are stated to be just that: Magi. The external evidence is strongly supportive of this. We have no way of authenticating the appearance of angels to Mary or the shepherds from historical records outside the Gospels – but the authenticity of the events we can check should encourage us to treat these other events as historically accurate.

Reference links

Who Were the Magi; Chuck Missler; *www.ldolphin.org/magi.html*

Background on the Parthian Empire in Wikipedia: *en.wikipedia.org/wiki/Parthia.* Also, Parthian horses and Parthian archers: *www.parthia.com/parthia_horses_burris.htm*

A list of Parthian rulers: *www.parthia.com/parthia_chrono.htm*

CHAPTER SEVEN

We Really Do Know the Time of John the Baptist

Now in the fifteenth year of the reign of Tiberius Caesar, Pontius Pilate being governor of Judea, Herod being tetrarch of Galilee, his brother Philip tetrarch of Iturea and the region of Trachonitis, and Lysanias tetrarch of Abilene, while Annas and Caiaphas were high priests, the word of God came to John the son of Zacharias in the wilderness.

Luke 3:1-2 (NKJV)

A court official in Abila

"It was a great honour for me to have served as chief scribe to King Lysanias. Now, indeed, I am old and the great emperor Claudius has made Agrippa king of this land, and others serve in my place – but I have been a most fortunate man. This may not be the largest or the wealthiest kingdom in the land of Syria, or even perhaps in the Decapolis, but we have a fine city, and King Lysanias, whose line is no more, was a descendant of the great rulers of Egypt. We have lived in peaceful times, thank God, not being troubled by events such as those that have afflicted the territories west of the Jordan. Abila (Abilene) may not be the greatest city of the region, but it is far more ancient than most of the others, excepting perhaps Damascus itself. We are a noble city with fine and ancient buildings, and a pure and dependable water supply, so we have fine wine and sweet fruit, and lack nothing needed for a civilised life.

"I think the trouble across the river is all rooted in the stupidity of King Herod Antipas – not a patch on his renowned father, Herod the Great. He should have known that taking his brother's wife would bring retribution from heaven. I never understood why he brought that crazy prophet John into his house. He should have left him, along with all those other fanatics at Qumran, to rant away in the desert. It was a great mistake to keep John in his own palace, knowing that he had offended heaven by taking his brother's wife. Why should anyone do that?

"Anyway, it was this John who proclaimed the man Yeshua (or, as we Greeks would say, Iesus) from Nazareth to be the Messiah long promised to the world. After that we saw such turmoil. Not far from here, it is said Yeshua cast a legion of devils out of one poor man, and sent them into a herd of swine. Imagine that! But now there are so many followers of 'the Way', as they call it, and there is trouble among the Jews. I believe they will end up rising against the Romans again, and who knows where that will lead except for bloodshed and destruction? Have they not seen enough of that in the past? Mind you, the followers of the Way who live here seem peaceable enough."

What are the facts?

Our fictional court official in Abila gives us a non-Jewish and non-Roman perspective on the time of John the Baptist. The two verses above from the beginning of Luke chapter 3 provide one of the most thorough cross-referencing of dates seen anywhere in ancient history. While we cannot be sure to within more than a couple of years or so when Jesus was born, Luke's Gospel tells us when the ministry of Jesus began (following the baptism by John). The lives and deaths of the Herods are all very well chronicled by Josephus. He makes no mention of this Lysanias, but the likelihood is that he is a son (or possibly grandson) of the Lysanias son of Pompey who became a ruler over a far greater territory which included Abila.

- The fifteenth year of Tiberius Caesar was 26 AD. He became co-regent with Augustus in 12 AD, from which time he had authority over the provinces (including Judea). He became sole ruler in 14 AD until his death in 37 AD). The 'Regnal year' count to 26 AD includes 12 AD.[9]

- Pontius Pilate was governor of Judea from 26 to 36 AD.
- Herod Antipas (son of Herod the Great) was tetrarch (minor king) of Galilee and Perea from 4 BC to 39 AD (when he was replaced by his nephew Herod Agrippa, who was also given Abila).
- Philip (son of Herod the Great) was tetrarch of Iturea and Trachonitis from 4 BC to 34 AD. He married Salome, the daughter of Herodias.
- An inscription found at Abila shows Lysanias was ruling there at a date sometime between 14 and 29 AD.
- Annas and Caiaphas were successive high priests. (Annas served from 6 to 15 AD, Caiaphas to 36 AD.) Caiaphas was son-in-law to Annas, so although Annas had been replaced, he continued to act as if he was high priest for the rest of his life. Five of his sons also became high priests.

These are six separate historical statements, which all interlock so that there can be no doubt about when the work of John the Baptist took place, and therefore when the ministry of Jesus began. The year was 26 AD. The most doubt in the past has been expressed about the identity of Lysanias, and it was suggested that Luke had mistakenly identified a ruler who was executed in 36 BC by Mark Anthony. The implication of that false allegation was that if Luke could have been mistaken about this detail, then many of the other things he wrote could be wrong.

Archaeological evidence now confirms that there was a ruler in Abila named Lysanias at the appropriate time, and Luke's reputation is vindicated. This short section establishes the historical accuracy of the

[9] For a full discussion of the dates of Tiberius' reign, see Ron Wallace's writing in the Bible Fragrances website:
www.biblefragrances.com/studies/tiberius.html
26 AD is the best option, though 29 AD remains a possibility. This would move the date of the crucifixion to 33 AD.

setting of Luke's Gospel. If he got these details right, then we can be comfortable that what he tells us about John and Jesus is accurate also.

There is archaeological evidence of early Christian churches at Abila, which would fit in with the references to the activity of Jesus in the region in Mark 5:14-20 and Mark 7:31.

During this era, communities of religious 'fanatics' lived around Qumran by the Dead Sea. Some were Messianic sects, with esoteric teachings which set them apart from mainstream Jewish beliefs and worship based on the Jerusalem Temple. Their lives and beliefs have been discovered with the finding of the Dead Sea Scrolls, many of which were written or maintained by these communities, and hidden in a time of trouble – probably between 66 and 69 AD – in the caves where they were found in the latter half of the 20th century.

Comment

The way of life adopted by John the Baptist is completely consistent with what is known about Judea at the time. There was a lot of interest in and enthusiasm for Messianic teaching, and the cults based at Qumran give a lot of evidence for this (in the Dead Sea Scrolls). The life and behaviour of Herod Antipas is well attested. We cannot independently confirm that John was cousin to Jesus, born six months earlier (because the Temple records which would have shown this were all destroyed in 70 AD), but we have enough historical cross-references to be comfortable that this narrative is an accurate record of what happened.

Reference links

John McRay's 2005 book, *Archaeology and the New Testament,* gives very comprehensive information on this subject. Summary details of his work are at: *historeo.com/web/?p=104*

Wikipedia gives a full overview of Lysanias: *en.wikipedia.org/wiki/Lysanias*

A review of archaeology finds at Abila up to 2004 is at: *www.bibleinterp.com/excavations/Abila_of_the_Decapolis.shtml*

Ron Wallace: *www.biblefragrances.com/studies/tiberius.html*

CHAPTER EIGHT

The Crucifixion of Jesus Really Happened on a Day of Earthquake and Darkness

Now when the sixth hour had come there was darkness over the whole land until the ninth hour. And at the ninth hour Jesus cried out with a loud voice saying, "Eloi, Eloi, lama sabacthani?" – which is translated, "My God, my God, why have you forsaken me?"

Mark 15:33-34 (NKJV)

A Christian woman in Pella, 70 AD

"People who have come from Jerusalem recently tell me that there are now hundreds of crucified bodies lining the roads leading out of the city. The Romans have taken a terrible revenge for the rebellion against their rule. And they say that all that was beautiful in the city is in ruins, and the Temple of our God is no more; even the very stones have been taken away because the soldiers wanted the gold that melted into them during the great fire. The 9th of Ab that happened, the very same day of the year that Nebuchadnezzar's army burned the Temple of Solomon all those centuries ago. And yet the cruelty of the Romans only follows the bloodshed caused by the Idumeans and even our own Jewish zealots, as they fell on one another in a time of blood and madness. They say the very Temple courts were awash with the blood of the slain. Many of those who tried to escape the fighting and famine inside the city were caught by the Roman soldiers and gutted like fish – do you know, the soldiers believed they had swallowed gold and silver coins?

"But why would any of us want to go back there now? Truly, the glory is gone from Jerusalem, and we have the commandments of our Lord Jesus to follow. And nothing that is happening now could be more terrible than that day forty years ago when they crucified our Lord. I was only a little girl, but my mother took me to see. There were many of our womenfolk who followed Jesus. Do you know that some of our great men of faith, even our apostles, had their courage fail them that day? But the women – the mother of our Lord, and his aunt and others he had blessed and ministered to – were there at the end. I remember the sky going dark. Do you know, we saw the stars shining as if it were night time, all that long afternoon? And the earthquake kept shaking and shaking the ground. Buildings fell in many towns and cities, I have heard, even as far away as Asia.

"That morning, my mother had taken me to the north side of the city, and we saw Jesus being brought out. There were crowds of women, and many wailed and cried out with grief when they saw him. I shall never forget what I heard him say, 'Daughters of Jerusalem, do not weep for me; weep for yourselves and for your children.'[10] The elders say that he also told the apostles that the Temple would be destroyed so that not one stone would stand on another. Now we know just what terrible things those prophetic words meant!"

What are the facts?

Our fictional (Jewish) Christian woman tells us what it was like to experience the crucifixion of Jesus at close quarters, and the fall of Jerusalem forty years later from a distance.

It is beyond reasonable doubt that Jesus was a man who lived in Galilee and Judea at the time the Bible says, and that he was crucified by the Romans. Writing around 49 AD, Suetonius reports troubles in Rome between Jews and Christians. Tacitus, writing about 112 AD, writes in detail about how Nero persecuted Christians in Rome in 64 AD. Josephus, writing his histories in the later part of the 1st century,

[10] Luke 23:28 (NIV).

also mentions Jesus, his crucifixion and resurrection, and the martyrdom of his brother James in 62 AD.

Several early Christian writers record the history of the church from these early days. Eusebius and Epiphanius both tell about how the Christians all left Jerusalem in 66 AD in response to their belief in a prophecy of Jesus:

> *For days will come upon you when your enemies will build an embankment around you, surround you and close you in on every side, and level you, and your children within you, to the ground; and they will not leave you one stone upon another, because you did not know the time of your visitation.*
>
> *Luke 19:43-44 (NKJV)*

In 66 AD the Roman army started besieging Jerusalem, exactly as described in this passage, but then left unexpectedly only to return less than four years later and finish the job. According to Eusebius, the Christians went first to Pella in Perea, to the east of the Jordan. The character in the story above is one of these people.

The fact that the Christians in Jerusalem all left the city when they saw the first encirclement by the Roman army under Vespasian in 66 AD meant that they were not present to experience the terrible scenes four years later, when Vespasian's son Titus returned to finally put down the rebellion. Forty years after Jesus was crucified, the entire city was destroyed in a horrendous bloodbath, with different groups within the city fighting each other viciously as well as the Romans.

The events of the day of Jesus' crucifixion are reported by the pagan historians Phlegon of Tralles, and Thallus. Both of them separately report a three-hour darkness during the time of Caesar Tiberius (Phlegon specifying the 18th year of Tiberius; i.e. 30 AD), which they both say was an eclipse of the sun, though Phlegon notes that it was during a full moon. The discussion of later Christian writers (Julius Africanus, Origen) about the testimony of these two writers centres on explaining the impossibility of a three-hour solar eclipse, and also the impossibility of a solar eclipse during a full moon. Phlegon mentions that the stars could be seen, meaning that the darkness was not caused by clouds, dust or smoke. We are left with a profound mystery if we want to explain what happened that day.

The earthquake is well-attested in secular records, and was felt as far away as the city of Nicea and region of Bithynia, both located in modern Turkey. Interestingly, these are places located at the far end of the major fault line that runs up the Jordan Valley past Jerusalem.

Given how few writings have survived from the world of the Roman Empire in the 1st century AD, how small a group of people the early Christians were, and what a seemingly minor person Jesus was (a poor builder...) the number of references from the non-Christian literature of this era is impressive.

Crucifixion as a method of carrying out the death penalty was used by the Romans until it was outlawed in 313 AD. Josephus records that, following the siege of Jerusalem in 70 AD, the soldiers used nails to fix the men to the crosses. He also says that they crucified so many men that they ran out of places to put the crosses and wood to make them with. His account of the fire which destroyed the Temple says:

> *The Temple Hill, enveloped in flames from top to bottom, appeared to be boiling up from its very roots; yet the sea of flame was nothing to the ocean of blood, or the companies of killers to the armies of killed: nowhere could the ground be seen between the corpses, and the soldiers climbed over the heaps of bodies as they chased the fugitives.*
>
> *Josephus, The Jewish War*
> *Transl. Williamson, G. A.*
> *Revised by Mary Smallwood (1981) p. 359*

The Romans removed all the stones of the Temple because of the gold which had melted into them, thus fulfilling the prophecy that Jesus had made as he looked across at the Temple Mount with his disciples:

> *Do you see all these great buildings? Not one stone shall be left upon another, that shall not be thrown down.*
>
> *Mark 13:2b (NKJV)*

The fact that it was forty years from when Jesus made this prophecy to when it was fulfilled is believed to have caused discouragement in the early church prior to 70 AD.

The details mentioned by the character in the story above are only a glimpse of the horrors recounted by Josephus from the siege of Jerusalem and its aftermath.

Comment

In recent times, many scholars have attempted to claim that the Jesus of the Gospels is a fiction. This is to fly in the face of some of the best evidence available for the existence of any historical character of ancient times. The events that took place during the crucifixion of Jesus (earthquake, darkness) are matters of independent record.

No feasible explanation can be given for a natural event which resulted in the three hours of darkness during the daytime when stars could be seen. This was no solar eclipse or passing thunderstorm. More striking than this, though, is the complete lack of any writer of ancient times attempting to claim that the resurrection of Jesus did not happen. If it had not taken place, and Jesus had died on the cross and remained dead, then the body would be available to deny the resurrection. Despite the very high level of official interest in the case, nobody attempted to produce a body (even falsely) to try and prove he had not risen from the dead. This is a case where the absence of evidence is the best evidence of all for the resurrection.

The date of the 9th of Ab is mentioned. This is indeed the date on the Jewish calendar when the first Temple was destroyed in 586 BC and again in 70 AD.

Reference links

Blood on the Mountain: A History of the Temple Mount from the Ark to the Third Millennium; Richard Andrews; BCA (1999).

Phlegon of Tralles on the passion phenomena:
www.textexcavation.com/phlegontestimonium.html

A good review of the historical sources mentioned above can be found at:
www.blueletterbible.org/Comm/mark_eastman/messiah/sfm_ap2.html

A summary of archaeological evidence for the early church, at:
www.uncover.org.uk/questions/does-archaeology-confirm-the-new-testament/

The Antiquities of the Jews; Josephus (translated by William Whiston, 1867); available at: *sacred-texts.com/jud/josephus*

Chapter Nine

Paul's Shipwreck on Malta

Now when the fourteenth night had come, as we were driven up and down in the Adriatic Sea, about midnight the sailors sensed that they were drawing near some land. And they took soundings and found it to be twenty fathoms; and when they had gone a little farther, they took soundings again and found it to be fifteen fathoms. Then, fearing lest we should run aground on the rocks, they dropped four anchors from the stern, and prayed for day to come. ... When it was day, they did not recognize the land; but they observed a bay with a beach, onto which they planned to run the ship if possible. And they let go the anchors and left them in the sea, meanwhile loosing the rudder ropes; and they hoisted the mainsail to the wind and made for shore. But striking a place where two seas met, they ran the ship aground; and the prow stuck fast and remained immovable, but the stern was being broken up by the violence of the waves.

Acts 27:27-29,39-41 (NKJV)

A girl on Malta

"Of course, now they call that place St Paul's Bay, but it had another name when I was a little girl. The word went out all around that there was a ship wrecked in the bay, and everyone hurried to get down there. We were hoping there would be good cargo washed ashore, but really, we could use practically everything that came off the ship except its main cargo, the wheat. And that's what there was lots of: wheat soaked in salt water. No use to man or beast! The amazing thing was, all those people got ashore safe, hundreds of them. Not one body floating in the surf. Not that bodies scared me, even then when I was little. I'd seen a few come in, and from the first they looked pretty harmless to me, I couldn't see how they could frighten anyone. Mind you, if the fish had been at their faces, you could get a bit of a shock when you turned one over!

"My first thought was how we would deal with all those people. They tell me now there were nearly three hundred, and winter was coming on and – where would there be food for them all? But we knew our gods and the honour of our people meant we had to be good to strangers and travellers. I had never seen a ship so big before – my father said it was 120 cubits long[11]. As the waves broke it up over the following weeks, so much good timber came ashore that several families were able to repair and add to their homes and barns. I could not understand what the people were saying, because I had not yet learned the Greek tongue.

"My mother explained they were saying it was a miracle they had all survived; a holy man on the ship had seen an angel. We got busy making fires to dry them all out; I was sent into the woods to get sticks. Then I saw that one of the travellers was bitten by a snake. It turned out he was the holy man, whom we learned later was St Paul. The second miracle was that he did not die from the snakebite, and the third was when he healed the father of our First Man who was dying from sickness. After that, all who were sick went to him for healing, and he told our people about Jesus Christ as he healed them.

"Publius, our First Man, became our Christian leader, and many of us became Christians after those days, even though many preferred to keep their allegiance with the old gods. We now call Publius our Bishop."

---

[11] Approximately fifty metres.

What are the facts?

This fictional girl helps us to get an idea what it would have been like to experience seeing the wreck of the great Alexandrian grain ship which Paul travelled on.

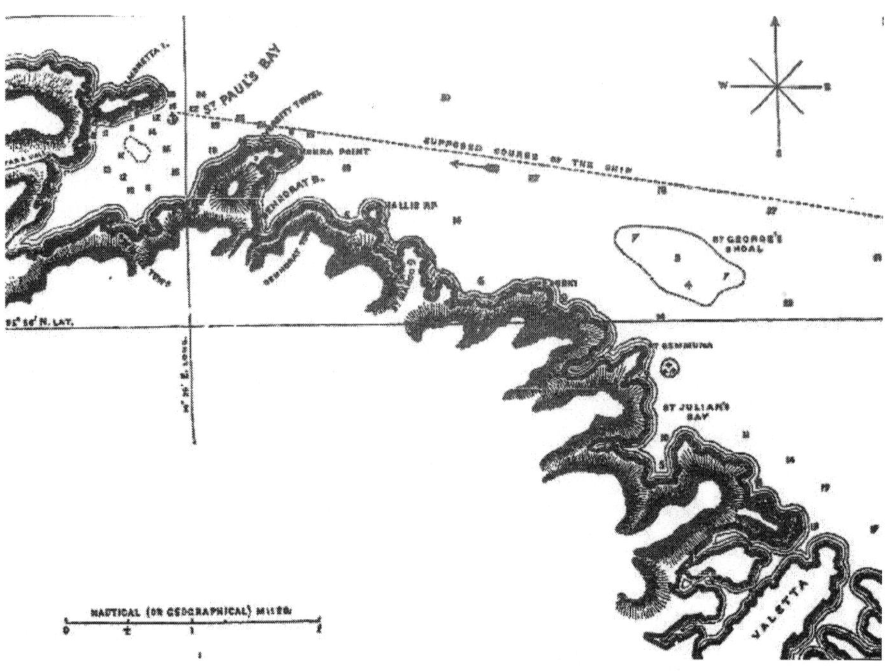

Figure 8. Probable final route of Paul's ship before being wrecked on Malta. Source: The Voyage and Shipwreck of St Paul; James Smith Esq. (1856); p. 124.

The whole account of this voyage that ended with the shipwreck in Malta has been checked against the prevailing winds and currents in the Mediterranean. The storm and the direction of the winds is exactly what would be expected, and in the storm conditions described, the drifting time between Crete and Malta has been calculated as thirteen days (a distance of nearly nine hundred kilometres). The size of the ship (big enough to carry a cargo and 276 passengers and crew) is consistent with the large Alexandrian grain ships. One third of all the wheat supply from Rome came from Egypt, and although the time of this voyage is after the normal 'end of season' for sailing cargo vessels on the Mediterranean, it is known that the Romans would pay a large bonus for extra cargoes delivered at this time, after the end of the main shipping season.

The details of the shipwreck itself tie in with the conditions in and around St Paul's Bay, Malta. A very similar thing happened to HMS Lively, a British navy 38-gun frigate, which was wrecked there on the night of 20 August 1810, also during bad weather and easterly winds. This sailing ship was a very similar size to Paul's ship, at forty-seven metres long with a twelve-metre beam and a full complement of three hundred men. The court martial records show that the lookout first warned of danger when he saw the surf breaking on Koura point, about four hundred metres off the course for St Paul's Bay. The sound of this surf breaking in the dark is almost certainly what the sailors on Paul's ship "sensed"[12]. Trying to anchor a drifting ship from the stern in a gale is a desperate measure, and with the stone anchors of the day (and a ship of that size) one not likely to succeed. The Lively's crew also tried this, but failed as they made the attempt farther out and the anchor did not hold. The Lively was then blown onto the rocks at Koura Point, and ran aground.

Exceptionally for the region, however, the seabed once inside St Paul's Bay itself is very firm clay, and an excellent anchorage. The risk of being 'pooped', when waves break over the stern and swamp the ship, remained high. Most ships are designed on the assumption that the bows will always be turned into any severe sea. The anchors meant, however, that the ship would not 'broach', or turn sideways to the sea – if this had happened it would have probably turned over and sunk quickly. The crew also appreciated that, with land so close, they would almost certainly not have sea room to turn the ship around, so they set it up to run ashore in the safest way possible. This plan was thwarted by a shoal some distance from the beach on which it grounded. The shoal had to be soft enough for the ship to slow and stop, rather than crash and break up. Again, there are two creeks flowing into St Paul's Bay which could have deposited mud, so even though there is not a shoal there now, the conditions are there which could have formed one in the past.

---

[12] Acts 27:27 (NKJV)

On Malta today there are no forests, nor any snakes. There is no sandy beach in St Paul's Bay. All these are features very likely to have changed over the course of two thousand years. The clearing of the forests could easily have eliminated the habitat for the snakes, and the soil erosion associated with deforestation at the time could well have accounted for a mud shoal in the bay which has since been washed away.

Archaeology has shown that the title given to the head person on the island was indeed 'First Man' (a literal translation of the words translated "chief official" in Acts 28:7). Throughout the book of Acts, the author Luke consistently shows his mastery of the many different titles of officials in every part of the Roman Empire, and this is no exception. The tradition on Malta is that the first bishop of the Christian church was Publius. Archaeology and contemporary histories cannot validate the report that Paul saw an angel, nor that he survived a snakebite, nor that he healed Publius' father. The reader has to weigh the reliability of the events that can't be validated against those that can and have been.

Comment

Scholars during the past 150 years have felt entitled to approach these narratives from a position of extreme scepticism, and to challenge the veracity of almost every part of the book of Acts and the life of Paul. Using these standards, virtually none of the surviving histories of the ancient world could be accepted. The detailed analysis of this voyage, based on a report by someone who is clearly not a sailor himself, shows that it is an eyewitness account. The earliest surviving document naming this place as 'St Paul's Bay' is some four hundred years later, but that is still very ancient testimony. The probable date of this shipwreck is early in November 59 AD.

Reference links

The main resource for this chapter is: *Evidence & Paul's Journeys: An Historical Investigation into the Travels of the Apostle Paul;* Jefferson White; Parsagard Press, Hilliard OH (2001). Details can be found at: *pauls-journeys.com*

A good short summary of the events leading up to Paul's wreck is at: *jeffersonwhite.com/pauls-journeys/pauls-shipwreck-2/*

A very full account of the voyage together with comparisons made by expert mariners of the 19th century can be found in *The Voyage and Shipwreck of St Paul* by James Smith, available for download at: *ia601405.us.archive.org/32/items/voyageandshipwr02smitgoog/voyageandshipwr02smitgoog.pdf*

Details of HMS Lively (Launched in 1804, and 10th ship of that name in RN service) can be found at: *en.wikipedia.org/wiki/HMS_Lively_(1804)#cite_note-LL051010-11*

CHAPTER TEN

The Seven Churches of Revelation Were in Real Cities

I, John, both your brother and companion in the tribulation and kingdom and patience of Jesus, was on the island that is called Patmos for the word of God and the testimony of Jesus Christ. I was in the Spirit on the Lord's Day, and I heard behind me a loud voice as of a trumpet, saying, "I am the Alpha and the Omega, the First and the Last," and, "What you see, write in a book and send it to the seven churches which are in Asia, to Ephesus, to Smyrna, to Pergamos, to Thyatira, to Sardis, to Philadelphia, and to Laodicea."

Revelation 1:9-11 (NKJV)

A boy in Ephesus

"The elders of the church had been busy for several days copying the vision our great apostle John has written down and sent to us from Patmos. It is called the *Apocalypse.* I shall never forget the night they first read it out to the whole church in Ephesus. Hundreds came to listen, and most were shocked into silence at the amazing things we heard that were to come. Many said they were greatly encouraged, for things have become very difficult for Christians under Caesar Domitian.

"We had to have enough copies to take to the other six churches. My name is Michael, and I was twelve years old when my mother agreed with my father that I was big enough to go and help him and the others on the journey. I was very excited; I had never left Ephesus before. Three of the elders of our church travelled with us, and we were away for nearly six weeks. The elders read out the *Apocalypse* in every church we visited, and gave a copy into the hands of the elders of each church.

"At Smyrna, I heard one of the men in the church there say to my father, 'Isn't that amazing, in the message to your church, the Lord is contrasting His cross as the true "Tree of Life" to the famous tree of Artemis, which the unbelievers worship in your city?'

"My father laughed, and said, 'Yes, and there are more of those words of wisdom hidden in the messages to all of our churches!'

"I went up to my father after he had finished speaking to this man, and asked him what these 'hidden words' were. He looked at me, and said, 'The word of God says, "It is the glory of God to conceal a matter; to search out a matter is the glory of kings."[13] I want you, son, to study the words the Lord says to the churches, and to study the cities and churches we are visiting, and tell me what you have found. Remember, this vision of the apostle John is called the *Apocalypse* (which means "uncovering/revealing") for this very reason.'

"Here is what I found. Although I had never been allowed by my parents to enter the temple of Artemis in Ephesus, we all knew that it was built around a sacred tree. They also sometimes called the sanctuary area of the temple, where thieves and robbers hid from justice, their 'paradise'. I thought that the 'seven stars' might also be connected to the seven lights on the Menorah, the lamp stand of the tabernacle of our God.

"I started looking more carefully at Smyrna, which was a city nearly as big as Ephesus. It had many beautiful buildings, and I discovered that it was famous for having come 'back to life' as a city after it was destroyed in ancient times. They also said that the city had always stood for faithfulness, and its very name, coming from Myrrha, the mother of Adonis, could remind us of the Myrrh given by the Magi as a symbol of grief and suffering. I also found out that in Smyrna, families like my own who are of Jewish descent but follow Jesus as our Messiah have

13 Proverbs 25:2 (NIV).

been treated badly by Jews of the synagogue. The synagogue Jews wanted to declare that the Christian Jews were not entitled to the Imperial protection given to those who were listed on the synagogue rolls. I was grateful for the good fellowship we have in Ephesus with the synagogue Jews. Later on during the journey, I discovered the same problem was happening in Philadelphia, and clearly the Lord mentions it in the letters to both those churches.

"When we got to Pergamos, a three-day journey up from Smyrna, I was amazed to see the great citadel-hill rising up out of the plain. It was a very hard walk up the steps to the top, one thousand feet. I started looking for 'Satan's throne', and first I thought it was the great temple of Zeus, on the citadel, especially when I found it was decorated with serpents. Then I discovered they had a great temple of Asklepios, who is the god of healing they also call 'Saviour', and whom they worship in the form of a serpent – surely reminding us of Satan in the garden with Adam and Eve.

Figure 9. Great Altar of Pergamon – Satan's Throne? Pergamon Museum, Berlin. © Martin Johnson.

"Then I learned that the temple of Caesar Augustus, whom they called the 'Saviour of Mankind', was ranked as foremost in our whole province. This temple was the reason that our fellow believers risked facing the sword of the magistrates, because of the bitter rejection by the synagogue Jews. I saw then the connection with the 'double-edged sword' of the word of Jesus.

"At Pergamos also, I heard our elders arguing strongly with their elders about Balaam. Then my father saw I was listening, and he sent me on an errand to look after our two donkeys. I remembered Balaam was the prophet of old who had instructed the king of Moab to send young women to have sex with the Israelite men, so they would cease to do the work of God.

"At Thyatira, I knew we would see the foundries from where the famous special brass is made. They have many metalworking secrets at Thyatira – some say they have been handed down from the ancient Trojans. This city was not large or beautiful as the others had been; it seemed devoted to business activities. I learned that there were many guilds, which controlled what happened in the city from behind the scenes.

"One of the boys in the church there told me it was impossible to survive in business in the city without upholding the traditions of the guilds, and they had secret ceremonies which outsiders were barred from. They were also proud of their prophetess, a Sybil, who had the ability to see into the future. One of the leading women in the church was also a wealthy businesswoman, and she was always saying that Christians could not be harmed by the rituals of the guilds.

"Sardis was a city that, while not as big as Ephesus, had some of the grandest streets and buildings I had seen. They were also famous for the strength of their citadel, which was said to be impossible to capture. The truth was, I discovered, that this 'impregnable' fortress had been captured twice, because the guards were sleeping. Earthquakes had also weakened it badly, and much of the original citadel had fallen onto the lower city.

"I also thought that when the Lord called them to be dressed in white, that referred as a contrast to the purple cloth they made there. I heard some of the legends about King Croesus, who turned everything into gold. I was hoping to see gold being gathered from the Pactolus River, but my father said this was done a long way out of town, and we did not have the time. There was a big Jewish community in Sardis, but our elders were concerned that the elders of the church in Sardis made too light of the ways in which their people compromised their belief in Jesus, so they could have an easy life.

"Philadelphia was the smallest of the cities we visited. We got there in two long days of travel, arriving just as night fell. The church there was very friendly and welcoming. There were no grand civic buildings – they had too many earthquakes, they said. They were also badly troubled by the synagogue Jews, as we had found in Smyrna. Not only were these synagogue Jews insisting that those who had become followers of Jesus had to pay the Jewish civic tax, they were also insisting that they must renounce Jesus. Many of the church people lived and worked outside the city, where the ground was very fertile. Because of the financial support they had received following a great earthquake two generations earlier, the city had a new name, 'Neocaesarea', in honour of Caesar Germanica. I don't imagine anyone around knows it as other than Philadelphia, the city of brotherly love, famed for the two brothers who founded it. It is still the newest of all the cities we visited, even so.

"By the time we got to Laodicea, we must have travelled about 240 miles[14], and we had 120 to go before we got home. It had been quite a climb up from Philadelphia into the hills, and we were grateful for the hospitality when we arrived. Church people came in from both Hierapolis and Colossae to hear the *Apocalypse* being read out by our elders. I had been tricked into taking a drink from a fountain on the way into the city. I discovered not only was the water lukewarm, it also tasted vile and made me throw up. I didn't think it was nearly as funny as everyone else did! What I did find out was that the city was famous for its natural black wool and its wealth.

"The history of Philadelphia was that they had needed financial aid to rebuild after the great earthquake, but in Laodicea they were rich enough to fund the rebuilding themselves, and were proud of the fact. There was also a medical school, with a teacher called Demosthenes, famous for curing diseases of the eyes.

"After we left Laodicea, I spent one evening explaining to my father all that I had found out, linking the letters to the churches with the

---

[14] The mile was a Roman unit of distance, 1,000 'paces' (actually two steps, left foot to left foot). Approximately 1,500 metres.

cities they were based in. He smiled at me, and said, 'Well done!' He told me I had made a good start on understanding the hidden wisdom in the *Apocalypse,* but there was much more left to discover. He reminded me of our Jewish tradition – that there are four levels to understanding the scriptures – and that this book was every bit as much a part of scripture as the writings of the great prophets of the past!

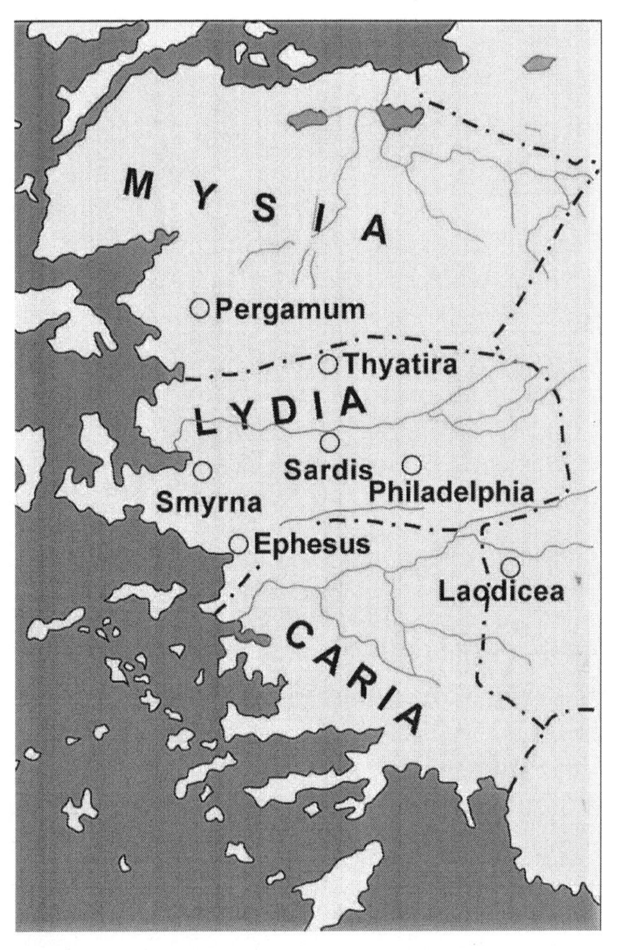

Figure 10. Location of the seven churches of Revelation in Asia Minor (modern Turkey). Courtesy: Bible History Online.

"Then he said, 'Our Lord said, "...the worker deserves his wages,"[15]' and gave me a silver coin. It was only after he left to talk to the other men that I looked at it and realised it was one struck in the year I was born, which I had often seen in the marketplace at Ephesus. It showed the infant son of the emperor, sitting on a globe and surrounded by seven stars. We are supposed to see this as showing how our emperor is the God of the whole world. John's vision of Jesus in the *Apocalypse* is a direct contradiction of this image and stands in opposition to all those who serve Satan from the throne of Imperial Rome!"

What are the facts?

Our fictional boy helps to walk us round the landscape of the seven churches listed in Revelation (*Apocaluptos* in Greek) chapters 2 and 3, on a route that corresponds with the natural roads of the region avoiding the high ground. It is highly probable that the vision received and recorded by John on Patmos would have been copied for circulation as soon as he got back to Ephesus.

The word 'Apocalypse' means the uncovering of things that are hidden, hence the title 'Revelation of St John' used for this book mainly in the Protestant tradition. The early church fathers all said that this book was written by the apostle John at a time when the emperor Domitian was on the throne of Rome, and that sets it at about 95 AD. Early tradition also holds that John died at great old age, about 100 AD, in Ephesus. Some argue that the persecution in view at the time was that of Nero, some thirty years earlier, but that makes no material difference to the details concerning the seven churches (and their cities).

The seven cities can all be easily identified on the landscape, and they would form a kind of circular tour, in the precise order they are listed. They can still be visited, and are now known by their Turkish names. Ephesus is close to Selçuk, Smyrna is Izmir, Pergamos is Bergama, Thyatira is Akhisar, Sardis is Sart, Philadelphia is Alaşehir, and Laodicea is Denizli. The total journey by road is now 752 kilometres, and should take eleven hours by car, according to Google

[15] Luke 10:7 (NIV).

Maps! The relationship of the geographical and historical reality of the seven churches of Asia to the things that are written in Revelation chapters 2 and 3 is very close, and far more detailed than the outline given in the story above. The book as a whole is written in a way that tightly links up with the Old Testament, with a traditionally Jewish use of symbols.

The reference to four levels of interpretation of scripture is part of the Jewish tradition now known as 'Kabballah'. These are:

- *Peshat,* the surface meaning of the text;
- *Remez,* allusions or allegories within the text;
- *Derash,* a rabbinic or midrashic way of reading new lessons into the text;
- *Sod,* the hidden mystical reading of the inner secrets of the text.

The information above includes several Remez-type allusions (e.g. "lukewarm" and "vomit" linked to Laodicea in Revelation 3:16), while understanding "Satan's throne" in Revelation 2:13 goes beyond allusions to local history, to the symbolism of the Roman rule and the emperor/state cult of worship.

It is probable that the "synagogue of Satan" at Philadelphia (Revelation 3:9, NKJV) "who say they are Jews and are not" refers to a group who have carried on the Samaritan form of Hebrew worship, which became corrupted with Babylonian practices including the use of pagan sexual practices in their cult.

Comment

The writer of this book was someone who himself was Jewish and had a very deep and thorough grasp of the Jewish scriptures, and yet was intimately familiar with these seven named cities of Asia Minor. The references to their history, geography, religion and culture are accurate and extensive. The narrative above only hints at the full extent of this. The setting in the changing scene of the Roman Empire towards the end of the 1st century AD is also absolutely authentic. Yet, while the book uses the Roman context as its base, it goes far beyond this in a way similar to the writings of Daniel and Zechariah.

Reference links

The main resource for this chapter is the book by *The Letters to the Seven Churches of Asia in their Local Setting;* Colin J Hemer; JSOT Press, Sheffield (1986). It can be found on Google Books at: *books.google.co.uk/books?id=r8_eBAAAQBAJ*

The Archaeology of New Testament Cities in Western Asia Minor; Edwin Yamauchi; Pickering & Inglis, Glasgow (1980); available at: *www.amazon.com/Archaeology-Testament-Cities-Western-Minor/dp/0720804825*

John McRay's 2005 book, *Archaeology and the New Testament,* gives very comprehensive information on this subject. Summary details of his work are at: *historeo.com/web/?p=104*

CHAPTER ELEVEN

Plate Tectonics and the Bible

Then God said, "Let the waters under the heavens be gathered together into one place, and let the dry land appear"; and it was so. And God called the dry land Earth and the gathering together of the waters He called Seas. And God saw that it was good.

Genesis 1:9-10 (NKJV)

You can see on any world map that there are the continents of North and South America, Europe, Africa, Asia (including the sub-continent of India), which extends all the way to the Kamchatka Peninsula, with Australia and finally Antarctica (bottom centre on nearly every map!)

The visible land is arranged in blocks. The big blocks are called continents and the smaller ones, islands. Maps of the ocean beds will show that there is a ridge running all the way through the middle of the North and South Atlantic Oceans. In the Pacific Ocean, there are several similar ridges, but also a major series of trenches. The Kuril-Kamchatka trench and the Japan and Marianas Trenches stretch south nearly to the equator. In the South Pacific, the Tonga and Kermadec Trenches continue southwards towards Antarctica. The great underwater ridges, mountains, volcanoes and trenches, "undersea features", were first identified in 1850, as a result of the many attempts to lay telegraph cables on the ocean beds around the world. The major feature between Tenerife and Barbados in the Atlantic, where the earth's mantle is exposed at the bottom of the ocean, was only explored for the first time in 2007.

By the beginning of the 20th century, a few scientists had noted that there were reasons to suspect that the lands on each side of the Atlantic Ocean had been connected at some previous time. The person who really triggered the debate was a young meteorologist called Alfred Wegener, based at the University of Marburg. He had gained his PhD in Astronomy at the University of Berlin. He became an expert in meteorology and climatology, and led many pioneering scientific expeditions on the Greenland ice cap where he met his death a day or two after his fiftieth birthday in 1930. His work in meteorology underpins current knowledge about the mechanisms by which raindrops form.

In 1915 Alfred Wegener published a book entitled *The Origin of Continents and Oceans,* which attracted little attention until its first English translation was published in 1922. In it, he details the wide range of geophysical connections between the coastlines of West Africa and South America and the Caribbean. They match closely to each other in shape. Even more compellingly, the rock formations and the fossils which they contain are the same on opposite sides of the Atlantic Ocean. Similar features are also evident when the coastlines of North America and Europe are compared; for example, the geology and geography of the Scottish Highlands closely resemble the Appalachian Mountains in the USA. An earlier theory of land bridges had been proposed to explain these features, in which the intervening terrain had at some time been washed away. Wegener showed how this theory could not be supported.

The real challenge was to find an explanation of how the land masses came to be separated. It was at this point that Wegener's ideas were challenged most strongly. He had thought that the continents were moving about on the earth's mantle rather like icebergs on the sea. The reaction of the leading international geologists to these ideas was extremely hostile, and led to Wegener being refused a professorship at his own university (Marburg), and being unable to get one anywhere else in Germany. He was finally appointed Professor of Meteorology and Geophysics at the University of Graz, in Austria, in 1924. In 1926 he presented his theory to an international symposium in New York, and faced hostility and sarcasm. While he was forced to conclude that the mechanisms causing continental drift had not been identified, he was sure they were the same forces responsible for producing the great fold mountain ranges such as the Himalayas and Andes, and other geological features such as earthquakes, volcanoes and the movements of the magnetic poles.

It was not until the 1950s, over twenty years after Wegener's death, that several geophysical discoveries convinced geological scientists that the continents did move, and that these movements did give rise to earthquakes, volcano eruptions, sea-level changes and the movements of the magnetic poles. The theory became known as Plate Tectonics. Wegener has now received posthumous recognition as the 'father' of this science.

Plate Tectonics theory assumes that all the continents of the earth were originally a single land mass (Wegener coined the tile 'Pangaea', now more usually spelt 'Pangea', which is Greek for 'every-land'). Around Pangea was a single ocean, 'Panthalassa' ('every-sea'). The continuing movement of the continents has been measured from space. The Atlantic Ocean is still widening very slowly by about fifteen millimetres each year.

Fernand Crombette, born near Lille in 1880, studied possible ways of 'reassembling' the land masses of today. He studied the outlines of the extreme edges of the continental shelves, where the depth of the ocean is two thousand metres. He found that if the contours of the oceans at this depth were compared, then an exact match could be made for all the continents. This resulted in a land boundary for Pangea that was a symmetrical shape, with eight scalloped edges, like the petals of a flower. This suggested to him that the original sea levels were two thousand metres lower than the present day. In the centre of this land mass, he noted, was Jerusalem. More recently, submarine drilling has confirmed that the two-thousand-metre depth level is where the edge of the continental granite shelf is to be found.

Figure 11. Crombette's reconstruction of Pangea.
Reproduced by kind permission of Ceshe.It.

There is also evidence that a very major population movement happened in extremely ancient times. Ancient written characters have been discovered in the Indus valley (in Pakistan) which are very similar to inscriptions found on Easter Island, literally on the opposite side of the world.

The Bible says...

Genesis 1:9 is quite unambiguous. It says that in the beginning when God created the world, all the land was in a single land mass – the original supercontinent now known as Pangea! Some people interpret Genesis 10:25 ("Two sons were born to Eber: one was named Peleg for in his days the earth was divided."[16]) as referring to the break-up of Pangea. Others take the view that this verse refers to the division into nations caused by the language break-up at Babel, and that the land break-up happened during Noah's flood. Either way, an enormous catastrophe is assumed to have taken place that resulted in the distribution of continents and islands which we know today.

Genesis 10:5 refers to 'the isles of the Gentiles': "From these the maritime peoples spread out into their territories"[17].

So, in between Genesis 1:9 (no continents, no islands, one land mass) and Genesis 10:5 (identified island-dwelling people across the sea) there has been a big change to the geography of the earth. Once there were no islands, now there are islands! The 'table of nations' in Genesis chapter 10 has been analysed and found to be a very accurate description of the origins of the known nations of the ancient world.

Crombette believed that Psalm 74:12 was an important clue: "For God is my King from of old, working salvation in the midst of the earth."[18] He reasoned that Jerusalem was the place where Jesus was crucified, and therefore the location at which God "worked salvation", and therefore the geophysical centre of the original world land mass.

Comment

Theories about what may have caused the land mass to break up vary, from an impact by a large asteroid or comet, to alternatively a basic geophysical instability related to density variations in the magma layers below the earth's crust, as well as various ways of combining these ideas. For the secular geophysicists, who prefer a very slow uniform rate of change, the date of this event is set approximately 250 million years ago (you get this date if you divide the width of the Atlantic Ocean by fifteen millimetres a year!)

The problem with uniform change is figuring out what started the continental drift. There is no credible evidence to support the idea that

---

[16] NKJV.
[17] NIV.
[18] NKJV.

the present rate of movement has been constant from the beginning, and much in geophysics that supports the idea of major changes beginning with sudden catastrophes. If the break-up of Pangea began with a catastrophe, then it is more likely than not that the initial rate of movement was far faster than anything that has been observed during the past century. In this case, the date of the break-up must be much more recent than 250 million years. As we will see, there is a strong bias within 'science' in favour of extending ancient dates back as far as imaginable.

The problem here is that the Bible has always contained this information. If the land break-up happened long before mankind existed, as some suppose, how did the writers of the Bible know about it? Indeed, the idea of an originally united land mass has only been confirmed by scientists in the past few decades. Moreover, amongst historical documents the Bible is unique in this information; you will not find any ancient creation legends from other texts that give information as exact and specific as this.

Imagine a time long ago, before anyone had mapped the world, before global travel by sea and air. How could people, with only the evidence of their own eyes of the lands and seas around them, have got such an idea that there was originally one united land mass with a single sea? But that is what the Bible has always taught.

Reference links

Overview of Plate Tectonics: *www.ucmp.berkeley.edu/geology/techist.html*

SC Links review Alfred Wegener: *www.pangaea.org/wegener.htm*

After the Flood: The Early Post Flood History of Europe Traced Back to Noah; Bill Cooper; New Wine Ministries (1995).

Review of Crombette: *crombette.altervista.org/en_index.htm*

CHAPTER TWELVE

The Bible and Cosmology

The heavens are telling of the glory of God;
And their expanse is declaring the work of His hands.

Psalm 19:1 (NASB)

It is hard today, when we have satellites out in space helping us navigate our cars and fill our TVs with hundreds of channels, to imagine how little mankind knew about space and the stars long ago. Nowadays, the moon landing projects of the 1960s are history topics for schoolchildren, and Google Earth gives us pictures of our homes taken from space, but as recently as five hundred years ago there were not even telescopes to look at the stars with.

Just standing on the ground, looking up at the sky, how much can a person figure out? What holds the earth up? What shape is it? Does the sun move around the earth, or the earth move around the sun? This kind of question has been occupying people's thoughts for a very long time.

From the 4th century BC through to the 16th century AD, a period of nearly two thousand years, the dominant view of the cosmos and its relationship to the earth was that of Aristotle and Claudius Ptolemaus. This held that the earth was at the centre of the universe, and that everything rotated about the earth. The universe was made up of a series of "celestial spheres", which held the planets and the stars. These spheres rotated around the earth. The mediaeval church adopted this view, because of the teachings of Thomas Aquinas (1225-1274), who was a priest. He became a highly-respected teacher in the church, and because he followed the philosophical teachings of Aristotle, so Aristotle's cosmology was adopted by the church. A consequence of this was that narrative statements in the Bible about the movement of the sun were interpreted as scientific truths. Therefore, if a scripture mentioned that the sun rose in the east and set in the west, then that was argued to prove that the earth did not move, rather than being a good description of how these events appeared to people on the ground.

In more recent times, the first person who challenged this cosmology was Nicolaus Copernicus, a gifted scholar scientist and astronomer from a part of Prussia (Germany) that is now in Poland. Copernicus worked in the early part of the 16th century AD. His book *De revolutionibus orbium coelestium (On the Revolutions of the Heavenly Spheres)* was printed in Nuremburg and published in the year he died (1543 AD). These ideas were picked up by Galileo Galilei (1564-1642). Galileo invented and developed several telescopes, so he could look at the stars and the planets. He believed that his observations validated the theories of Copernicus, and this led to a major controversy within the Church at Rome. Galileo was put on trial for heresy in 1633, as he was refuting the teachings of Aquinas, and he was forced to recant his belief that the earth circled the sun. It took another hundred years for the Church authorities to finally admit that Galileo's teachings were correct. He has since been called "the father of modern science" by Albert Einstein and others.

The Bible says...

> *He stretches out the north over empty space, and hangs the earth on nothing.*
>
> *Job 26:7 (NASB)*

The first part of this verse can be shown firstly to refer to the movement of the earth on its axis about the North Pole, orientated, as the ancients knew, to Polaris the pole star. This is the only star that does not move relative to the earth. Job says here that the north-pointing axis of the earth extends to Polaris through empty space. The word translated "empty space" is 'tohu', the word translated as "formless" in Genesis 1:2. Here it indicates the emptiness of space.

The second part of the verse is completely unambiguous: there is "nothing" supporting the earth. This statement can be categorised as a factual proposition about the planet. There is no hint here of "celestial spheres", or the arguments rehearsed by the ancient Greek philosophers or their followers in mediaeval Europe. This book of the Bible is estimated to be around 3,600 years old, so therefore this teaching has survived countless changes in the understandings and teachings of centuries of philosophers. And yet, how could a man from millennia before the age of telescopes and space exploration have known this?

> *And He took him outside and said, "Now look toward the heavens, and count the stars, if you are able to count them." And He said to him, "So shall your descendants be."*
>
> *Genesis 15:5 (NASB)*

> *As the host of heaven cannot be counted...*
>
> *Jeremiah 33:22a (NASB)*

Galileo is credited with inventing the first astronomical telescope in 1609, although there is evidence that telescopes had been made long before then. Isaac Newton invented the first reflecting telescope in 1668, and this became the dominant pattern in astronomical observatories for the next three hundred years. The challenge for a long time was how to make the biggest possible reflecting lens, in order to see more and more of the fainter stars. The biggest astronomical telescope to date is the six-metre diameter one at the Special Astrophysical Observatory in Russia, which opened in 1974, but the most expensive so far is undoubtedly the Hubble telescope in earth's orbit.

The Hubble telescope has a three-metre lens, and by being positioned outside the earth's atmosphere it can view the stars better and more clearly than any previous telescope. As each newer and better telescope has come into use, astronomers have been able to see more new stars and galaxies. Galileo's telescope increased the number of stars he could observe from about 3,000 to 30,000. The Milky Way galaxy where earth is located, is now estimated to contain 200,000,000,000 stars ($2x10^{11}$). With the help of Hubble, it is now thought there could be hundreds or even thousands of billions of galaxies in the universe.

The Hubble telescope helps to confirm that it is not possible to count even the number of galaxies in the universe, and since every galaxy is made up of vast numbers of stars, so the impossibility of ever counting the number of stars has been confirmed. Each advance in technology serves only to make the size of the problem more obvious. Hubble has even shown ever more clearly that each star is unique, varying in colour, size and intensity, confirming what Paul wrote in 1 Corinthians 15:1: "For one star differs from another star in glory..."

Figure 12. "Pillars of Creation".
Hubble public picture.

COUNTING STARS!

In Genesis 15:5 Abraham is challenged by God to count the stars. This challenge is affirmed in Jeremiah 33:22:

> *I will make the descendants of David my servant and the Levites who minister before me as countless as the stars of the sky and as measureless as the sand on the seashore.*[19]

Science has validated this biblical challenge in a way and to a degree that would have surprised the ancients. They would probably have imagined (before telescopes) that counting the stars could possibly be achieved if a man had enough time and was able to travel to the southern latitudes, to see the stars in those parts of the sky not visible to them. It has taken modern astronomy to confirm the absolute truth of these statements recorded some 2,500 and 3,600 years ago. The first half of this verse is a prophetic statement that is probably fulfilled nowadays for practical purposes: the spread of the Jewish people, including the descendants of David and the Levites, has been to just about every country in the world. Identifying all their descendants would now be impossible.

> *He counts the number of the stars;*
> *He gives names to all of them.*
>
> *Psalm 147:4 (NASB)*

The difference between God and mankind is plainly stated. Even though men will never even be able to count the stars, God not only knows their exact number, but He has named every one of them!

GOD'S PURPOSE FOR THE STARS

What is God's stated purpose for the stars?

[19] NIV.

Then God said, "Let there be lights in the expanse of the heaven to separate the day from the night, and let them be for signs and for seasons and for days and years; and let them be for lights in the expanse of the heavens to give light on earth"; and it was so.

Genesis 1:14-15 (NASB)

The stars are intended to be:

- lights which are separating day and night;
- for signs and seasons;
- marking days and years;
- for giving light on earth.

From the earliest times, the stars have been used as a calendar, which was vital for farming communities. They have also been used for navigation, especially at sea. The story of the Magi indicates that they were used as "signs" for special events, and indeed their light reaches the earth (when the light pollution afflicting our developed countries permits!) At first sight these are simple statements of fact, but they also set limits on the purposes of the stars, which has been exceeded from ancient times by the use of astrology, a form of divination.

AN EXPANDING UNIVERSE

Who alone stretches out the heavens...

Job 9:8 (NASB)

It is He who sits above the circle of the earth,
And its inhabitants are like grasshoppers,
Who stretches out the heavens like a curtain
And spreads them out like a tent to dwell in.

Isaiah 40:22 (NKJV)

Thus says God the LORD,
Who created the heavens and stretched them out...

Isaiah 42:5a (NKJV)

He has ... stretched out the heaven by His understanding.

Jeremiah 51:15b (NKJV)

Thus says the LORD, who stretches out the heavens...

Zechariah 12:1b (NKJV)

There was much scientific debate about whether the universe was static in size, expanding, or even prone to implode under its own gravity, until 1929. In that year, Edwin Hubble showed that galaxies were moving away from the earth and each other. This meant that the universe is indeed expanding, and has been from the start. Just as stated in the Bible.

Einstein's General Theory of Relativity triggered interest in the possibility that gravity propagates as waves through the space-time continuum, and they were first observed and measured in September 2015. Their discovery – or confirmation – did not so much solve a problem as create more: how is it that gravity waves can transport massive amounts of energy through a vacuum? The puzzle is to find out just what structure, fabric or field exists in space-time for this effect (gravity!) to work, highlighting just how much is not yet known about the universe!

Comment

The history of Western cosmology has been very turbulent, and scholars have attempted to use and abuse the Bible in support of their own beliefs. "He hangs the earth on nothing" (Job 26:7) is a simple factual statement. It should not be compared with verses beloved of the flat-earthers, such as Isaiah 11:12 and Revelation 7:1, which refer to the four corners of the earth.

In Isaiah, the prophet writes of the regathering of the people of Judah "from the four corners of the earth", and in Revelation the prophet sees "four angels standing at the four corners of the earth". People have tried to argue that the references to "four corners" mean that the Bible writers thought the earth was square (and flat), but this is an unreasonable interpretation of language. If we now refer to the "ends of the earth" or the "four points of the compass" using English, we would not expect people to infer that we were ignorant of the spherical shape of the planet.

Figure 13. Image of Earth from space, showing Arabia and Middle East. Courtesy: NASA.

Elsewhere in Isaiah (40:22) God is described as sitting enthroned "above the circle of the earth", which is an accurate literal description of the appearance of the earth from space, and implies a spherical shape.

> *Hubble's mission in space is to explore the solar system, and measure the age and size of the universe. Hubble's giant telescope searches for our cosmic roots, and charts the evolution of the universe. It also tries to unlock the mysteries of stars, planets, galaxies, and life itself.*[20]

This quotation, from one of the websites explaining the Hubble telescope, gives a clear indication of what many of its supporters hope to achieve. The importance of these projects can be gauged by the enormous sums of money spent on them. Six billion dollars could have made a vast improvement to the lives of people in several undeveloped

[20] *www.ezinearticles.com/?The-History-and-Achievements-of-the-Hubble-Telescope&id=35411*

countries, or contributed to eliminating one of the major diseases. Instead, it has been spent on this one aspect of space research. If you trust the Bible, you don't actually need to spend vast amounts of money to search for "cosmic roots" or "the mysteries of ... life itself". But, the Hubble project has unwittingly given an even clearer understanding of the statements in the Bible that mankind cannot count the stars.

Modern astronomy and ancient astrology are both attempts to divert the attention of people from God's original purposes in filling the heavens with stars.

The challenge in looking into a biblical cosmology lies not between 'scientific' propositions and the use of an everyday language. It comes when the Bible describes events that are obviously impossible on any rational scientific basis. This includes the 'long day' in Joshua 10:11-13, and the reversal of the sun's shadow in 2 Kings 20:9-11. You either have to accept that the Bible writers are truthfully recording what happened, and the happening has to be classed as a miracle, or that they invented fiction and intended to delude and deceive.

Reference links

For a discussion on the use of biblical language and cosmology, see: *www.answersingenesis.org/creation/v2/i3/genesis.asp*

For a history of Thomas Aquinas and his work, see: *plato.stanford.edu/entries/aquinas*

Martin Luther's approach to science in the Reformation: *www.leaderu.com/science/kobe.html*

Counting the stars: The vastness of the universe is cause for joy, not loneliness; Werner Gitt; Creation 19(2):10-13 March 1997. Available at: *www.answersingenesis.org/creation/v19/i2/stars.asp*

The website for Hubble gives amazing pictures of the universe: *hubblesite.org*

For a discussion of the expansion of the universe: *www.physicsoftheuniverse.com/topics_bigbang_expanding.html*

A brief summary of the Gravitational Wave measurement system, LIGO: *space.mit.edu/LIGO/more.html*

CHAPTER THIRTEEN

The Bible and Oceanography

Have you entered into the springs of the sea?
Or walked in the recesses of the deep?

Job 38:16 (NASB)

Despite several imaginative and highly dangerous underwater experiments, the first practical submarines did not appear until the late 1890s. World War 1 was the event which forced a rapid development in these craft, though it would be decades later before submarines capable of descending more than a hundred metres or so below the surface of the sea were made. Diving developed with other naval technology in the 19th and early 20th centuries, but divers could only go down to about a hundred metres at most until more recent times. This meant that, apart from shallow coastal waters, men's activities have been limited in the main to the top layers of oceans that go down many thousands of metres.

The first true deep-diving machine, William Beebe's Bathysphere, descended to about one thousand metres in 1934. Not until 1960 did Jacques Piccard and Donald Walsh descend in the Bathyscaphe Trieste to the bottom of the Challenger Deep near the Marianas Islands, which is more than 10,900 metres deep. More recently, the deep-sea submersible Alvin has made many dives to depths around 1,800 metres. What has been found on the ocean floors has startled scientists. The Alvin's missions have resulted in the discovery of 4,700 new species of marine life, including giant tubeworms on the floor of the Pacific

Ocean; and even locating the wreck of the Titanic in the Atlantic. The two-thirds of the earth's surface that was hidden beneath the oceans held many more surprises.

Springs of the sea

By the 1930s it was suspected that submarine volcanoes might be emitting water, and in the 1940s the development of sonar systems ('echo sounding' – developed to detect submarines) meant that many undersea volcanoes were being located. The first shallow-water hot springs were identified along the coast of Baja California in the late 1960s. The first deep-sea springs were located on the Mid-Atlantic ridge in 1973, and then some spectacular springs were found using the Alvin on the Galapagos rift in 1977. Some of these are spouting superheated water at temperatures up to 400°C (water at temperatures far above its normal boiling point is possible because of the high pressures at the ocean floor). It has been estimated that as much as 160 cubic kilometres of water (forty cubic miles) flow out of earth's oceanic springs each year from these 'vents'.

Figure 14. 'White Smoker' undersea vent.
Courtesy: US NOAA.

Paths of the sea

Matthew Maury (1806-1872) was a US Navy officer who founded modern oceanography. He studied a vast amount of material, including thousands of ship's logs, reports of the sightings of whales, and the results of 'drift bottles', bottles designed to drift with the ocean currents. His work was recognised internationally, and by encouraging ship's captains to understand the currents he had identified flowing in all the oceans of the world, they were enabled to reduce their sailing times by days and even weeks when crossing the oceans.

He began this research because he had read Psalm 8:8: "...and the fish of the sea that pass through the paths of the sea."[21] He deduced from this verse that there were "paths of the sea", regular routes where water flowed consistently. This simple insight was the basis of the science which followed.

The Bible says...

FOUNTAINS OF THE GREAT DEEP

> *In the six hundredth year of Noah's life, in the second month, on the seventeenth day of the month, on the same day, all the fountains of the great deep burst open...*
>
> *Genesis 7:11a (NASB)*

Not only does the Bible say that there were "fountains" under the oceans, but that these were the primary cause of Noah's flood. Creationist scientists have speculated that these could have resulted from water below the earth's crust being forced out under considerable pressure as the crust split.

Recent reports from NASA using images from the Hubble telescope have suggested that water plumes have possibly been observed erupting through splits from under the thick ice crust on Europa, a moon of Jupiter, jetting up to 190 kilometres into space. The photos taken in 2014 show this happening around the south pole of Europa. Could these be similar events to the "fountains of the great deep" during Noah's flood?

---

[21] NKJV.

Figure 15. Photos of possible water plumes from Europa. Courtesy: Hubble/NASA.

SPRINGS OF THE SEA

> *Have you journeyed to the springs of the sea or walked in the recesses of the deep?*
>
> *Job 38:16 (NIV)*

This passage explicitly links the bottom of the oceans to the location for the "springs of the sea". Given that these have only been identified in recent decades, we must conclude that the writer of Job had access to accurate geophysical knowledge only recently recovered by mankind.

Job 38:16 contains a challenge: "Have you ... walked in the recesses of the deep?" No man who has ever lived could yet answer yes, unless they only mean the shallowest coastal waters. The deep-diving submersibles have carried men down to the depths of the main oceans, but the conditions and technology available are such that it is still impossible for men to get out and walk. Men have walked on the surface of the moon, but not yet on the floor of the deep oceans of the world.

PATHS OF THE SEA

Matthew Maury is a wonderful example of a man who, believing his Bible was true and accurate when it spoke of the physical world, built a science which has benefited sailors and travellers for the past one and a half centuries.

FROZEN OCEANS

Can you imagine if you had never been to the Arctic or Antarctic, and had never seen books or films about these places? If someone at the seaside pointed at the sea, with waves pounding in towards the beach, and told you that it could all freeze, how easy would it be to believe them?

Job 38:30 says:

> *The waters harden like a stone and the surface of the deep is frozen.*[22]

The book of Job was written, as has been noted earlier, about 3,600 years ago. The setting for Job and his life, the land of Uz[23] is widely agreed to be in Arabia. While it is not unlikely that Job may have seen the sea, this would have been the Persian Gulf, the Red Sea, the Indian Ocean, or just possibly the Mediterranean. How would such a man know that the sea could freeze?

Comment

We can take time to study and think about whether the "springs of the sea" with their present flow rate of 160 cubic kilometres of water each year are related to the "fountains of the great deep" that caused Noah's Flood and were then "stopped" (see Genesis 7:11; 8:2). To reflect on this passage, we must consider that the only survivors of the flood were closed up in Noah's Ark, and therefore were poorly placed to see what happened. They also started their journey with the Ark on dry land. How did they know first that there were "fountains" under the deep ocean, and that these helped to cause the flood?

Similarly, we must ask if Job was a witness to an ice age – but the ice caps are believed never to have been as far south as Uz. And while some ancient seafarers may have told David, the author of Psalm 8, that they used predictable currents in their sailing, even they could not have known that these applied all over the world. The accuracy of each these statements is far beyond the likely knowledge or experience of any

---

[22] NKJV.
[23] See Job 1:1.

contemporary people, and yet they are accurately recorded in writings dating from around 3-4,000 years ago.

Reference links

Oceans – the Sea Floor: www.bbc.co.uk/dna/h2g2/A2082962

Europa plume observations report in The Guardian:
www.theguardian.com/science/2016/sep/26/jupiter-europa-water-plumes-nasa

Dr Walt Brown has calculated the possible pressures involved if there had been large volumes of water beneath the earth's crust, and the conditions that could have caused the crust to split: *www.youtube.com/watch?v=sD9ZGt9UA-U*

Springs of the Ocean, by Steven Austin at: *www.icr.org/article/180*

The Remarkable Record of Job; Henry Morris; Master Books, Green Forest AR (2000); available at: *www.amazon.co.uk/remarkable-record-job-henry-morris/dp/0890512922*

A History of Matthew Maury, Wikipedia:
en.wikipedia.org/wiki/Matthew_Fontaine_Maury

More on Maury at: *www.answersingenesis.org/creation/v11/i3/maury.asp*

CHAPTER FOURTEEN

The Bible and Meteorology

When it is evening you say, 'It will be fair weather, for the sky is red'; and in the morning, 'It will be foul weather today, for the sky is red and threatening.'

Matthew 16:2-3a (NKJV)

In Matthew's Gospel, Jesus quotes one of the oldest known weather sayings, which is generally true, as the red sky at night usually means that bad weather is moving away to the west, leaving better weather behind it, while red sky in the morning usually means a weather front is moving towards you, carrying bad weather with it. On another occasion, he cites a weather proverb concerning the south wind, which clearly applies to the territory of Galilee and Judea (as a south wind will have travelled across a lot of very hot and dry land first):

And when you see the south wind blow, you say, 'There will be hot weather'; and there is.

Luke 12:55 (NKJV)

Modern meteorology can be much more precise, using observations of the movements of air masses, with details of the amounts of moisture they are carrying, and their temperatures and pressures. Central to all of this are two main factors: the circulation of the air masses and the winds they cause; and the 'water cycle'. This is the term for the way water evaporates from the oceans and seas, is carried up into the sky where it will form clouds, which will then under the right conditions precipitate, giving rain, hail or snow. This falls to earth, where ultimately it travels into the river systems and thereby back into the oceans. Thus, all the water in the rivers derives (one way or another) from precipitation from the clouds, and the water cycle is the complete description of how water circulates from sea to land and back again

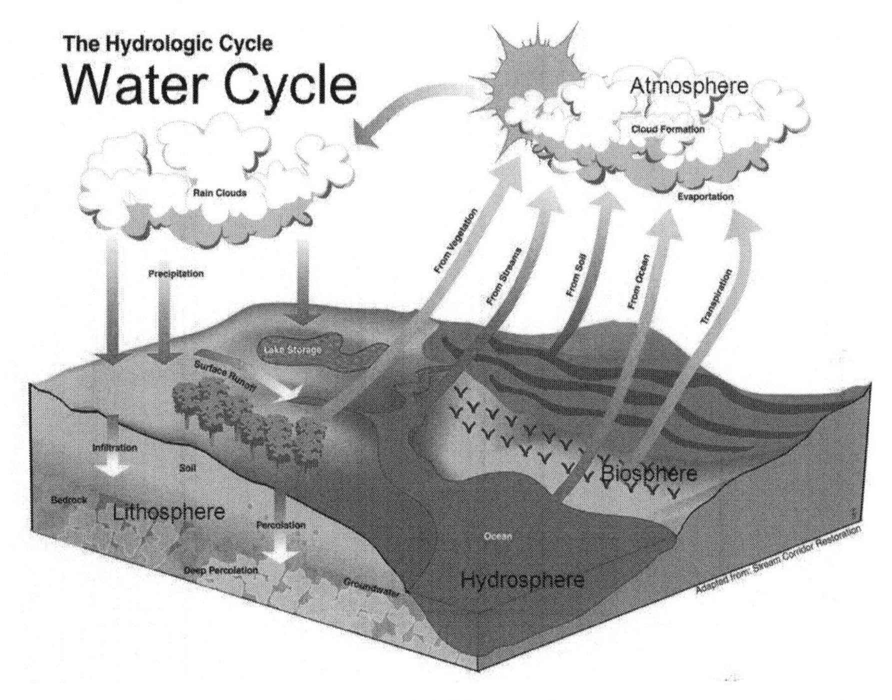

Figure 16. Water cycle.

It may seem obvious to us now, but in modern history this was first stated by Bernard Palissy, around 1580 AD. It took nearly a hundred years before Pierre Perrault tested this scientifically, and even then, this did not achieve mainstream scientific acceptance until the early 19th century. Until this time, it was generally held that rain via the water cycle produced insufficient water to feed all the rivers, and that water arose from below ground to feed them. This view can be found in Homer (ca. 800 BC) and even Leonardo da Vinci (1500 AD). We now know that springs of water emerge from geological strata after water has filtered down through the rocks from ground above where it first arrived as rain or snow. The existence of springs, however, is enough to make the older beliefs not appear illogical.

The Bible says...

For He draws up the drops of water,
They distill rain from the mist,
Which the clouds pour down,
They drip upon man abundantly.
Can anyone understand the spreading of the clouds,
The thundering of His pavilion?

Job 36:27-29 (NASB)

All the rivers flow into the sea,
Yet the sea is not full.
To the place from which the rivers flow,
There they flow again.

Ecclesiastes 1:7 (NASB)

These two statements, from around 1,600 and 1,000 BC fully encapsulate the water cycle. As opposed to the teachings of men for the best part of two thousand years (at least) the water cycle does not rely on subterranean springs arising from below the earth, almost in contradistinction to the fact that there are indeed springs feeding the bottom of the main oceans! There are also some interesting verses which indicate the weight of water held in clouds, though this could readily be derived from observation and experience (i.e. rainwater gathered up can be heavy...), but this in turn means that the atmosphere itself has enough substance to hold the clouds up:

He wraps up the water in His clouds,
And the cloud does not burst under them.

Job 26:8 (NASB)

Also with moisture He loads the thick cloud...

Job 37:11 (NASB)

When He imparted weight to the wind...

Job 28:25 (NASB)

The Bible also describes the circulation of the atmosphere:

> *Blowing towards the south, then turning toward the north; the wind continues swirling along, and on its circular courses the wind returns.*
>
> *Ecclesiastes 1:6 (NASB)*

This statement from three thousand years ago again could have been based on careful observation and reflection, but it does betray assumptions about the size and shape of the earth, and is a long way from the personification of the winds in popular culture (e.g. "The north wind doth blow and he doth bring snow," etc.).

Galileo and Torricelli between them established that air did have weight, and that this amounts to just over 1 kg per square metre mass (1.225 kg/m^3). You can see the gap between science and practice here, though, as sailors from the beginning of time used the fact that wind exerts pressure to drive their ships, and any experienced sailor would have a very good idea of just how much force wind could exert against a sail.

The experience of a storm on Lake Galilee gave rise to this comment, reporting the view of the apostles who included a group of experienced sailors, describing the effect of a "contrary" wind lifting the water into waves, thereby demonstrating the power and force of wind:

> *But the boat was now in the middle of the sea, tossed by the waves, for the wind was contrary.*
>
> *Matthew 14:24 (NKJV)*

The statement in Job, "he imparted weight to the wind", combines this knowledge with the assumption that air itself has mass.

Comment

We can see that some of the most ancient texts in the Bible speak accurately of the water cycle, and the nature and movement of the atmosphere, and this would hardly be cause for comment except when contrasted against the incorrect views of 'scientific authorities' until much more recent times.

Reference links

'Red sky at night' and other sayings: *www.metoffice.gov.uk/learning/learn-about-the-weather/how-weather-works/red-sky-at-night*

A good article on the operation and history of the water cycle: *en.wikipedia.org/wiki/water_cycle*

The weight of air, in nature: *www.nature.com/nature/journal/v78/n2022/abs/078294a0.html*

CHAPTER FIFTEEN

What About the Age of the Earth?

First of all, you must understand that in the last days scoffers will come, scoffing and following their own evil desires. They will say, "Where is this 'coming' he promised? Ever since our fathers died, everything goes on as it has since the beginning of creation." But they deliberately forget that long ago by God's word the heavens came into being and the earth was formed out of water and by water. By these waters also the world of that time was deluged and destroyed.

2 Peter 3:3-6 (NIV)

When Charles Darwin wrote *The Origin of Species* (published 1859) he said in his foreword that anyone who "does not admit how incomprehensibly vast have been the past periods of time may at once close this volume". It has become axiomatic that the evolution of species has taken place over thousands of millions of years. Nowadays, vast periods of time such as the earth having been formed 4,500 million years ago, the universe being 13.8 billion years old, or even the dinosaurs having been wiped out 65 million years ago are stated as established facts.

It comes as a surprise to modern readers with scientific training to discover that the theory of evolution is still unproven. For example, Professor Harrison Matthews FRS, a leading British evolutionary biologist, in his foreword to the 1971 edition of *Origin of Species* wrote:

> *Belief in evolution is thus exactly parallel to belief in special creation – both are concepts which believers know to be true but neither, up to the present, has been capable of proof.*

The main basis for deciding a 4.5-billion-year age for the earth is radiometric dating, while the main estimates for the age of the universe derive from its recently-measured rate of expansion, supported by cosmic background radiation.

It is generally assumed that there is a firm scientific basis for determining the age of the universe and the earth, and that the dates assigned to rock formations are indisputable. What we shall see is that the preferred dating system is the one that gives by far the greatest range of ages, and that in turn it is based on a very short series of experimental data, a set of assumptions that may not be correct and some very contradictory evidence.

In his book *How Old is the Earth,* Dr A J Monty White, one of many modern scientists who have reached similar conclusions, examines the various dating systems by which it is possible to date our planet. Measurements of the rate of decay of the earth's magnetic field, for instance, show that 10,000 years ago at the present rate, the magnetic field would have been far too strong for life to exist. Of all the available systems, the only ones which give dates in the order of millions of years are those based on the decay of radioactive minerals such as uranium. Here we will take a look at the science involved.

How good is radiometric dating of rocks?

Early work in nuclear physics indicated that the nuclear decay parameter (I), was a constant. Radioactive decay is believed to be a spontaneous, random event that is not affected by the age of the decaying atom. It was, and is, generally believed that decay rates are unaffected by external parameters, such as:

- pressure;
- temperature;
- electromagnetic fields; and,
- differing chemical environments.

Accurate measurement of nuclear decay has taken place only since the beginning of the 20th century, with experimental data recording decay rates at up to three or sometimes four significant figures. This experimental data itself indicates a degree of variation in decay rates, which typically can be up to one part per thousand per year. If the rates of nuclear decay are, in fact, variable, then ages for rock formations and the earth as a whole which are based on these must also be variable. Just how sure can we be that nuclear decay is indeed constant?

And if it may have changed, then how much impact could that have on the estimates for the age of the earth?

The case for a changing nuclear decay parameter

- External parameters can affect nuclear decay by as much as 5%.[24]
- Radioactive decay is not actually a spontaneous event, but is triggered by neutrinos from the neutrino sea.[25]
- Radiohalos in minerals such as mica indicate a change in decay rate with time.
- Some investigators claim there is experimental evidence that the speed of light may have been faster in the past. The energy of emitted particles from an atom's nucleus is related to the speed of light; the half-life of an atom is related to the energy of the emitted particle by the empirical Geiger-Nuttal relationship. Therefore, it follows that if the speed of light is slowing down, then so is radioactive decay.
- Experimental data into the measurement of the half-lives of long-lived isotopes has a precision of around one part per thousand. This is not important when short time periods are involved, but is when the length of time is greater. For example, a one part per thousand variation in a million years means a

---

[24] *Thousands, Not Billions: Challenging an Icon of Evolution: Questioning the Age of the Earth;* Donald B DeYoung; New Leaf Publishing Group (2005). Recommended reading for anyone wanting to study the details of nuclear decay data.

[25] *Michelson's Hunch was Right;* H C Dudley; Bulletin of Atomic Scientists, University of Illinois Medical Centre (1975).

variation of one thousand years if decay is a linear arithmetic progression.

Theory

Consider these three possible cases for the pattern of radiometric decay:

- the disintegration index, I, is constant;
- the disintegration index, I, varies linearly with time (i.e. the rate of change is constant);
- the disintegration index, I, varies exponentially with time (i.e. the rate of change is itself changing).

When each case is modelled mathematically, the variation between the various models is shown as Figure 17. This graph shows a plot of half-lives ($T\frac{1}{2}$) versus the decay constant (α).

Also shown on Figure 17 are the most important radionucleides used in radiometric dating (U238, K40, Ru87 and C14). These four radionucleides are said to have half-lives of 4.5 billion years, 1.2 billion years, 47 billion years and 5.73 thousand years respectively.

Figure 17 describes the values for the half-lives of these radionucleides for constant, linear variation and exponential variation.

With the possible variation in the precision of the decay constant, it is quite possible that an exponential variation of the decay constant exists. This means that the rate of decay itself is changing, so what appears to be a slow rate of decay measured at a late stage in the process could actually show a much greater rate of decay at an earlier stage. The amount of radioactive decay that took one hundred years at the end of the process could have happened in ten years, or one year or even a few hours at earlier stages in the process.

The difference between the constant model and the exponential model is described most clearly in the case of U238, where it is seen that the half-life is reduced by orders of magnitude. For constant decay, the half-life of U238 is 4.7 billion years; the exponential case indicates a half-life for U238 of 10,000 years.

We have insufficient data to validate the assumptions.

If this small amount of exponential variation does occur in the nuclear decay index, then the half-lives of the radionucleides may reduce by several orders of magnitude.

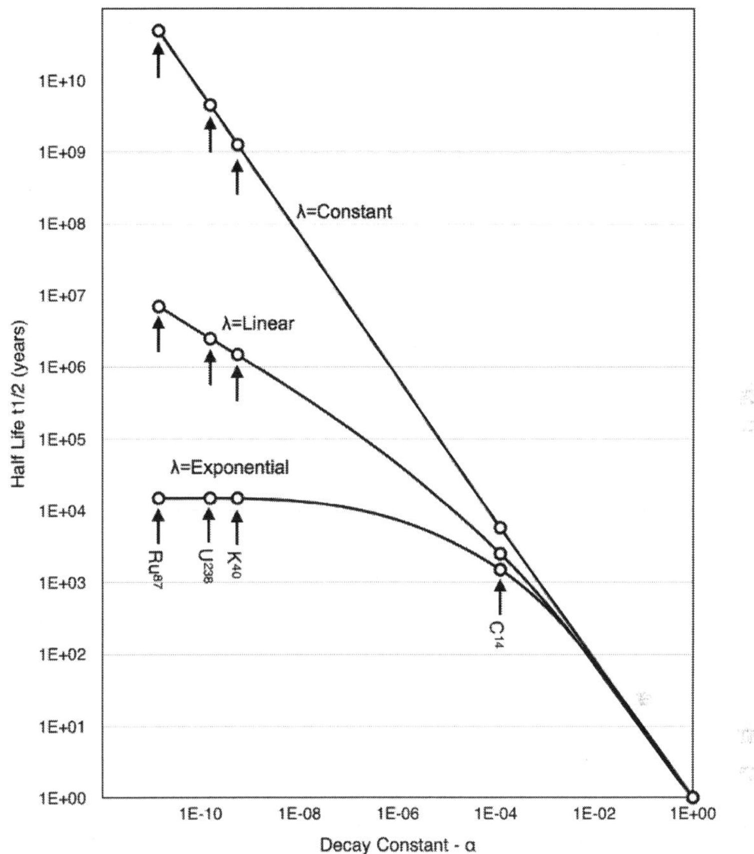

Figure 17. Y (vertical) axis: 1E+04= 10,000 years; 1E+10 = 10,000,000,000 years.

As can be seen in Figure 17, the same sets of measurements can, with different sets of assumptions about the nature of radioactive decay rates, produce ages ranging between around 10,000 years (10^4) and 10 billion years (10^{10}). In his book, A J Monty White cites some examples of rock formed (from volcanic eruptions) within the past few hundred years which have been found to have radiometric ages dated in excess of one million years, so at the very least, there is cause for doubt. These include two-hundred-year old lava near Kilauea, Hawaii radiometrically dated at 22 million years, and volcanic rocks from Faial Azores, Tristan da Cunha and Vesuvius formed within the last few hundred years radiometrically dated in excess of 100 million years.

Studies into the rates of erosion on the Hawaiian Islands show a great disparity between radiometric dating and what is actually happening (current measured rates of erosion indicate the islands can only have been there a few thousand years, rather than the radiometrically-measured age of many millions of years).

The Bible says...

As noted in 2 Peter 3:3-5 above, it was foretold that people would deny the validity of the biblical account of creation and flood, and use this to attempt to discredit the teaching of Jesus, especially regarding His return as judge of all mankind. The Genesis record does not support an age for the planet greater than ten thousand years (unless major violence is done to the plain meaning of the Hebrew text). The apostle Paul wrote:

> *...nor to devote themselves to myths and endless genealogies. These promote controversies rather than God's work – which is by faith.*
>
> *1 Timothy 1:4 (NIV)*

The "endless genealogies" relate to Eastern religious thinking, which some Christians were attempting to 'blend in' with Christianity in a heresy called Gnosticism. They implied a never-ending passage of time, in a similar way that can be found in modern Hinduism. The question of origins has always been, ultimately, an argument about belief. The Bible says that we have to choose what to believe by an exercise of faith, which implies that evidence will always be contentious.

Comment

Several of the scientists working at the time of Darwin had as their main objective the denial of the story of the worldwide flood of Noah. This was because they wanted to deny the existence of the God of

Abraham, Isaac and Jacob – and Jesus. There is no doubt that Darwin's teachings were seized on by many who wanted to promote social evolution, such as Karl Marx, and also the evolutionary racism of Hitler's Nazi Party. Yet the scientific study above shows that the same evidence regarding nuclear decay can be used to support an age for Earth of 4.7 billion years or of 10,000 years.

There is probably no other arena of work where data gathered over a relatively short period of time would be allowed to be extrapolated 45 million times (100 years into 4,500,000,000) to produce a publicly accepted figure as has been done with radiometric dating of rocks.

Reference links

A useful resource on methods of dating the age of the earth can be found in *How Old is The Earth?* Dr A J Monty White; Evangelical press, Welwyn (1985). He gives some background to his views at: *theevolutioncrisis.org.uk/testimony1.php*

A brief history of the discovery of radioactivity: *way2science.com/radioactive-decay*

Consequences of Time Dependent Nuclear Decay Indices on Half Lives; Rybka; Impact No. 106 (1982); at: *www.icr.org/article/200*

Age of the universe: *www.space.com/24054-how-old-is-the-universe.html.* Also in Wikipedia: *en.wikipedia.org/wiki/age_of_the_universe*

Age of the earth, a summary in Wikipedia: *en.wikipedia.org/wiki/age_of_the_earth*

Overview of radiometric dating: *en.wikipedia.org/wiki/radiometric_dating*

Several more anomalies in radiometric dating are provided in: *creation.com/radioactive-dating-anomalies*

A discussion of the implications of the decay of the earth's magnetic field: *www.icr.org/article/9695*

Minuscule Erosion Points to Hawaii's Youth; Tim Clarey, Ph.D. in: *www.icr.org/article/9751*

CHAPTER SIXTEEN

Light Moves

Then God said, "Let there be light," and there was light. And God saw that the light was good, and God separated the light from the darkness.

Genesis 1:3 (NASB)

The closing years of the 20th century and the first decade of the 21st century have been exciting times for those physicists working in fields connected with the speed of light. In January 2003, the New Scientist reported a successful experiment by Ed Formalont and Sergei Kopeikin who had become the first people to measure the speed of gravity. They showed that (within the limitations of the experiment) gravity travels at the same speed as light. This had been suspected for a long time, but never demonstrated until then. The speed of light was proposed as a constant by Einstein in 1917 which relates to a very wide variety of other things in the physical universe (such as the viscosity of fluids and the rate of decay of radioactive minerals).

In February 1999, Lene Hau, a scientist at the Rowland Institute in Cambridge Massachusetts reported how she had led a team which created a new state of matter. This state of matter, called a Bose-Einstein condensate, involves ultra-high vacuum and super-low temperatures, causing an extreme density of atoms. Although Albert Einstein and the Indian physicist Satyendra Nath Bose had proposed that this new kind of matter was possible in 1924, it was first created in 1995. The 1999 report by Lene Hau explained how they had used a

Bose-Einstein condensate to slow light down from its normal speed of 299,792 kilometres per second to 60 kilometres per hour. Subsequent experimenters have managed to slow it even further. In 2003, Mikhail Lukin reported that his team of scientists had managed to completely halt a beam of light using this technology.

In a different type of experiment, in 2015, Dr Jacqueline Romero and Dr Daniel Giovanni at Glasgow University reported that they had managed to slow photons down using a masking device so that they continued travelling at the slower speed even when they were returned to free space. They said they had achieved this by "altering the shape" of the photon.

The idea that light could exist in the form of "packets" was first proposed by Max Planck in 1901, and these were described as "quanta" soon afterwards by Albert Einstein (1905), giving rise to what is now known as 'quantum physics'. The word 'photon' as applied to discrete 'particles' of light became widespread after being used by Arthur Compton in 1928. So light could be conceived of as both a wave and a particle.

And while nothing can travel faster than the speed of light, a number of physicists have proposed that the speed of light itself may have changed. In his 'Variable Speed of Light' (VSL) theory, Professor Joao Magueijo argues for just this, with light possibly travelling up to sixty times its present speed in the past. This theory is an attempt to overcome anomalies in the 'Big Bang' cosmological model currently dominating this field, including that the universe has expanded a lot further than it appears to have had time for (this is known as the 'Horizon Problem').

In any event, there is now universal agreement that light travels, even if what it is and how it operates seems to become ever more bewildering for the non-physicist.

For much of history, however, famous philosophers held to the view that light did not move – or that it was infinitely fast (which is the same thing, for practical purposes). This shows the influence of Aristotle in scientific thought. Galileo (1564-1642) reported an experiment to test the speed of light, but said all it showed was that light travelled at least ten times faster than sound. Isaac Newton (1642-1727), who is credited with 'discovering' gravity, and creating the laws of mechanics, agreed that light moved, but thought that gravity was static (or "instantaneous").

A series of experimenters, beginning with the Danish scientist Ole Römer in 1676, devised methods to measure the speed of light. Römer's experiment using Io, a moon of Jupiter, was flawed because of inaccurate measurements of the solar system, but by about 1850 two French scientists, Fizeau and Foucault, both produced results close to modern measures. Albert Michelson, a US Navy researcher, produced a figure of 299,940 kilometres per second in 1879. Improved techniques are now recording a speed of 299,792 kilometres per second.

The Bible says...

There is a surprisingly large number of references to light in the Bible, many of considerable spiritual importance (light can refer to the presence of God, the "garment" of God, the role of God's word, the presence of Jesus, the presence of the people of Israel, the presence of those who follow Jesus etc.).

The 'physics' of light in the scriptures, though, are very consistent.

- *Light is created by God.* See Genesis 1:3 (above). It is formed by God; Isaiah 45:7 says, "I form the light..." 'Forming' here is the Hebrew word 'yatsar', meaning that it has form or substance and can be shaped – as is now being done by experimenters.
- *Light moves.*
    - It is "sown" (i.e. scattered) in Psalm 97:11.
    - It travels (Hebrew word 'derek', meaning 'to journey') in Job 38:19,24.
    - It is "sent" (Hebrew word 'shalach' meaning 'send forth, send out') in Psalm 43:3.
    - It "rises" or "comes forth" or "comes in" (Hebrew words 'zarach' and 'bo') in Psalm 112:4 and Isaiah 60:1.

These features of light contrast strongly with the biblical view of darkness, which only "resides" (Job 38:19), and although it can be "created" by the absence of light, is everywhere dispelled by the arrival of light.

I have come as a light into the world, that whoever believes in me should not abide in darkness.

John 12:46 (NKJV)

Comment

It has taken brilliant minds to work out what light is, and the rules it operates by. Even now, this is a field of developing science. The assumptions of a decade or so ago, that light moved at a fixed speed which had been constant for all time and was unchangeable, are being challenged. Many scientists are now being careful to point out that nothing they are discovering denies Einstein's theories, but they are also looking for new fundamental laws of physics to explain how the universe works.

Before the discoveries of the past century, people did not have any idea that light could be a kind of substance which could be formed, as is now understood. It is only in the past five hundred years that people have even understood that it travels and has finite speed.

The Bible was never offered as a manual on quantum physics, but its observations on the nature of light, while today uncontroversial, have been at odds with the scientists' opinions for about 1,800 of the past 2,300 years.

Reference links

Speed of gravity: *www.newscientist.com/article/dn3232-first-speed-of-gravity-measurement-revealed.html*

Electrical pulses faster than light: *physicsworld.com/cws/article/news/3630*

A review of Variable Speed of Light theories:
en.wikipedia.org/wiki/variable_speed_of_light and
www.dailygalaxy.com/my_weblog/2012/08/light-traveled-faster-in-the-early-universe-todays-most-popular.html

Critical geometry of a thermal big bang; Niayesh Afshordi and João Magueijo; Phys. Rev. D 94, 101301(R), 18 November 2016; at:
journals.aps.org/prd/abstract/10.1103/PhysRevD.94.101301
and a good lay explanation of the issues at:
www.dailymail.co.uk/sciencetech/article-3978402/Was-Einstein-WRONG-speed-light-New-theory-completely-change-view-universe.html

Glasgow 2015 experiments slowing light:
www.bbc.co.uk/news/uk-scotland-glasgow-west-30944584

Photons: *en.wikipedia.org/wiki/Photon*

Discussion of problems with (creationist) Speed of Light theories:
www.answersingenesis.org/docs2002/0809_cdk_davies.asp

CHAPTER SEVENTEEN

Information is the Key to Life

> *For you created my inmost being, you knit me together in my mother's womb. I praise you because I am fearfully and wonderfully made; your works are wonderful, I know that full well.*
>
> *Psalm 139:13-14 (NIV)*

Twins! Their parents' delight and joy, the two babies are gleefully investigating the new world around them. Created by the splitting of a fertilised egg soon after conception, virtually every single cell in the bodies of the two babies contains identical copies of DNA, the code that contains all the information needed for life. This code is composed of sequences of molecules called nucleotides, or bases, and these in turn are attached to long sugar phosphate strands that form the backbone of DNA. These strands of DNA ultimately form pairs, with bonds between the bases on opposing strands acting like 'rungs' on a ladder. Bound together in this way, the long strands of DNA twine around each other in a double helix formation. As the twins play and discover their own hands and fingers, they have no idea that the intricacies of their bodies are made possible by the most efficient information system known on earth. In fact, if the total knowledge contained in all the world's libraries (about 10^{18} bits) could be sorted using DNA, it would use only 1/100th the volume of a pinhead.[26]

The twins are also unaware of complex systems needed to translate the genetic information contained in their DNA into all the processes necessary to sustain life. Working unceasingly in their cells are large, complex protein molecules called enzymes. It is these enzymes that are able to 'unravel' the DNA helix to allow other enzymes to create the 'messenger' RNA that can be translated into all the proteins that the cell needs to maintain life. Of course, depending on where a cell is located (internal organs, connective tissue, skin etc.), it will only need to 'decode' certain parts of the DNA it contains in order to fulfil its function. Not only that, but this genetic information will only need to be expressed at certain times in the cell cycle. This is a very complex, self-regulating, self-regenerating and self-replicating system! It is also remarkably robust with editing and self-repair processes to weed out errors and damage to the DNA strand that results in mutations. Occasionally, however, non-repairable damage occurs and these mutations are almost invariably harmful, causing diseases such as cystic fibrosis, haemophilia and sickle-cell anaemia. Information has been lost, leading to disease and loss of viability. Conversely, there is no record of new genetic information arising spontaneously and no known way of producing new, meaningful genetic information.

Now the babies grow older and as features such as eye and hair colour emerge, the parents and wider family note familial resemblances and traits. These physical characteristics are caused by the expression of certain portions of DNA, known as 'genes'. As the children grow older still and enter into adulthood, people around them will notice some differences emerge, even though genetically they are still identical. This is due to the complex interplay between their 'genes', the non-coding portions of their DNA (previously called junk DNA) and their environment. This is the emerging field of epigenetics, where traits that cannot be explained by changes to the DNA sequence can be passed on to offspring. Although humans have been shown to carry only

[26] Information on the amazing information storage capacity of DNA can be found at: *reasonandscience.heavenforum.org/t2052-the-amazing-dna-information-storage-capacity*

approximately 35,000 genes, proportionally our complexity as living organisms is far, far greater. For instance, one gene present on the DNA strand may be affected by other genes or even a portion of non-coding DNA at a far distant site. The whole system is reliant on the information already present and the ability to 'read' and express that information. Without every part present and correctly functioning, the system will inevitably fail.

The Bible says...

By the word of the LORD were the heavens made,
their starry host by the breath of his mouth.
He gathers the waters of the sea as into a heap;
he puts the deep into storehouses.
Let all the earth fear the LORD;
let all the people of the world revere him.
For he spoke and it came to be;
he commanded, and it stood firm.

Psalm 33:6-10 (NIV)

Just as we have now learned that the information coded in DNA is part of an intricate information system, which orders the whole growth of a person, so the Bible says that God created the universe by a "word". In fact, the Bible says that information generation is an intrinsic aspect of God.

In the beginning was the Word, and the Word was with God, and the Word was God.

John 1:1 (NIV)

Using English, we tend to think of a word as a small set of letters which make up a single piece of information. The Greek word 'logos' translated "word" in John 1:1 and the equivalent Hebrew word 'dabar' mean not just the information, but also the delivery of that information. And the information content can be far greater than just one word, up to the complete set of instructions for the entire universe and everything in it.

We are now used to information as a concept distinct from the means of recording or delivering it. Up until the late 20th century, people would have found it hard to separate the information content of an encyclopaedia from the large quantity of heavy books it comprised. Today we can easily consider the difference between a blank DVD and one containing 8 gigabytes of information (e.g. a normal full-length film). We can see that information has no weight, is independent of time and space, and can vary in quantity or quality, so is dimensional. We are also familiar with how the enormous amount of information in a programme such as a Microsoft operating system is required to organise the component parts and systems of a computer in order that it will function as we want it to.

The proper application of 'dabar' or 'logos' constitutes 'wisdom'.

> *I, wisdom, dwell together with prudence; I possess knowledge and discretion ... The LORD possessed me at the beginning of his work, before his deeds of old; I was appointed from eternity, from the beginning before the world began ... I was there when he set the heavens in place, when he marked out the horizon on the face of the deep ...Then I was the craftsman at his side, I was filled with delight day after day, rejoicing always in his presence, rejoicing in his whole world and delighting in mankind.*
>
> *Proverbs 8:12,22-23,27,30-31 (NIV)*

A quotation attributed to one of the 'fathers' of modern evolutionary thought, T H Huxley, is that if a hundred monkeys had a hundred typewriters, eventually they would type out the works of Shakespeare. The famous science writer, Stephen Hawking, in his book *A Brief History of Time* modified it slightly to say, "...the well-known hordes of monkeys hammering away on typewriters ... very occasionally by pure chance will type out one of Shakespeare's sonnets."

Another scientist, Gerald Schroder, considered this statement, noting there are not quite five hundred letters in the sonnet *Shall I Compare Thee to a Summer's Day.* With a choice of twenty-six letters available for each space, the chances of the first letter typed being the right one is one in twenty-six. The odds of the second letter being the right one becomes one in 'twenty-six times twenty-six', and so on for every letter that follows. The odds of producing a complete sonnet from random typing then become a very, very big number – one with seven hundred zeros after it, 10^{700}! The size of this number can be better appreciated by noting that the estimated weight of all the matter in the universe is 10^{56} grams, while the number of basic particles (protons, neutrons, electrons, muons) in the universe is 10^{80}. Roughly speaking, there's a 10^{600} difference between all those subatomic particles and this single sonnet coming about by random chance. Unimaginably vastly remotely unlikely!

This simple fact has not put people off – there have been some attempts to demonstrate that random chance can produce intelligible text. Students at Plymouth University reported in 2003 that they had supplied a monkey house at Paignton Zoo with a computer keyboard, and let the six monkeys hammer away on it for a month. In that time, they failed to produce a single English word – not even 'A' or 'I' (on the basis that to be a word these letters need a space each side of them), let alone anything remotely intelligible. After one month the monkeys had broken the keyboard and were using it as a toilet...

A later 'test' by Jesse Anderson was reported in the Daily Telegraph in 2011, "Monkeys at typewriters 'close to reproducing Shakespeare'." In this test, however, they had confined the "virtual monkeys" (millions of small computer programs) to producing nine-letter sequences, with the system looking for words within those nine-letter sequences that appear anywhere in Shakespeare's works, and then matching them. They claim to have thus produced "99.9% of Shakespeare". A moment's thought will show that this exercise is flawed – as he needed to work with only 5.5 trillion permutations in the nine-character sets. The design of the experiment thereby reduced the scale of the problem by 10^{688}! And think about the intelligence and information that had to be applied to set the experiment up!

If it is inconceivable that random chance can produce a set of intelligible information even as short as a 500-letter text, then how could DNA have ever come about by chance? No-one would dream of suggesting that the operating system for the computer being used to produce this text could come about by random chance, rather than by teams of expert programmers. The only rational conclusion must be that all the information in the universe has an intelligent source. The smallest particle of matter operates according to its programming, and interacts with other particles according to strict rules, which is the only reason we can begin to understand how everything works.

> *By faith we understand that the worlds were framed by the word of God, so that the things which are seen were not made of things which are visible.*
>
> *Hebrews 11:3 (NKJV)*

The modern scientists exercise their faith in the intelligibility of the universe in their quest to better understand its workings and all the laws it operates by. If they did not believe that the universe is able to be understood, science itself would be pointless. The laws of science are a clear example of God's 'framing' the universe, showing that information in its various forms comes before everything else.

Comment

The Bible says that the whole creation process involved God, with Wisdom not only bringing everything into being, but also rejoicing in the creation. Proverbs 8:30-31 describes Wisdom in the same way as the Logos in John 1:1 – creating the world, with God, but also part of God. The whole of creation is therefore an information process. The nature of DNA, with its awesome data storage capacities, and its role at the core of all life's processes, is just one aspect of this.

Reference links

Information on the amazing information storage capacity of DNA can be found at: *reasonandscience.heavenforum.org/t2052-the-amazing-dna-information-storage-capacity*

God According to God; Gerald Schroder; Harper One (2009).

Monkeys and typewriters: *en.wikipedia.org/wiki/infinite_monkey_theorem*

A report on the attempt to use millions of "cyber monkeys" to recreate Shakespeare is at: *www.telegraph.co.uk/technology/news/8789894/Monkeys-at-typewriters-close-to-reproducing-Shakespeare.html;*
and its criticism:
www.cnet.com/uk/news/virtual-monkeys-recreate-shakespeare-methinks-not

Chapter Eighteen

Life is Still a Mystery

Remember him – before the silver cord is severed,
and the golden bowl broken;
before the pitcher is shattered at the spring,
or the wheel broken at the well,
and the dust returns to the ground it came from,
and the spirit returns to God who gave it.

Ecclesiastes 12:6-7 (NIV)

For decades, medical researchers struggled to find how to propagate human cell tissue *in vitro* (i.e. in a glass jar). Cells would live for a short while, but not replicate. Then, perhaps, they divided a few times and died off. In 1951, a breakthrough took place. While she was being treated for cervical cancer, in February 1951, doctors took a tissue sample from the cervical cancer of Henrietta Lacks. Henrietta lived in southern Virginia, and was thirty-one years old when she died eight months later in the segregated ward for blacks at the John Hopkins Hospital, leaving five children.

Henrietta's tissue sample was the first in medical history that kept dividing, continuing to live and propagate. This strain of cells, known as 'HeLa', has become famous in the history of cancer research, and provided the means for many medical breakthroughs including the development of the polio vaccine by Dr Jonas Salk. The descendants of the original cells are now in use in several research institutes around the world. Nobody knows for sure, but the total amount of tissue growing from these cells today is estimated to be vastly greater than the weight of Henrietta when she was alive.

Figure 18. Henrietta Lacks, born 1 August 1920, died 4 October 1951.

The profound paradox remains that, although Henrietta Lacks died in October 1951, human tissue with her DNA that was part of her has continued to live ever since. There is no suggestion that the living tissue has the 'personhood' of Henrietta, resembles her in any meaningful way, or has even attempted to grow as any form of identifiable human organ. But it lives on, and Henrietta is dead. There were (at least) two different forms or levels of life present in Henrietta Lacks, one of which survives and *is not her.*

Where life comes from and what it is continues to perplex scientists. In mediaeval times, it was assumed that human life would emerge if you mixed human semen with various materials (e.g. blood, flesh, even an egg). The alchemist Paracelsus (early 16th century) is one of many who claimed to have created a miniature 'synthetic' human known as a 'Homunculus' using these methods. Louis Pasteur was the leading scientist in the 19th century who demonstrated conclusively that life only came from living matter, and could not generate spontaneously.

We owe to him the medical technique of vaccination that protects us from many infectious diseases.

Even as Pasteur's work was going forward, a new philosophical problem was emerging, with the growing popularity of the theory of evolution. For this theory to be accepted, it was important to believe that life could come from non-life. There has been an enormous amount of research to try and identify conditions in which molecules could be formed that could ultimately become alive. This has even involved a range of experiments which would have been familiar in principle to Paracelsus, using chemical mixtures of different descriptions.

Current 'models' for the spontaneous creation of life include a range of different chemical mixtures and conditions. Possible conditions suggested have been a world rich in iron and sulphur; the inside of a deep-ocean vent ('black smoker'); a depth of several kilometres below the earth's crust; an oily bubble environment in a primordial ocean; and the "organic filling in a multilayer sandwich of mica sheets". None of the experiments arising from this work have shown any positive results.

Many respected scientists have reviewed this work, and argued that the propositions are impossible, either on the grounds of statistics or chemistry. The alternative solution proposed (e.g. by Sir Fred Hoyle) is that life originated somewhere else in the universe under conditions never found on earth and arrived here attached to space debris.

The important thing to understand is that, despite an enormous amount of scientific research and a considerable exercise of scientific imagination, life has never been observed to come from non-life. The story of Henrietta Lacks, while exposing another paradoxical situation, also shows the tremendous problems the scientists have had in trying to propagate and sustain life from living human cells.

Living organisms are present in abundance everywhere on earth, in the deepest oceans and deep under the ground, but it seems we do not even know what Life is. A creature that is alive is identical in the moment after it is dead in all the obvious ways we can measure. It has the same chemical composition, temperature etc. Except that a decay has begun which will see the body deteriorate in a very short space of time, and something has gone which cannot be weighed, measured or counted, called Life.

We have learned the techniques in intensive care wards of keeping the blood circulation and breathing going of someone who might otherwise be dead. These techniques have facilitated life-saving treatments, but have also created ethical dilemmas: at what point do you switch the machines off? But delaying death is completely different from creating life.

The Bible says...

The passage above from Ecclesiastes is typical of the biblical view: all life comes from God, and returns to Him. The reference to the "silver cord" has been compared to near-death experiences, where people have sometimes claimed to have seen something like a 'silver thread' connecting them to their bodies, before they return to life. This passage may contain more information than many realise.

> *And the LORD God formed man of the dust of the ground and breathed into his nostrils the breath of life; and man became a living being.*
>
> *Genesis 2:7 (NKJV)*

This verse carefully separates the formation of Adam's body from the material he was made of and the way he was brought to life. This strongly suggests that life is not an intrinsic property of the material world, but enters separately.

More prosaically, the Bible has always asserted that life relies on the circulation of blood. "For the life of a creature is in the blood..."[27]; "...the blood is the life"[28]. This points to the work of William Harvey, who is credited as the first person to have discovered the circulation of blood, with his publication in 1628, *On the Motion of the Heart and Blood.*

The word for "life" in these passages is 'nephesh', which is understood also to include the meanings of 'soul', a 'breathing being', the abode of 'emotions and passions'. Thus, blood and breath and personhood are intimately combined in the biblical view of what comprises life. A more abstract word, 'chayyim', is usually also

---

[27] Leviticus 17:11 (NIV).
[28] Deuteronomy 12:23 (NIV).

translated 'life', and this is found in passages such as "...the breath of the Almighty gives me life"[29]; "For with you is the fountain of life..."[30]. 'Chayyim' is more about the condition of being alive rather than coming to life. The word used for "spirit" in Ecclesiastes 12:7 (above) is 'ruach', which is also sometimes translated as "wind" or "breath". In the Bible 'life' refers both to the personhood of an individual and the means of animation. Paul, in his letter to Timothy, gives a clear summary of the traditional Jewish belief that God is the giver and source of life (in all its forms):

I urge you, in the sight of God who gives life to all things...

1 Timothy 6:13 (NKJV)

Does the Bible give any encouragement to those scientists who are trying to find ways of creating life from non-living materials? Is this an area where someone may use a biblical text as a clue to discovery? Proverbs 5:6 looks as if it could be directed specifically at such scientists: "Lest you ponder the path of life, her ways are unstable; you do not know them."[31] This seems to suggest that people will never find out how to bring something to life that has started as non-life; all their efforts will be futile, as this is something that can only be done by God. This is supported by five hundred years of failed scientific effort in this direction.

Ecclesiastes 3:21 says: "Who knows the spirit of the sons of men, which goes upward, and the spirit of the animals, which goes down to earth?"[32] This hints at different categories of life between people and animals, and is possibly supported by the Henrietta Lacks story. Life seems to have different categories, both in the Bible and as shown in recent scientific work.

Comment

Life is a force which is present everywhere on earth, and which is able to organise inorganic materials into living organisms. These living

---

[29] Job 33:4 (NIV).
[30] Psalm 36:9 (NIV).
[31] NKJV.
[32] NKJV.

organisms everywhere work against the second law of thermodynamics, by increasing the organisation and order of the material environment around them. Consider perhaps how a plant assembles water gases and minerals into sugars and other nutrients using the energy of sunlight, or how cattle rearrange the material contained in plants into their own ongoing mammalian life, which itself supports much wider ecosystems.

The question of the origin of life is being pursued with extremely dogged determination. Some of the sources listed in *Reference links* show how much time, energy and money is being invested in this quest. The philosophical paradox that does not seem to be explored is what it might mean if the means of creating life are discovered. We have a tremendous dependence (in areas such as medicine and food hygiene) on the fact established by Louis Pasteur that life does not come from non-life. Why should anyone assume that scientifically created life would be benign rather than harmful?

The real possibility that must be considered is that life enters the material dimensions from a dimension outside those of the material universe: space and time, matter and energy. It is as if the life researchers are people searching inside a room for the source of its light, which all the time is shining through the window from outside.

Reference links

The Cultivation of Human Tissue in Vitro; Joseph Loser and Albert Ebeling (1914);
jem.rupress.org/content/jem/19/6/593.full.pdf

The Henrietta Lacks story reported by the Smithsonian magazine:
www.smithsonianmag.com/science-nature/henrietta-lacks-immortal-cells-6421299

A background on attempts at creating 'Homunculus' in Wikipedia, at:
en.wikipedia.org/wiki/Homunculus

Review of theories of the creation of life:
www.answersingenesis.org/articles/ee/origin-of-life
en.wikipedia.org/wiki/origin_of_life
and from Science Daily:
Life On Earth May Have Originated As The Organic Filling In A Multilayer Sandwich Of Mica Sheets: www.sciencedaily.com/releases/2007/12/071204102500.htm

An account of the discovery of blood circulation by William Harvey, in Wikipedia at:
en.wikipedia.org/wiki/William_Harvey

CHAPTER NINETEEN

Food, Hygiene and Health

And the pig, though it has a split hoof completely divided, does not chew the cud; it is unclean for you. You must not eat their meat or touch their carcasses; they are unclean for you.

Leviticus 11:7-8 (NIV)

Are you feeling well? Perhaps you are experiencing nausea, and fatigue, feeling a bit feverish, sweating profusely, with pain and swelling around your eyes? Is your skin feeling itchy? Maybe you have a problem with constipation or diarrhoea? Getting a bit of chest pain? If the answer is yes, the doctor might ask you if you have eaten any undercooked polar bear lately! She might explain that, while your condition is quite treatable, if it is not treated you could die a horrible death.

The disease that gives rise to these symptom is called trichinosis, and it is caused by a parasite that is found primarily in bears, felines and other common carnivores such as the fox, dog, wolf, seal or walrus. The most common animal that is prone to being infested with the Trichinella worm is, however, the pig. While the disease is endemic in the Arctic, and has been held responsible for the deaths of all the members of at least one polar expedition who did eat infected polar bear, it used to be far more common in America and Western Europe. Modern animal husbandry has helped almost eliminate the problem in these areas, but it is still prevalent in pigs in the territories to the east of Europe.

The Trichinella parasite was discovered by researchers James Paget and Richard Owen, in 1835. It is still regarded as a significant public health issue, as some of the links in the *Reference links* section show.

The Bible says...

Leviticus 11:7-8 (above) says, don't eat pigs! In Deuteronomy 14:4-6 the food instructions state what is permissible to eat – ox, sheep, goat, deer, and their wild kin – but nowhere on this list are any of the carnivores such as lion, wolf or dog. Following these instructions will make it unlikely that you become infected with the Trichinella parasite.

DON'T EAT VULTURES!

> *...they shall not be eaten, they are an abomination: the eagle, the vulture, the buzzard, the kite, the falcon, after its kind, every raven after its kind, the ostrich, the short-eared owl, the seagull, and the hawk after its kind, the little owl, the fisher owl, and the screech owl; the white owl, the jackdaw, and the carrion vulture, the stork, the heron after its kind, and the hoopoe and the bat.*
>
> *Leviticus 11:13-18 (NKJV)*

Apart from the ostrich, this list of birds contains many of those that will feed on carrion (dead animals), and are likely to be disease-carriers, as are the insects in verses 20 and 21.

WATCH OUT FOR SHELLFISH!

Small marine plants called dinoflagellates or diatoms produce a range of poisons which can produce paralytic, neurotoxic, diarrheic or amnesic symptoms. In non-technical terms, this means that if you eat these poisons you are likely to experience:

> *...tingling or numbness of the face, arms, and legs, followed by headache, dizziness, nausea, and loss of muscle coordination. In cases of severe poisoning, paralysis and*

respiratory failure occur, and death may follow in 2-25 hours.[33]

These symptoms are virtually identical to the effects of nerve gas poisoning!

EAGLES AND CRABS: NOT TO BE EATEN!

Figure 19. An eagle and a crab.
© Martin Johnson.

Since eating microscopic marine plant life is not something people are prone to do, you need to be aware that these are a part of the regular diet for shellfish (oysters, mussels, lobsters, crabs, prawns etc.). Luckily for residents of the developed world, the creatures producing these poisons generally prefer warmer waters, and the husbandry of shellfish commonly practised in Western countries helps to eliminate the risks involved. This is just as well for those of us who like to eat seafood, as these toxins (unlike Trichinella) cannot be eliminated by cooking. Warmer waters would include most of the seashores around the areas the Israelite people were going to live for the next two thousand years.

FOLLOW THE INSTRUCTIONS!

Leviticus 11:9-12 distinguishes between seafood that is generally safe to eat and that which is likely to prove lethal:

---

[33] Medic8 travel guide 2007.

> *Of all the creatures living in the water of the seas and the streams, you may eat any that have fins and scales. But all creatures in the seas or streams that do not have fins and scales – whether among all the swarming things or among all the living creatures in the water – you are to detest. And since you are to detest them, you must not eat their meat and you must detest their carcasses. Anything living in the water that does not have fins and scales is to be detestable to you.*[34]

Wherever you are in the world, if you are not sure of the safety of your food you can follow these simple guidelines. By so doing, your risk of serious harm is greatly reduced. This is not to say that other types of food poisoning may not affect you, but again, further study of the biblical personal and food hygiene laws should stand you in good stead (especially ensuring that those people preparing your food have washed their hands and equipment properly!)

It is probably significant that the Hebrew word translated "unclean" in these passages has the fuller meaning of 'contaminated' or 'defiled', implying contact with foul things (hence, by implication, carriers of contamination or disease). The word translated "detestable" however, comes more simply from the prime root meaning 'filth', i.e. something which is itself bad.

HYGIENE AND HEALTH

In Leviticus 13-15 there are several instructions dealing with infectious diseases (the word translated "leprosy" appears to refer to some different conditions), and a number of principles are clear. These include quarantining the sick person, which reduces the risk of spreading the disease, and washing not only the infected person but also the clothes and things he or she may have been in contact with. The modern confirmation that infections could spread through contact, and that antiseptic procedures could prevent this, is now credited to the Austrian doctor Ignaz Semmelweis (1818-1865), and his story is mainly about the extreme difficulty he had in persuading other doctors to adopt simple hygiene practices such as handwashing which we now

---

[34] NIV.

take for granted in health care. And yet they are plain in Leviticus, written more than three thousand years before his time.

Comment

We live in an era where food shortages do not seem to be a problem even for the poor in the Western world. Instead, the news is about the problems of obesity. We need to try and understand how people can be hungry enough to try eating whatever they find. These are the circumstances in view behind the food laws in Leviticus.

Trichinosis was not understood until 1835, and the operation of nerve toxins on the human body only became an object of scientific study in the 1930s. The Bible does not explain the nature of the problems caused by such things, but it does offer a simple way of reducing or eliminating the risk of these natural parasites and toxins harming people. Normally we expect to understand the science first before we can devise the protective measures, but the Bible supplies us with the protective measures first. This implies that the science of the Trichinella parasite and dinoflagellate nerve toxins was understood by the author of these laws in Leviticus.

The spread of Trichinella in pigs is a result of their indiscriminate eating habits, and the feeding to pigs of remains of infected animals. A more recent parallel is the spread of Bovine Spongiform Encephalopathy (BSE and its link to New-Variant Creutzfeldt-Jakob Disease – nvCJD). This has happened because farmers were encouraged to save money by feeding their cows (and sheep) with the ground-up remains of infected animals, and many people have died as a result. What has happened here is that, in effect, farmers have tried turning herbivores into carnivores (and cannibals, at that) with disastrous results.

In the natural environment, there is no possibility that cows or sheep would eat animal remains; it took food-processing technology to convert animal products into food acceptable to these creatures. The Bible presents the concept of a natural order in the world that is to be respected, and supplies guidelines in those situations where boundaries are hard to distinguish. The Israelites did not need to be told not to feed animal remains to their cattle, but they did need help about what wild animals, birds and seafood were safe to eat. The biblical guidelines provided 3,400 years ago remain valid, and science now gives us a way of understanding the logic behind the laws!

Perhaps more surprising is how recently medical practitioners agreed to adopt basic hygiene measures when caring for the sick, and especially those with infectious diseases. No other ancient writings and particularly from other religions contain such simple and explicit instructions on how to manage food hygiene and health care to reduce the risk of harm in the way the Bible does.

Reference links

A history of Trichinella at: *www.trichinella.org/history.htm*

Dinoflagellates and poisoning: *www.ncbi.nlm.nih.gov/pmc/articles/PMC2525493*

The story of Ignaz Semmelweis: *en.wikipedia.org/wiki/Ignaz_Semmelweis*

CHAPTER TWENTY

What About the Dinosaurs?

Behold now Behemoth, which I made with thee; he eats grass as an ox. Lo now, his strength is in the navel of his belly. He moves his tail as a cedar...

Job 40:15-17 (KJV)

The challenge is often made, "If the Bible is true, then what about the dinosaurs?" This assumes that there are no creatures in the Bible that can be compared with dinosaurs. Part of the problem is that the word 'dinosaur' was not coined until 1842, by Sir Richard Owen. The word means 'terrible lizard', and it followed less than twenty years from the discovery of the first such creature, the Iguanodon, by geologist Gideon Mantell in 1825. His discovery was soon followed by several more, and the science of palaeontology (literally: Ancient-Bone-Study) was begun. The belief in the 19th century was formed that these were creatures never before seen by mankind, and their existence became one of the pillars of the theory of evolution.

In the Bible, however, from about 1,600 BC we find the description of the Behemoth (Job 40:15). Some Bible versions may carry a footnote suggesting this could be a hippopotamus or elephant. The word remains usually untranslated because of this uncertainty and the plain mismatch of the description of its tail with that of either the hippopotamus or the elephant, both of which have very small tails. "He moves his tail like a cedar." The cedar tree is well-known for its wide spreading large branches. The word itself is a form of superlative, and derives from

'Behemah', or 'beast', the generic term for cattle, like the ox. So this is the biggest, grandest of the grazing animals, with a very large, strong tail. The description is an excellent fit for a dinosaur like the apatosaurus.

Job has a vivid description of a huge water monster:

> *Can you draw out Leviathan with a fishhook or press down his tongue with a cord? Can you put a rope in his nose or pierce his jaw with a hook? ... Can you fill his skin with harpoons or his head with fishing spears? ... His back is made up of rows of shields...*
>
> *Job 41:1-2,7,15 (ESV)*

Here is a creature no man can capture or kill, making it bigger than a crocodile and fiercer by far than any whale. It is also able to emit fiery breath. Leviathan sounds very much like the classic dragon of myth and legend. But they never existed, except in the imagination, or so we are told. However, a search of the Internet for 'sea serpents' will throw up many reports of such creatures which have been seen, supposedly, even in the last hundred years.

The odd thing is that the existence of 'dragons', as large, fierce reptilian creatures, is recorded in the cultures all over the world, and with a remarkable degree of commonality. In his book *Dragons or Dinosaurs,* Darek Isaacs identifies many examples from all over the world, with both narrative accounts and artistic representations – from cave paintings to church carvings. Bill Cooper, in his analysis of the Anglo-Saxon epic poem *Beowulf* identifies up to five different types of dinosaur from the poet's descriptions. These include a raptor of some kind (Grendell) and one or more big flying creatures. The Beowulf epic is only one among several Nordic sagas describing the killing of large reptilian monsters. He has gone on to identify some eighty places in the UK where there are reports from the last 1500 years of dinosaur-type creatures.

The simple fact is that cultures worldwide have many stories of creatures that are remarkably like many of the dinosaurs that have been unearthed in the past two hundred years, and which in English we have named 'dragons'. They vary in size, some can fly, they are reptiles which lay eggs for reproduction, and they were generally perceived as a threat to people and cattle. And European records report their activity within the past five hundred years (*Beowulf* is set about 1,400 years ago).

The earlier historians whose work we have seen in other contexts – Pliny, Herodotus, and Josephus – all record stories involving 'dragons' as actual creatures. The only problem here is the insistence that all such creatures died out "65 million years ago"[35], and this stance is necessary to maintain a sense of authority for the theory of evolution. The photographs below show carvings of unknown horned beasts from Yemen, at the southern end of the Arabian Peninsula, made six hundred years apart, in about 300 BC and 300 AD. You can see three different types of unknown horned creatures, one very like a classical dragon.

Figure 20. Carvings of unknown horned beasts, Yemen, ca. 300 BC (left) and 300 AD (right); Fitzwilliam Museum, Cambridge. © Martin Johnson.

Much more recently, there has appeared a powerful new challenge for the claims of great age. Since 2005, there have been several discoveries of soft tissue remains inside some fossil dinosaur bones. These have included blood cells and vessels, collagen and even possibly DNA. The first finds have not been subjected to carbon dating (C-14), but samples from a triceratops and a hadrosaur have been. The 2009 report assigns C-14 dates to these samples of approximately 31,000 years and 23,000 years respectively. There are several explanations how C-14 dating might overstate the age of a sample, meaning they could

---

[35] e.g. *www.newscientist.com/article/dn9936-top-10-dinosaur-myths*

easily be younger than the ages given, but they cannot be older than these ages. The mere existence of C-14 in these samples utterly disproves any age of millions of years for these fossils.

As if this C-14 dating were not enough, the discovery of six different types of proteins and tissues in fossil samples over recent years should be more than enough to dispel the idea that fossils could even be one million years old, as there is no possible way they could have survived enormous lengths of time. These include pigments still bright enough to reveal the feather and skin colours of some birds and dinosaurs, chitin (a tough tissue found in many sea creatures), haemoglobin from dinosaur blood, ovalbumin from dinosaur eggs, collagen from bones and skin, and even whole soft tissue sections.

There are two conflicting world views: an immensely old earth, and a young earth. The first, claiming immense ages for the dinosaurs, is maintained because of its importance to the theory of evolution. To sustain this view, it is necessary to deny the relevance of stories from cultures all over the world, often accompanied by paintings and carvings accurately representing dinosaurs, and claim this is all mythology. The fact that these stories contain accurate descriptions of creatures, including their skin, colour and behaviour, which conforms closely to the dinosaurs that have been uncovered has to be ignored.

The amazing discovery of tissues inside fossils that had not completely decayed has become the focus of extremely imaginative explanations as to how decay could have been thwarted – just in these cases. On the other hand, if the earth is only a few thousand years old, and if dinosaurs were preserved on Noah's Ark, we would expect records of their existence to have survived. If the creatures were as dangerous and obnoxious as they seem to have been, we would also expect them to have been wiped out sooner or later!

So where are the rest of the dinosaurs in the Bible?

The answer is that there are several references in the Bible to 'dragons', apart from Behemoth and Leviathan, and you will find them in older versions, particularly the King James. A problem exists because translators at the end of the 19th century and the early 20th century were clearly embarrassed by the word 'dragon' and struggled to find alternatives. They did not see the possibility that dragons were references in many instances to dinosaurs.

The key Hebrew word is 'tanniyn' or its plural 'tanniym/tannynim'. So "great whales" in Genesis 1:21 (KJV) ('tannynim gadolim') is generally now better translated as "great sea monsters" (NASB) or "great sea creatures / great creatures of the sea" (NKJV/NIV). As we have seen, this could also read 'great dinosaurs' or 'great dragons'. The implied location of the sea indicates why "sea monsters" or "sea creatures" is a probably the best choice, but it does tend to obscure the possible link with those great sea creatures found in the fossil beds.

There are twenty-eight occurrences of this word in the Old Testament, 29 if the lone variant 'tannah' in Micah 1:3 is included[36]. The way tanniyn has been translated varies considerably. For example, where most modern translations will now have 'serpent' in Deuteronomy 32:33, the Jewish translators of about two thousand years ago used the Greek word 'drakon', exactly the word translated only as 'dragon' in the New Testament in English, as they also did for the creature that Aaron's rod turned into before Pharaoh in Exodus 7:9,10,12. Since the boundary between the idea of a 'serpent' or a 'dragon' is fairly flexible, there is no real problem with these choices.

What is bizarre, however, is how English-speaking translators have adopted the word 'jackals' as an alternative for 'dragons'. The words 'tanniyn' and 'tanniym' occur twelve times in Isaiah and Jeremiah, all translated "dragon/s" in the KJV, but replaced in nine out of twelve cases in the NIV and NKJV – as most recent translations – with the word 'jackals', and 'serpent' or 'monster' for the remaining three cases.

If you do a web search for 'Hebrew for Jackal', you will now be offered the word 'tan', which does not exist in the Bible as a noun in the singular, i.e. there is no lone 'jackal' = 'tan'. One commentator describes the choice of 'jackals' to translate 'tanniym' as a good guess based on Isaiah 43:20 with its reference to "the beasts of the field"[37], which could include a very wide range of animals. These creatures live in wild and remote places (Isaiah 34:13; 35:7; 43:20; Jeremiah 9:11;

[36] The old suggestion was that 'tannah' was a feminine singular of 'tan', which was then thought to mean 'elongate, draw out'.
[37] NASB.

10:22; 14:6; 49:33; 51:37; Micah 1:8; Malachi 1:3), and their behaviour includes hissing (Jeremiah 51:37), making a wailing noise (Micah 1:8), and sniffing up the wind (Jeremiah 14:6). Wolves may howl, and foxes may make a screeching noise, but mostly dogs are known for barking. They definitely do not hiss, nor do they normally sniff up the wind (which describes a lifting up of the creature's head to pick up a scent, as opposed to lowering their heads to trace a scent near the ground as dogs characteristically do). However, all these behaviours are in the range of activity for reptiles, and palaeontologists are now of the view that dinosaurs would have been capable of making a wide range of noises.

Figure 21. Horned Lizard, Uluru Australia, sniffing the wind.
© Martin Johnson.

The possibility that this word could mean 'jackals' does not seem to have occurred to translators much before the end of the 19th century. A 1906 Bible Dictionary suggests that:

> *[The word tanniym,] always in the plural ... is always applied to some creatures inhabiting the desert, and we should conclude from this that it refers rather to some wild*

beast than to a serpent. The Syriac renders it by a word which, according to Pocock, means 'a jackal'.[38]

So serpents – snakes and lizards even – don't live in the desert? And this always-plural 'jackals' creature becomes "a jackal"? And finally, the evidence this interpretation never was based on Hebrew shows it relies on a speculative back-translation from the Syriac Bible.

To underline this matter, there are three types of canine animal always acknowledged to exist in the Hebrew Bible: the dog ('keleb'), the fox ('shual') and the wolf ('z'eb'). These nouns are found in both singular and plural forms throughout (altogether, forty-five canine references in the OT), and between them these terms cover all the normal range of canines. There is no warrant for adding a different canine into the Bible. A jackal as now known is simply a medium-sized type of dog, though it may look a bit like that other well-known canine, the fox.

Figure 21. Coyotes (N. American Jackal) in Death Valley, California. © Martin Johnson.

[38] *A Smaller Dictionary of the Bible for the use of schools and young persons;* Sir W Smith; John Murray London (1906 edition); p. 136.

Conversely, the decision to introduce 'tanniym=jackals' leaves the odd situation that we now have 'tanniyn=dragon' without a plural. There become no plural 'dragons' in the Bible (except for Genesis 1:21), only singular ones.

It may be argued by Hebrew scholars that the correct plural for 'tanniyn' should be 'tannynim' (as in Genesis 1:21) rather than 'tanniym', but this is the sort of contraction that pops up many times in Hebrew usage. So turning dragons into jackals, and that as a brand new translation after many hundreds of years, has no reasonable explanation other than that the translators were trying to avoid dragons!

Translation is often a challenging matter, but it seems we are now served with the creatures the modern translators think should have been around two and three thousand years ago rather than those that actually were. Dinosaurs (as dragons, serpents or other reptiles) appear to have been largely edited out of the Bible, and where they are the best explanation for the descriptions given, as with Behemoth and Leviathan, we are asked to consider creatures like the hippopotamus and crocodile respectively, which plainly don't fit the bill.

Comment

In a way, this is the opposite story to most of the others we have seen in the Bible and Science chapters. In this instance, a new branch of science, palaeontology, has arrived, finally proving beyond doubt the existence of the great reptilian creatures mentioned and described many times in the scriptures. Unfortunately, this has resulted in the Bible being altered to hide this fact.

For many centuries people everywhere have maintained detailed descriptions of large reptilian creatures that used to be well-known, and terrifying, but have not been seen for a very long time, and these creatures from China through Asia, Europe and Africa to North America all fit the description of dinosaurs. There used to be many plain references in the bibles then in use to dragons, which was the normal word for such creatures, in all their variety, accepted as reasonable by translators for several centuries until just over one hundred years ago.

Despite the fact that examples of such creatures have been dug up in almost every continent, the rise of palaeontology alongside the theory of evolution has seemingly required us to jettison these worldwide historical records, merely because the dates don't fit the theory. That the latest scientific evidence has shown unequivocally that at least some of these creatures became fossilized only thousands of years ago should be enough to overturn many evolutionary assumptions, which does not appear to be happening. That doesn't sound like the objective scientific approach you would expect in most fields of enquiry!

Reference links

Sir Richard Owen, inventor of 'dinosaur':
www.bbc.co.uk/news/uk-england-lancashire-31623397

Dinosaur images: *www.creation.com/dinosaurs-in-noahs-vineyard*

Dragons or Dinosaurs; Creation or Evolution; Darek Isaacs; Bridge Logos (2010)

After the Flood; the early post-flood history of Europe traced back to Noah; Bill Cooper; New Wine Press (1995); some details at: *www.ldolphin.org/cooper*

Dinosaur soft tissue reports; John Morris (2005): *www.icr.org/article/2032*

Dinosaur DNA research; James Johnson et al. (2009):
www.icr.org/article/dinosaur-dna-research-tale-wagging

Recent C-14 dating of fossil tissues: *www.sciencevsevolution.org/Holzschuh.htm*

There is fascinating information on the biological evidence in *Six Fossil Timers Stun Secular Scientists* by Brian Thomas, M.S., at: *www.icr.org/article/9753*

Alternative views of tannin/tanniym translations: *www.answersingenesis.org/dinosaurs/tannin-sea-serpent-dinosaur-snake-dragon-or-jackal*

Reptile noises: *www.youtube.com/watch?v=7YFLzQYriEw*
and: *www.scholastic.com/teachers/article/what-sounds-did-dinosaurs-make*

Dinosaurs disprove the Bible? Further discussion, some images of apatosaurus-type creatures from ancient Mesopotamia: *www.icr.org/article/9967*

CHAPTER TWENTY-ONE

Solid Literature

Oh, that my words were written! Oh, that they were inscribed in a book! That they were engraved on a rock with an iron pen and lead, forever!

Job 19:23-24 (NKJV)

The evidence in Genesis shows it was compiled from documents written on clay tablets, from the very earliest period of human history.

The British Royal Air Force (RAF) was playing a key role keeping the corrupt Iraqi government in power. The country had descended into murder and chaos with terrorism and warring factions everywhere. The year was 1922. The leaders of the RAF, which had only been created as an independent force four years earlier from Naval and Army air arms, had accepted a role which involved the RAF in bombing villages and farms to subdue the rebellious factions among the Iraqi people in the hope of ensuring survival as an independent force. Iraq was the former Ottoman province of Mesopotamia, a colony now of the British following the defeat of Turkey. It was also on a direct overland route to India and the Far East, where the British Empire still thrived, and there were hopes of developing air transport routes, using airships or even long-range aircraft.

Into this setting, in 1931, came a very experienced senior RAF officer, Percy J Wiseman. He had served through World War 1, and had done a previous tour of duty in the region in 1923-5, when many major air operations were carried out. While the strength of the RAF had fallen by 90% in men and 95% in aircraft in 1919, he had shown the skills and capabilities needed by the service. Not only had he been retained when most of his colleagues had been discharged, he had done very well and been promoted. Before he retired a few years later he reached the rank of Air Commodore (1-star General) and was honoured by King George VI.

During his first tour of duty in Iraq, in 1923, he visited the excavations at Ur of the Chaldees. This was the birthplace of Abraham, and had been recently discovered by Leonard Woolley. He became fascinated by the archaeological work going on in the area, and especially by the discovery of bricks and tablets with cuneiform (wedge-shaped letters) writing on them, dating before 2000 BC.

Now, in his mid-forties, he looked forward to the opportunity to put his off-duty time to good use. He had been 'bitten' during his earlier tour by the opportunities for archaeology in the region, and become an 'amateur' archaeologist in the best sense of the word (which means doing something for the love of it). The more peaceful situation prevailing in Iraq during the 1930s meant that he was able to explore and visit the principal excavations underway at the time. These were by the British Museum, the University Museum of Pennsylvania, and Oxford University, with leaders including Leonard Woolley and Professor S H Langton.

The first important fact that impressed itself on Wiseman was the age of the written texts being found all over the region. If writing was prevalent in the millennium before Abraham, reasoned Wiseman, how could the biblical scholars continue to support the Documentary Hypothesis proposed by Wellhausen and Graf some fifty years earlier? This hypothesis said that because writing did not exist before about 1,000 BC, the Bible could not have been written as early as was traditionally believed, and must have been made up from folk stories and legends handed down by word of mouth. Moses, therefore, could not possibly have written the first five books of the Bible, as tradition held. It was argued that the real authors could never be known, but they came from groups of people such as priests and those who originally worshipped God by different names, such as 'Elohim' and 'Yahweh'.

As a senior RAF administrative officer, Wiseman had been trained in the rules of evidence applied in courts of law. He could see that the evidence of a highly literate society over a thousand years before Moses then appearing from the sands of Mesopotamia should have demolished the Documentary Hypothesis for good. The RAF was very methodical in its storage of documents (filing systems), and that is possibly where Wiseman gained his second fundamental insight into the nature of Genesis. Every documentary storage system has identifying codes, showing the key information about the document. This was seen to be true of even the most ancient clay tablets, which often had a strip of writing up the edge indicating the authorship and contents of the tablet. This was to make it easier to identify them when they stood side by side on shelves in the palace libraries.

Figure 22. Selection of clay tablets inscribed with cuneiform script, dates ranging from ca. 500 to 2050 BC. Sizes range from 5 to 10 cm tall approx. Fitzwilliam Museum, Cambridge.
© Martin Johnson.

The method of making clay tablets was by writing in the soft clay with a hard stylus which made wedge-shaped impressions. The smaller the stylus, the more words could be recorded on a tablet. The tablets were then either baked in ovens or allowed to dry in the sun. This made them resistant to fire and most forms of decay. Clay tablets fell into disuse with the development of vellum (calf or goat's skin) and then papyrus as writing media, which were easier to use and more portable, but a lot less permanent.

Figure 23. Cuneiform tablet recording a loan of 3 shekels to buy sesame, with index script on side, ca. 1733 BC. Approx. 5 cm x 6 cm. Fitzwilliam Museum Cambridge. © Martin Johnson.

Who were the writers of Genesis?

Jewish tradition holds that the first five books of the Bible (the Torah) were the work of Moses, but that he compiled Genesis using earlier records. It also holds that Moses wrote the Torah on vellum. Traditionally, the Torah was always maintained as a single document. The break-up into the five books with the chapter and verse divisions we are familiar with was done by Christian scholars in the 13th century AD (2,700 years after Moses).

Wiseman noted that periodically in Genesis, a repeated form of text appeared. These are the phrases translated as “these are the generations of...” (KJV) or “this is the history of...” (NKJV) or “this is the account of...” (NIV). These are translations of the Hebrew word ‘toledoth’, which contains this range of possible meanings. The final appearance of a toledoth statement is at Exodus 1:6, just before the story involving Moses begins. This shows that by the 13th century when the book, chapter, and verse divisions were introduced, mediaeval Christian authorities assumed that the toledoth statements introduced the passages that followed. Bible scholars have struggled since then to make sense of the way they are used.

Wiseman noted that the scribes of tablets were methodical with their indexing, and he suspected that the toledoth statements were the title code at the end of each tablet set, indicating the author or owner. A problem at first sight reading the Bible in English is that some of the toledoth statements appear in the middle of verses. This is explained by the fact that the Bible (both Old and New Testament) was written book by book in continuous strings of letters. The scribes had to know where each word started and finished, both in Hebrew and Greek, and so they introduced verse and chapter breaks as seemed logical to them.

If we note that each section at the end is attributed to the leading individual(s) present throughout that period, and accepting that the creation account must most probably have been told to Adam or one of the other early Patriarchs, then the probable breakdown of the authorship of Genesis is:

Tablet	Start verse	End verse	Owner or writer
1	Genesis 1:1	Genesis 2:4a	God himself?
2	Genesis 2:4b	Genesis 5:1a	Adam
3	Genesis 5:1b	Genesis 6:9a	Noah
4	Genesis 6:9b	Genesis 10:1a	Shem, Ham and Japheth
5	Genesis 10:1b	Genesis 11:10a	Shem
6	Genesis 11:10b	Genesis 11:27a	Terah

Tablet	Start verse	End verse	Owner or writer
7	Genesis 11:27b	Genesis 25:19a	Isaac
8	Genesis 25:12	Genesis 25:18	Ishmael, through Isaac
9	Genesis 25:19b	Genesis 37:2a	Jacob
10	Genesis 36:1	Genesis 36:43	Esau, through Jacob
11	Genesis 37:2b	Exodus 1:6	Jacob's twelve sons

Figure 23. Possible tablet sets within Genesis.

This analysis indicates that the shorter tablets of Ishmael and Esau were incorporated into the tablets of Isaac and Jacob respectively, with their identifiers retained.

A good brief explanation of this has been written by Curt Sewell. Wiseman's theory has been edited and published by his son, Professor Donald Wiseman, who became Professor of Assyriology at London University.

More than 150 years after the first version of the Documentary Hypothesis was proposed, no tangible evidence of any kind has yet been found to support it. Even worse, the clear evidence against it seems to be widely ignored, and it is still being taught in theological colleges in the 21st century.

The Tablet Theory, on the other hand, is soundly based on the evidence of vast numbers of tablets found during the 20th century and the internal structure of Genesis. The end of the toledoth statements at the beginning of Exodus is probably due to Moses moving on from transcribing the tablet libraries in front of him to the story he was personally involved in. He also most likely did not himself write on tablets, but a more portable form of written record, such as vellum (originally calf skin). The ancient Jewish tradition is that the Books of Moses always have to be copied onto vellum.

The debate as to whether the toledoth statements refer to the preceding or following passage still continues. One criticism is that these statements do not contain the full range of information found in such 'colophon' lines in other tablets now known. This is an argument based on the doubtful idea that all cultures in the area had to have used the same filing system. Other points include what people think each owner/author would have done (e.g. Would the moon-worshipper Terah have maintained his genealogy from the godly Shem? Well, yes, if he was like people in a vast range of cultures down to the present day.) Another criticism is that Moses "would not have been able to read the early tablets, not knowing the language or script"[39], so therefore could not have been the transcriber and translator. But he is on record as having been raised a prince in the court of Egypt, and is therefore likely to have been trained in at least in Egyptian hieroglyphics and hieratic script, Cuneiform scripts (for foreign correspondence), and as writer of the Torah, Palaeo-Hebrew too, plus about four different languages, making none of this improbable.

What is not now at issue is the plain evidence within Genesis that it has been transcribed very carefully from records that were mostly very ancient even then. The fact that in Genesis 1:16 the "great lights" that we call the sun and moon have no titles or names is striking evidence that this record pre-dates the era of Abraham, when they had already become deified and would have invariably been referred to by their pagan titles. Similarly, the direction in Genesis 10:19, "...as you go towards Sodom," a place which by Moses' day had long vanished, demonstrates the extreme respect for the original text.

Comment

Percy J Wiseman, during his long RAF career, would have had to take part in several courts-martial and summary trials of airmen who had fallen foul of Air Force Law. He knew about the standard of evidence required in a court of law. The Tablet Theory is robustly supported, and by far more evidence than has been shown here. The attraction of the Documentary Hypothesis was (and is) that those who follow it could pick and choose what parts of scripture they feel are authentic for their purposes.

If scripture is largely the invention of (albeit well-intentioned) men, then it can be superseded by whatever value system a later generation

---

[39] *www.apologeticspress.org/apcontent.aspx?category=13&article=36*
Also see 'Theories now obsolete' in *Clues to creation in Genesis;* P J Wiseman; Marshal, Morgan & Scott, London (1977); pp. 75-78.

chooses to adopt. The Tablet Theory does not provide this kind of latitude! Genesis was clearly compiled from the most reliable and ancient records known to anyone.

Reference links

RAF Operations in Mesopotamia:
www.rafmuseum.org.uk/documents/Research/RAF-Historical-Society-Journals/Journal_48_Seminar_the_ME_Mespot_Iraq_NW_Frontier_4_FTS.pdf

The Tablet Theory of Genesis Authorship; Curt Sewell; Bible and Spade, Winter 1994, Vol.7, No.1, and available at: *www.ldolphin.org/tablethy.html*

Clues to Creation in Genesis; P J Wiseman; Marshall, Morgan & Scott, London (1977); some details at: *intelligentchristian.grahamclinton.com/christianresources/clues_to_creation_in_genesis.htm*

CHAPTER TWENTY-TWO

The Torah Codes

It is the glory of God to conceal a matter; to search out a matter is the glory of kings.

Proverbs 25:2 (NIV)

Behold, You desire truth in the inward parts. And in the hidden part You will make me know wisdom.

Psalm 51:6 (NKJV)

The existence of the Torah codes reveals that the author of the Torah used encryption techniques only decipherable since the invention of modern computers.

During an October evening in 1944, the learned Rabbi Weissmandel took the hacksaw blade out of the loaf of bread where he had been hiding it and began sawing through the lock on one of the windows of the cattle car. With a breaking heart, he made his last farewells to his wife and five small children, and climbed out of the window. He waited for the train to slow down before he jumped into the darkness. He was knocked unconscious by the fall. He was found by some local people, who kept him hidden and cared for him until he was well enough to travel secretly back towards Bratislava.

In the new hiding place, his comrades say that he just wept for days and nights on end, in sorrow for his family who had all by then died in the gas chambers of Auschwitz. This man, whose efforts had saved tens of thousands of Jewish people during the previous two years, had not been able to save those dearest to him. He had also spent the time sending messages out to England and America informing them of the death camps, using eyewitness reports from escapees, and had also trained the younger men how to escape from the death trains in the way he himself had ended up doing. It is reported that he still suffered agonies of grief years later, tormented by the thought that he might, with a bit more effort, have saved at least one of his children.

Auschwitz, Enigma and the Torah codes

Weissmandel's hope that the allies would bomb Auschwitz and put it out of action had come to nothing. It was finally revealed in 1996 that the real reason had been that they were frightened of compromising the fact they had cracked the German's Enigma code. Many authorities on World War 2 affirm that the success of the allies in the West had depended very heavily on their skill at code-breaking, and a most important aspect of code-breaking is not letting your enemy know that you have broken their codes. Through Enigma the leaders of the Allies had been receiving full details of the German activities in murdering millions of people in the death factories they had built. The Allied authorities feared that if they attacked Auschwitz, the Germans would not believe they had been informed from Jewish sources in central Europe, but had instead got the information from the Enigma codes, and they would in turn change their coding systems to ones that could not be broken.

A cruel irony is that the study of the Torah codes over the previous millennium had provided the intellectual basis for the code breaking at Bletchley Park in England where Enigma had been broken. In 1945 Rabbi Weissmandel was probably the last surviving Jewish expert on the codes within the Torah.

Shortly after Weissmandel's family were murdered, a rebellion at Auschwitz which destroyed one of the gas chambers led to the other gas chambers and crematoria being blown up, in an attempt to destroy the evidence of what had happened. On 27 January 1945, the Red Army captured and liberated Auschwitz. There were only 7,600 survivors still there, abandoned by the retreating Germans.

Enigma, statistics and the first computers

The essential science behind breaking the Enigma codes was statistics, the study of probabilities. The mathematical underpinning of the work at Bletchley Park had been prepared by Alan Turing, a mathematical genius who had developed a conceptual design for computing machines capable of the range and quantity of calculations involved. This is why the code-breakers at Bletchley Park built the world's first electronic computer, known as Colossus.

By 1945, there were ten of these top-secret machines running, and they showed the capability of cracking even the most high-level German ciphers. When the war ended, the British government, showing typical lack of foresight, decided to save costs by dismantling the whole project. They destroyed the Colossus machines (except for one, sent to the USA). In the USA, on the other hand, it was felt that the risks in the world were not finished with the defeat of Hitler, and the National Security Agency (NSA) was founded using the code-breakers who had served the US war effort.

The origin of the Torah codes

The rules for copying the Torah were extremely rigorous. This is because the ancient Jewish tradition held that the Torah had been written down by Moses in the Hebrew language (which has no vowels) by dictation from God. Many of the most eminent Jewish teachers over the past thousand years and more have affirmed the status of divine authorship for the Torah. Typical of many of these most learned men, Rabbi Elijah Solomon of Vilna (1720-1797, 'the Vilna Gaon') said, "All that was, is, and will be to the end of time is included in the Torah, the first five books of the Bible."[40]

After the war, Rabbi Weissmandel settled in New York State where he slowly formed a new Yeshiva (training college) and went to work to restore his study material that had been destroyed. This included a collection of cards, which contained all the 304,805 letters of the Torah (the first five books of the Bible) in blocks of ten letters square (a handy

---

[40] Vilna Gaon; quoted from *The Truth Behind the Bible Code;* Dr Jeffrey Satinover; Sidgwick & Jackson, London (1997); p. 2.

size for spotting simpler codes). This was a method he had learned from his study of the writings of the ancient sages.

Weissmandel taught his students about the codes he had found in the Torah. The method he taught was based on Equidistant Letter Sequences (ELS). This involves treating a piece of text as a single string of letters, with no gaps between words or punctuation marks. You are looking for a series of letters, an equal distance apart, which make another word within the text.

An illustration of Equidistant Letter Sequences (ELS)

Consider the following statement, produced by the present author solely for this book:

"The stories only show to people few aspects of the greater picture. The scriptures seem important!"

The 81 letters can be set into a 9x9 grid:

T	H	E	S	T	O	R	I	E
S	O	N	L	Y	S	H	O	W
T	O	P	E	O	P	L	E	F
E	W	A	S	P	E	C	T	S
O	F	T	H	E	G	R	E	A
T	E	R	P	I	C	T	U	R
E	T	H	E	S	C	R	I	P
T	U	R	E	S	S	E	E	M
I	M	P	O	R	T	A	N	T

Figure 23. A hidden message within a piece of text.

Encoded in ELS at a nine-letter interval, you can now see diagonally from top left to bottom right the words "TOP SECRET" (which is the typical security grading for decoded work from the NSA!) If this were a text from the Torah, the code scholars would have been alerted by the slight awkwardness in the language: why put "to" before "people" – a bit pedantic, isn't it? And shouldn't there normally have been the word "a" before "few"?

This was the principle Weissmandel followed. He taught his students among other things that he had found references to hundreds of the great sages (scholars) and famous people of Jewish history. This claim went far beyond the more basic codes, because it meant that the Torah had recorded details about people long before they had lived!

Even the 'basic' codes seem very improbable. For instance, in the passage about the garden of Eden, Genesis 2:4-17, the word "Eden" occurs three times. Hidden in the text, though, at various ELS distances, it appears another nineteen times, a frequency not found for this word in any other passage.

Genesis 1:29 says:

> *Then God said, "I give you every seed-bearing plant on the face of the whole earth and every tree that has fruit seed in it. They will be yours for food."* [41]

In this one verse are encoded the names of the seven species of seed-bearing plants grown for food in Israel: barley, wheat, vine, date, olive, fig and pomegranate. If the passage is extended to include Genesis 3:3, it turns out to include all twenty-five species of trees known for Israel.

The question is, how real an effect is this? If we use our short English text, in addition to the planted code, we can start finding many other word combinations. "HER" at a nine-letter skip, "PEG" at an eight-letter skip, and "SET" at a seven-letter skip are highlighted in the grid overleaf. This could conceivably be interpreted as some kind of message. While it is moderately difficult to design a grid around a planted code, and combine it with a meaningful and relevant message, it is the sort of task most people could do.

The second factor is then finding other words. The text in use was only built around the words 'top secret', but it should be possible to find a large number of words in any grid such as this. The question then becomes, how likely is it that we can find words (especially short three-

---

[41] NIV.

or four-letter ones) in a grid such as this? The answer is – almost certainly, and with a bit of ingenuity you could try and create some meaning from these random words made of random letters. And what about the use of Hebrew? Given the lack of vowels, it should be even easier to find word combinations in a Hebrew letter grid than it is in English. What should be our measure of something out-of-the ordinary?

T	H	E	S	T	O	R	I	E
S	O	N	L	Y	S	H	O	W
T	O	P	E	O	P	L	E	F
E	W	A	S	P	E	C	T	S
O	F	T	H	E	G	R	E	A
T	E	R	P	I	C	T	U	R
E	T	H	E	S	C	R	I	P
T	U	R	E	S	S	E	E	M
I	M	P	O	R	T	A	N	T

Figure 24. 'Coded' words appearing by chance in the text.

The arrival of modern computers

This is the stage at which work on the Torah code spread outside the world of the rabbinic scholars. The arrival of digital computers, and then personal computers, accelerated the process. In 1983, the existence of the codes was brought to the attention of one of the world's top mathematicians, Professor Eliyahu Rips. He was a non-believing Jew who had escaped from Russian-controlled Lithuania to Israel. He started working with Doron Witzum, a physicist who gave up physics to devote himself to full-time study of the codes, and Yoav Rosenberg, a computer scientist.

First Rips explored the probabilities of some of the phenomena such as the name of Eden, and the trees. Given that 'Eden' in Hebrew has only three letters (עדן) the odds against it appearing in ELS forward or reverse nineteen times anywhere in the fourteen verses of Genesis 2:4-17 is 'only' 1/100 (a hundred to one against). Unusual and unexpected, certainly, but not enough to convince a statistician that it could not have been arranged by a clever (human) author with plenty of time to spare.

The discovery of the twenty-five trees in a passage about one thousand letters long, most at short ELS distances, was not odds of a hundred to one against, but one hundred thousand to one against. And these odds would only apply to the appearance of that specific set of words in a random passage of that length. When the fact that the appearance of the 'trees' code is related to a passage speaking on that precise subject, and that other contextually relevant codes also appear in the text, the odds become astronomical. The flaw was that this type of discovery did not meet the methodological requirements of statistical science, as it is an attempt to apply a test 'after the fact'.

What was needed was a method of testing that would stand up to scientific scrutiny, where the conditions for the test could be agreed in advance, and the expected results could be specified before testing began, but the results could not be known in advance. Discussions were held with top statisticians and mathematicians.

The test they devised was to use the Encyclopaedia of Great Men in Israel, and make a list of the thirty-four most famous (by length of citation) and for whom dates of birth and/or death were listed. If the teachings of Weissmandel and the sages of the past were true, then these names with the key dates in close relationship should appear within the Torah.

What was revealed was astonishing. The name of every great man appeared in ELS code with the required date close by. In the language of statisticians, the results showed "a very strong tendency for the names of the personalities to converge with their associated dates". The sceptics were shaken, but not convinced. One of the key reviewers, Professor Per Diaconis, an eminent (and very sceptical) statistician from Harvard, proposed additional tests, including increasing the list of personalities from the initial thirty-four up to sixty-six, by adding the next thirty-two most famous men on the same basic criteria.

Another person to get involved was Harold Gans, a Senior Cryptologic Mathematician for the NSA, one of the most expert code and cipher specialists of his day. He ran a parallel test, adding a search for the cities associated with the sixty-six men, which was successful. The possibility of these connections between the great men, their names, dates and cities, all embedded near each other in the text, arising by chance was vanishingly small.

The work by Witzum, Rips and Rosenberg passed all these tests with flying colours. Their paper on the great sages was published by the journal Statistical Science in 1994 (a shorter preliminary paper had been published in 1988 by the Journal of the Royal Statistical Society).

While this paper had been in preparation, work on the codes had increased and been taken up by a number of other highly qualified mathematicians and statisticians. The effect on Eliyahu Rips had been profound: no longer a "strict atheist"[42] he had become a dedicated follower of the Jewish faith. This happened to many of the scientists who decided to engage with the codes. By the early 1990s, several references had been found to historical figures (ranging from emperor Franz Ferdinand of Austria to Anwar Sadat, assassinated President of Egypt) and events (including the Holocaust and the 1991 Gulf War).

Cross-checking, controversy and sensationalism

It must be understood that the key issue is not the existence of words found by manipulating the text of the Torah (so much easier now computers are readily available), but probability. There have been several strong challenges to the work of the codes scientists. The typical allegations are that they have produced the results by manipulating the source data: perhaps the selection of people, the spelling of their names or the choice of dates have helped to 'improve' the results. This has gone beyond the realms of scientists thinking of ever-tougher ways of testing the ideas, or others attempting to replicate the tests and produce the same results, to what amounts to saying, "They cheated, they must have done; there's no other explanation." A search of the web will produce a good idea of the issues involved. However, all the serious

---

[42] *The Truth Behind the Bible Code;* Dr Jeffrey Satinover; Sidgwick & Jackson, London (1997); pp. 34,131.

challenges and criticisms have been met squarely, and (at the time of this book's publication) the basic position is still the same as in 1996, if not more strongly reinforced.

This does not include the other direction that 'codes research' has taken. You can now buy Torah codes systems from the Internet, to run yourself. It obviously helps a lot if you have a good standard of Hebrew, but a range of other texts are available (the Bible, in various English translations, or in Greek or Hebrew, and many other books). One journalist, Michael Drosnin, published sensational claims which effectively said he was using the codes to foretell the future. He claimed to have predicted the assassination of the Israeli Prime Minister, Yitzhak Rabin in 1995. This produces two problems:

- *Statistical probability.* As noted above, the validity of the codes does not rest on the coincidence of words in the text, but how probable any specific convergence is. This is where the arguments have raged for a decade or more, between very highly qualified mathematicians, statisticians and others of their ilk. Any claim to have identified new codes in the Bible is virtually meaningless unless it passes this level of testing.
- *Biblical directions on fortune-telling (divination).* Deuteronomy 18:10-11 says: "Let no-one be found among you who sacrifices his son or daughter in the fire, who practices divination or sorcery, interprets omens, engages in witchcraft, or casts spells, or who is a medium or spiritist or who consults the dead."[43] This warning appears several times throughout the Hebrew scriptures. It is hard to see how using a personal computer and Torah codes programme to try and foretell the future would not be included as divination under the prohibition of this law. There must be a conflict in trying to use the Torah to do what the Torah tells you not to do!

'Jesus' codes

Some writers claim to have identified references to Jesus in key Hebrew texts, including Isaiah 53, especially 53:10, where "Jesus is my

---

[43] NIV.

name" appears in the verse about the suffering of his servant. These claims are fiercely contested, especially by conservative Jewish scholars; to a Christian, it would be probable if there is a code throughout the Hebrew scripture that mention would be found of Jesus. Conservative Jewish scholars should be expected to take a different line, but this divergence only reflects the earlier arguments about the validity of a code which appears to reveal events centuries and millennia after it was recorded. It should be kept in mind that the only section of the Bible for which there has been any tradition of a letter code is the Torah.

Implications of the Torah codes

The key issue is, what do the codes imply? At the first level (e.g. the lists of fruits and trees etc.) they appear to form a consistent 'watermark' behind the text. By the time the prevalence and complexity of this type of code in the early chapters of Genesis is considered in totality, it is hard to imagine how any person could have produced them. Modern computers reveal them, but the challenge of writing texts with that level of embedded letter complexity really is mind-boggling. Taken as a whole, though, even this effect should readily demolish any residual belief in the Documentary Hypothesis, of multiple authorship of the Torah some one thousand years after Moses.

One of the heroes of the Manhattan Project, the construction of the atomic bomb at Los Alamos, was John von Neumann. He had studied the work of Alan Turing, the mathematical genius behind the work at Bletchley Park. He knew that making an atomic bomb required solving mathematical problems that had never been solved before. This required a convergence of statistics, cryptology and quantum physics, and this is what led to the creation of the modern computer.

An important effect within the Bible code can be illustrated by the codes apparently referring to the Scud missile attacks on Israel at the outset of the Gulf War in 1991. Witzum & co. had no difficulty identifying several possible convergences involving 'Tel Aviv', 'Saddam Hussein', 'Scud' and 'missile'. A key area of interest was the date of the first missile attack. There were three dates in close connection with the convergences of these words, and the first attack took place on one of those. It seems from this that there were a range of possibilities – the future was not fixed until it happened. This would support the findings from quantum physics etc. that the material universe is not operating on a pre-determined basis, but is governed by probabilities and by factors outside the four primary dimensions of space-time. Only after an event can you look at the Bible code and recognise links to an event. However, the number of times this has been done in a credible way is startling.

How reliable is the Torah text?

If the Torah contains code in the form of ELS, then how much damage would it have to suffer before the code was destroyed? Looking at Genesis, it has been calculated that deleting seventy-eight letters would remove the code completely. In code terms, this would be described as 'transmission damage' – where the text containing a code has become damaged while en route to its recipients. Of course, not all transmission damage involves missing letters; some damage could occur when an individual letter has been changed in copying to a different letter. While deleting a letter changes the position of every letter that follows, corrupting all the text 'downstream', substituted letters would not have the same impact. The text downstream would remain unchanged. The traditional (Koren) text used by Jewish scholars clearly has far fewer than seventy-eight letters missing from Genesis.

The Biblia Hebraica Stuttgartensis (BHS), the Hebrew text used by most non-Jewish Hebraists for translations, has 130-plus letter-level differences from the Koren text across the whole of the Torah. Use of the BHS text for the Great Sages experiment reduced the p-value from <0.000002 to <0.002 (2/100,000 down to 2/1,000). This is a reduction of a factor of 100, but still a very strong result. Tests with the Samaritan Torah (Pentateuch) showed the code effect disappeared. There are about six thousand letter differences involved. This is a branch of Israelite religion that diverged about 500 BC. There are three different Torah versions in use by the main different Jewish groups around the world (Ashkenazi, Sephardi, and Yemenite). There are only nine letter-level variations between these three versions.

In Matthew 5:18, Jesus says:

> *For assuredly, I say to you, till heaven and earth pass away, one jot or one tittle will by no means pass away from the law till all is fulfilled.*[44]

The "law" here means the Torah. "Jot" means the letter 'yod', the smallest letter in the Hebrew alphabet, while "tittle" means the smallest stroke in a Hebrew letter.

Comment

Atheist scientists with world-level reputations in their fields have examined the Torah codes and been so impressed they have returned to their ancestral faith. Others have been raised to a level of fury in their determination to deny the effects. The result has been that the opposition is reduced either to saying, "It can't be," or to focussing their attacks on the enthusiastic and sensational (but often misguided) proponents of codes whose efforts haven't stood up to statistical analysis.

There have been many attempts to find codes in other books of the Hebrew Bible, but the transmission (copying) rules for the Torah were far stricter than for the other books, so the effect is not likely to be so clear, even if it exists. Those wishing to test it for themselves are recommended to learn Hebrew thoroughly, and then become statistical scientists. There are no reliable reports of ELS codes in the New Testament books, though several examples of numeric patterns have been discovered.

There is plenty of material available now on the codes, and it shows a number of things. One is the consistency of the underlying authorship of the Torah, and another is that whoever composed the text literally knew "the end from the beginning"[45]. And, if it has taken the arrival of modern computers to find most of these codes, what was the literary and intellectual capability of whoever wrote it?

Finally, the ancient Jewish tradition spoke of alternative ways of interpreting the Torah, four different levels. All the work discussed here

---

[44] NKJV.

[45] Isaiah 46:10 (NASB).

has been about Equidistant Letter Sequence analysis of the plain text. This is just one method of decrypting a text. It is therefore likely that there are other levels and types of code in this document.

Reference links

Story of the world's first computer, Colossus, at Bletchley Park:
www.picotech.com/applications/colossus.html

Jeffrey Satinover: *The Truth Behind the Bible Code* (1997); *Cracking the Bible Code* (1998); background on Jeffrey Satinover is on Wikipedia:
en.wikipedia.org/wiki/Jeffrey_Satinover

Cosmic Codes; Chuck Missler (1999). Chuck has material on YouTube:
www.youtube.com/watch?v=0IqsfwYcK1s

Chapter Twenty-Three

Genesis 23 – A Real Estate Deal

> *So the field and the cave in it were legally made over to Abraham by the Hittites as a burial site.*
>
> *Genesis 23:20 (NIV)*

Genesis records a land sale with a race of people lost to history, whose existence was only proved in the 20th century.

"So what is this law about 'adverse possession'? Do you really mean that if I use a piece of land belonging to somebody else for twelve years without their permission, I can claim it as my own?"

"Well, yes, there's a little bit more to it than that, procedures to follow, you know, but that is the law. In England and Wales, anyway. But don't think about trying to do that in Thailand, say, or Mexico. Or perhaps Indonesia. As a foreigner, it's very unlikely you'll be allowed to own land in those countries; you can't even buy it. And watch out if you buy a house in the Valencia region of Spain. They've got a law which allows the local authority to take a piece of your land for what they call 'communal development', and then make you pay for a share of the costs of roads and drains, and so forth! Tricky business, this property law! There is one thing I can guarantee is universal, though: Wherever you own property, the government will want you to pay tax."

What lies behind this strange chapter, Genesis 23? Abraham has lived in the area near Hebron, on and off, for over sixty years. He's wealthy and powerful, he has defeated a major military power that invaded the region, but somehow he goes into a negotiation where it looks as if he ends up paying maybe a hundred times the value of a piece of land just so he can bury his wife. This is a tiny plot in the middle of a whole territory which God promised to him, and where he's been grazing his flocks and herds for decades, and yet he does this deal.

Firstly, as this was Hittite territory at the time, it was governed by Hittite law. This meant that foreigners could not own land. This was normal in many Near Eastern societies – you had to be a member of the tribal family which controlled the territory concerned. This is why Abraham opens the negotiation with, "I am an alien and a stranger among you."[46]

Although he has lived there for decades, and is well known to them, this gives Abraham's legal status. The important factor which appears to have a bearing on this is the purpose for which he wants the land: "Sell me some property for a burial site here so that I can bury my dead."[47] Even today, in Middle East countries, the practice is often to try and bury dead people within twenty-four hours. There were no refrigerated mortuaries then! Abraham is under pressure to find a burial plot quickly, and all concerned know this.

Then there is the status of the dead person: Sarah was the wife of a great, wealthy man. In European aristocracy ranks she would have been regarded as a duchess or a princess. Her husband was not a man to offend! The purpose for buying the land could provide a reason for 'overlooking' the law. Therefore, the Hittite elders respond, "You are a mighty prince among us. Bury your dead in the choicest of our tombs. None of us will refuse you his tomb for burying your dead."[48] The first part of the statement looks like respect being given, but the punchline is "among us" – not 'of us'. "Yes, Lord Abraham, you *are* an alien!"

The offer of a free tomb for Sarah looks generous, but it does not square with the promises in earlier chapters, that all this land was destined for Abraham's descendants (Genesis 12:7; 13:15; 15:18; 17:18). It seems that Abraham has determined that Sarah will be buried

46 verse 4a (NIV).
47 verse 4b (NIV).
48 verse 6b (NIV).

in land that will belong to their descendants, as heirs of Abraham. In declaring much earlier that Sarah was his sister (Genesis 12:13), it is also possible that Abraham was conferring on her an equal rank to his own.

> *"If you are willing to let me bury my dead, then listen to me and intercede with Ephron son of Zohar on my behalf, so that he will sell me the cave of Machpelah, which belongs to him and is in the end of his field. Ask him to sell it to me for the full burial price as a burial site among you."*
>
> *verses 8-9 (NIV)*

Abraham has done his homework and knows what property is available for sale. The comment in verse 10, "Ephron the Hittite was sitting among his people," indicates he was the ruler of the city, which would make him of an equivalent social rank to Abraham.

Then follows a dialogue which confuses modern minds, where Ephron appears to offer the land as a free gift.

> *"No, my lord," he said. "Listen to me; I give you the field, and I give you the cave that is in it. I give it to you in the presence of my people. Bury your dead."*
>
> *verse 11 (NIV)*

This looks like the second offer of free land. But there would be problems for Abraham in accepting it as such. Firstly, it would put him under obligation to Ephron, and he would be expected to make a generous gift in return, and given the law about land ownership, there was no guarantee that his title to the land would be honoured by a future ruler. The additional possibility is that accepting the land may require him to be subject to Ephron under Hittite laws. Ephron, however, has 'upped the game' by adding the field into the negotiation. He obviously wants more cash than just a cave would fetch! There is an alternative possibility, and that is the law could continue to require that he paid tax on the whole field, even if he had sold off a part. This has been noted in Hittite territory in later times.

Abraham is determined to obtain the burial place, and presumably knows of no other available properties for sale that day.

> *"Listen to me, if you will. I will pay the price of the field. Accept it from me so I can bury my dead there."*
>
> *verse 13 (NIV)*

Given that Abraham knew the land was available for sale beforehand, it is unlikely he had not found out about the price involved. Although archaeologists have found evidence to indicate that an acre of land (about the size of an average field in the area) normally sold for four shekels of silver, what Ephron said next was probably a bigger surprise to the elders in the gate than it was to Abraham.

> *"Listen to me, my lord; the land is worth four hundred shekels of silver, but what is that between me and you? Bury your dead."*
>
> *verse 15 (NIV)*

So the deal is done, and the price is paid. It is possible that the shift in address (from "my lord" to "me and you") indicates that Abraham has in effect been adopted into Ephron's family for land ownership purposes. The price may be high but worthwhile, because title to the land is secure. Evidence of 'sale adoption', the process whereby an outsider could pay to be adopted by a family member and circumvent the ban on his buying land, has been seen from the records at Nuzi. If this is what happened here, it explains why the parties had to be Ephron and Abraham, because of their relatively equal social status.

Comment

This passage, the first acquisition of title to property in the land of Canaan by Abraham and his descendants, has puzzled many commentators in the past. Clay tablets, the very earliest examples of written documents, have been recovered from the civic and palace archives of several city states from Babylonia and the land along the seaboard of the Eastern Mediterranean. The tablets show that administrative and legal details of land ownership and taxation were recorded with scrupulous care, and there was very close attention paid to civil law in all its aspects.

The negotiation between Abraham and Ephron reflects this respect for law and civil behaviour from the dawn of history. It is likely that

Ephron surprised Abraham by including the whole field in the sale, but Abraham understood the logic and did not challenge it. While some commentators take the view that Abraham was being tricked into buying more than he needed, it is also possible that by only asking for the cave, Abraham knew that he was trying to duck a tax liability.

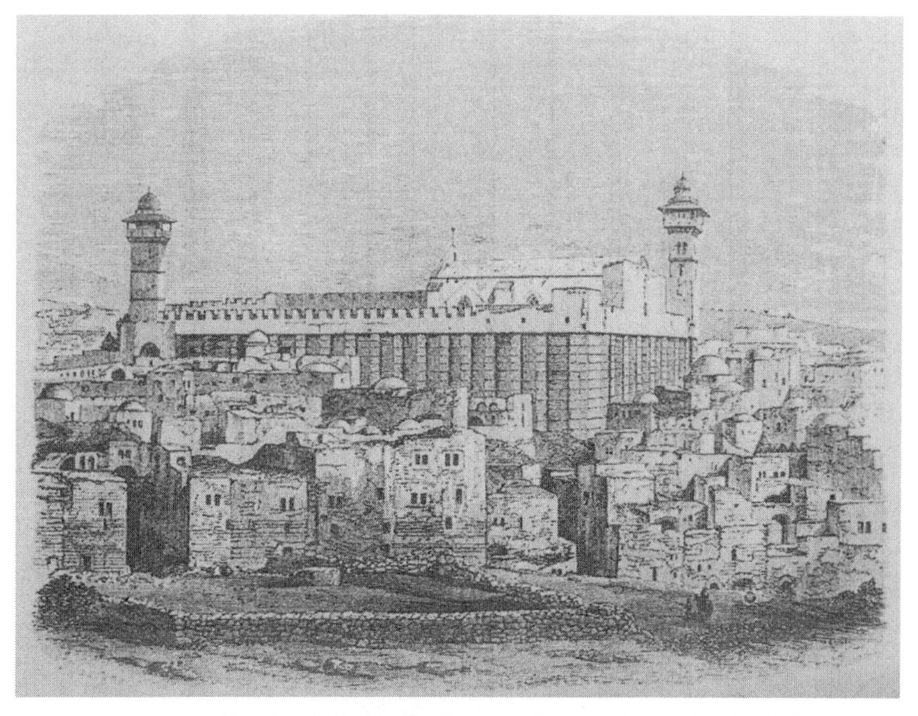

Figure 25. Tombs of the Patriarchs, covering the Cave of Machpelah, Hebron. 19th century engraving.
Source: A Smaller Dictionary of the Bible; Sir W Smith (1906 edition); p. 207.

The history of the developed world in the 19th and 20th century has many examples of people's property rights being ignored and denied, particularly in the colonies of the European countries and territories conquered in the many wars. The idea that people were so attentive to keeping the law and recording such things as land title, especially involving people of different nationality, thousands of years earlier seemed very unlikely to many scholars. This passage may well be a summary of the transaction recorded at the time in the town archive of

Hebron. This is a prime witness for the very early date of this section of the Bible. Within a few hundred years, the Hittites themselves had disappeared from historical record. They were only 'rediscovered' during the 20th century.

Access to the cave of Machpelah is currently barred, as the Moslem authorities who control the mosque which today stands above the cave believe that graves should be treated with the highest respect. It is probable that the remains of Abraham and Sarah, together with Isaac and Rebekah, and Jacob and Leah, are still buried there (the only one missing, so to speak, is Rachel, who is buried near Bethlehem). The people living nearby, whether Jewish or Palestinian, can all trace their ancestry to Abraham, so his heirs and successors remain in control of this piece of land. The title that Abraham took so much care to buy is still valid after four thousand years! The ancient Jewish perspective was that the Hittites, being from Anatolia (modern Turkey) are Greeks (i.e. everyone west of Syria on the north coast of the Mediterranean). They suggest that this negotiation sets a pattern for harmonious relationships between Israel and the West!

Reference links

Abraham and Ephron, a curious negotiation, Rabbi Yitzchak Etshalom; at: *www.torah.org/torah-portion/mikra-5773-chayeisarah*

Hebron: Tomb of the Patriarchs:
www.jewishvirtuallibrary.org/jsource/Judaism/machpelah.html

Covenant: See Robert Bradshaw (1998), at:
www.biblicalstudies.org.uk/article_covenant.html

Abraham in History and Tradition, Part II Abraham the Prince; Donald J Wiseman; Bibliotheca Sacra 135 (July-September 1977) 228-37; available at: *pdfs.semanticscholar.org/55c8/414586e3913cc84b8620d21b5ff35381874e.pdf*

CHAPTER TWENTY-FOUR

Numbers in the Bible

Teach us to number our days aright, that we may gain a heart of wisdom.

Psalm 90:12 (NIV)

The consistent use of numbers though the Bible suggests that the authors have all been collaborating. This isn't possible.

Seven

Why are there seven days in a week? It seems such an awkward number. Most months have thirty or thirty-one days – seven doesn't go into that without leaving a few days over. There are 365 days in a year, so there's always one day over there (except for leap years, when there's two). Look at lunar months – 29.5 days or thereabouts, so seven doesn't go into that, either.

There was a brief time when ancient Egypt had ten-day weeks, nice and neat, three weeks to a month (nice and close to lunar months) and twelve months to a year with only five-and-a-quarter days to juggle with every year. Perhaps that wouldn't work so well, either... Another country which tried ten-day weeks was revolutionary France, and they abandoned the experiment. The Lithuanians had a nine-day week before becoming Christian, and Soviet Russia experimented with five and six-day weeks for a couple of years between 1929 and 1931, but gave up.

It appears that the seven-day week was in use in ancient Mesopotamia and (apart from the interlude mentioned) in ancient Egypt. It was linked by the Egyptians to the sun and the moon together with the five visible planets: Mars, Mercury, Jupiter, Venus and Saturn (in that order). Possible evidence for the truth of this is that many countries either name the days of the week according to these heavenly bodies, or to the pagan gods that were associated with these planets.

The odd ones out are the Jews, who have always named their days 'first day', 'second day' and so on until they get to the seventh day, which they call 'Sabbath'. The pattern for numbering days one to seven is found in Genesis 1, following the six days of creation and the day of rest.

The purpose of the sun, moon and stars is plain:

> *And God said, "Let there be lights in the expanse of the sky to separate the day from the night and let them serve as signs to mark seasons, days and years."*
>
> *Genesis 1:14 (NIV)*

It seems that at some point, people stopped seeing the sun, moon and stars as markers for days etc. and declared them to be gods instead!

One consequence of Britain and other European countries becoming Christians is that the seven-day week became the Europe-wide standard. The influence of the empires of the European countries over all the other continents of the world means that the seven-day week is now the global standard.

Seven as a number permeates the Bible from end to end. It is said to signify spiritual perfection (because of the seventh day of creation). People who are interested in numbers claim to have found many examples within the text of the Bible, using a technique based on the fact that all the letters in both the Hebrew and Greek alphabets (in which the Bible is written) have a numerical value.

The only place known in all ancient literature, myth or legend where seven days is stated as a basic time period is in Genesis chapter one. It seems the whole world, in using the seven-day week, is acknowledging the seven days of creation.

Gematria

The original name for the study of number values in the text of the Bible is Gematria. This begins with observations about plain numbers in the text and then moves on to the number values of words. So, where in Genesis 14:14 it says Abraham had 318 servants, and the value of the letters in "Eliezer" (Genesis 15:2) is found to also be 318, this is held to be significant as he was Abraham's chief servant.

In Esther 3:11, the word for "the money" promised to Haman for destroying the Jews in the Persian empire has the same number value (165) as the word for "the gallows" on which he was to be hanged (Esther 9:25).

There are a several more examples like this. However, the rules that have developed for Gematria permit a wide range of changes and substitutions of letters, and reading words that have the same number values as if they may have the same meaning. This effectively invalidates it as a technique for forensic study. It also can have exponents arguing that words in the text may mean something completely different to their natural meaning.

Numerology

Numerology is really an occult activity, which can be traced all the way back to Ancient Babylon, in which numbers have significance in themselves, and is used to attempt to foretell the future in a similar way to modern astrology. The numbers in a date of birth, for example, may be used to predict the life events of an individual. This is obviously a form of divination. Some of the attempts to explore number in scripture seem to move in this direction, particularly when they claim to interpret prophecy in ways that do not relate to the plain meaning of the written words, and offer interpretations of scripture that can only be understood using these methods.

Numbers in the Bible text

At the end of the first word in Genesis is the first letter of the word 'Torah', which is 'tau'. At an Equidistant Letter Sequence (ELS) skip of forty-nine, the remaining letters of the word 'Torah' are spelt out. 49 is, of course, 7x7, or 7^2. The same feature is found at the beginning of Exodus, and then 'Torah' appears spelt backwards in the same intervals at the start of Numbers and Deuteronomy. In the corresponding place in Leviticus is the word 'Yahweh'.

49 years, or seven sevens, is the period of Jubilee[49], the year of release and rejoicing. This is also the period of days between the Feast of First Fruits, following Passover, and the Feast of Weeks (or, Pentecost).

This embedding of key words in each book, with its numerical significance, is a feature which could easily have been designed by a human author, but it does show careful design of each book and thus indicates the probability of a single author for all five Books of Moses.

Studies into sevens and forty-nines show a lot of possible connections with names and words. Ivan Panin published his study into the appearance of sevens in Matthew 1[50]. A similar feature is relevant in the studies done by many into the use of 153 in John 21:11 for the number of large fish caught. The most likely explanation for this is that tax was due on all 'large fish' caught, so John as a commercial fisherman would automatically keep track of such a number! The desire to find significant numbers is very strong among some people. Ivan Panin has described a considerable range of number patterns that he has unearthed in the New Testament books, as have other writers, which they judge to be beyond the capability of human authors to have constructed. He has demonstrated, for example, that the closing passage of Mark chapter 16, which some scholars believe not to be an original part of that Gospel, does in fact fit in with the hidden number patterns of that book, and is therefore original.

Universal constants

Dr Peter Bluer is a mathematician who has studied Ivan Panin and attempted to apply some critical tests to the question of Bible numbers.

---

[49] See Leviticus 25.

[50] Ivan Panin's response to a critic in the New York Sun in 1899 supplies 22 uses of 7 in the structure and vocabulary of the first 17 verses of Matthew 1, and this only begins his analysis of the complex use of numbers in the passage: *www.telusplanet.net/public/tsgibson/panin.pdf*

For example, Ivan Panin shows the numerical value of Genesis 1:1 (2,701) is unusual because it contains the prime factors of 37x73. 37 is the 12th prime number, and 73 is the 21st prime number. So, 37 and 73 are reflections of each other, but so also do they mirror their positions on the table of prime numbers. Three and seven are both regarded as significant. Mathematician Dr Peter Bluer shows that the factor 37 occurs far more frequently than it should by chance in Bible numerics, and that there is very unusual mathematical symmetry in the number values involved. Panin had noted similar and interlinked features between Genesis 1:1 and John 1:1.

These observations about 37 in the Bible mirror one that was recently made by cosmologist Maxim Makukov in respect of 37 appearing in the genetic code, which it does far more frequently than it should by chance. The genetic code is a complex set of rules by which DNA is translated into proteins. This has led to the suggestion that 37 is "the answer to life, the universe, and everything", and even suggestions that life originates with aliens from outer space...

Peter Bluer discovered that if the following equation was applied to Genesis 1:1, it produced the value of Pi (Π) accurate to within one thousandth of one per cent of the currently known value (3.14159 etc.; i.e. far more accurate than when derived from 22/7). The equation is:

$$\frac{\text{[The number of letters] x [The product of the letters]}}{\text{[The number of words] x [The product of the words]}}$$

or

$$\frac{28 \times 2.3887872 \times 10^{34}}{7 \times 3.0415352578417576 \times 10^{34}}$$

The significance of Pi is that it is required for virtually all calculations involving circular and spherical geometry, two and three-dimensional space. It is found in Genesis 1:1, the key verse describing all creation. "In the beginning God created the heavens and the earth."[51]

The test of this, Bluer felt, would be the other single Bible verse linked to creation, John 1:1: "In the beginning was the Word, and the Word was with God, and the Word was God."

Applying the same equation to this verse produced another universal constant: e (2.71828...) The accuracy of the value for e produced by John 1:1 is also within one thousandth of one percent. This is the exponential constant, which was first discovered in the 16th century and is also known as Euler's number. Pi, in contrast, was known to the ancient Greeks. e is the base for natural logarithms, and is used in equations for waves, the distribution of prime numbers, electrical theory and pure mathematics, among other things. The significance of e in wave functions is that these are essential for quantum descriptions of matter, and thus lie at the heart of the 'reality' of matter (or, perhaps, its lack of ultimate reality!) The appearance of this constant hidden within this verse is an indication that logos, or 'information', lies at the heart of all reality, and points to the mysteries at the heart of the material world that so far remain unresolved by physics.

Oddly, there have been critics who say that the Bible cannot be regarded as true because it contains an incorrect value for Pi. This is because in 1 Kings 7:23 the manufacture of a large brass bowl, or "Sea"[52] is described. The text says it was:

> *...Ten cubits from one brim to the other; completely round, it was five cubits high; and a line of thirty cubits measured its circumference.*[53]

Verse 26 says it was a "handsbreadth thick". The cubit was the measure from elbow to fingertip, and is estimated to have been about 46 cm. The handsbreadth is about 10 cm. So at first sight, it seems to say of this object that it had a circumference of about 13.8 metres and a diameter of about 4.6 metres, implying a value for Pi of 3.00 instead of 3.14. This argument seems to take no account of the difficulties of

---

[51] NIV.
[52] NKJV.
[53] NKJV.

casting an enormous bronze object 3,000 years ago. The sheer weight of molten bronze could easily deform the mould a little, enough to make this a poor choice of item for determining Pi. The difference needed in diameter to achieve Pi in this calculation is only about 20 cm, less than 1½% of the diameter of the vessel. However, the people making this objection really do want to argue that this verse proves the Bible is inaccurate.

Moreover, this criticism overlooks the thickness of the vessel. If the measurement is of the diameter from outside to outside while the circumference measure is the inside of the rim, as would be logical if you wanted to know the volumetric capacity of the vessel, then the ratio becomes not 10:30 but the inside diameter of 9.55 cubits to 30, or 3.14, an acceptable value for Pi (using outside diameter less twice the thickness). They could have easily measured the inner circumference by measuring the outside of the mould that they cast the bowl on, while the diameter would have been measured across the finished bowl.

Forty

The use of 40 in the title of this book reflects the many times it appears in the Bible (145) for so many different purposes. For instance, there are 22 references to periods of 40 days, and 42 references to periods of 40 years. Of the latter, 18 refer to the time the Israelites spent wandering in the wilderness, of which 11 are in the Old Testament, and 7 are in the new. 22 is the number of letters in the Hebrew alphabet while 7 is a number we now know well. There is little basis here to draw any firm conclusions on the meaning of 40, but many have tried!

Comment

Numbers play an intricate part in the Bible, and they validate the text in two ways. The first is the coherence of their plain use throughout, as if many of the thirty-three or so authors over a period of 1,500 years were all collaborating with each other. The second is that there are many examples which are clearly beyond the capability of human authorship – and the values of Pi and e in the two key verses about creation are among these.

Bible numbers is, more than most fields of study, a refuge for some very doubtful work. However, some critics are less than scrupulous and sometimes plain dishonest in their attempts to discredit those working in this field. Chuck Missler provides a lot of good information. The information resources listed in *Reference links* are worth exploring for those who want to find out more about the subject.

Reference links

Gematria in the Jewish Encyclopedia: *www.jewishencyclopedia.com/search?utf8=%E2%9C%93&keywords=gematria&commit=search*

Why are there seven days in a week? Cecil Adams (1973); a concise summary at: *www.straightdope.com/classics/a2_166.html*

Chuck Missler, a short summary of Ivan Panin's work: *www.khouse.org/articles/1995/102*

An alternative link for: *The Inspiration of the Scriptures Scientifically Demonstrated,* Ivan Panin (1899) at: *www.biblebelievers.org.au/panin.htm#Letter%20to%20the%20New%20York%20Sun*

Is the answer to life, the universe, and everything 37? *www.lehigh.edu/~dwp0/Assets/images/Is%20the%20answer%20to%20life,%20the%20universe%20and%20everything%2037%3F%20-%20space%20-%2022%20December%202014%20-%20New%20Scientist.pdf*

A Proof Set in Stone; Peter Bluer; at: *www.biblemaths.com*

An explanation of e, the exponential constant; in *en.wikipedia.org/wiki/E_(mathematical_constant)*

Materialism's Fatal Flaw Is... Matter; Astrophysicist Adam Frank. See more at: *www.evolutionnews.org/2017/03/astrophysicist-adam-frank-materialisms-fatal-flaw-ismatter/#sthash. WTmBmWeT.dpuf*

The Jewish value of Pi: 1 Kings 7:23,26; *www.purplemath.com/modules/bibleval.htm*

CHAPTER TWENTY-FIVE

The Great Isaiah Scroll

The scroll of the prophet Isaiah was handed to him. Unrolling it, he found the place where it is written, "The Spirit of the Lord is upon me, because he has anointed me to preach good news to the poor. He has sent me to proclaim freedom for the prisoners and recovery of sight for the blind, to release the oppressed, to proclaim the year of the Lord's favour." Then he rolled up the scroll, gave it back to the attendant and sat down.

Luke 4:17-20 (NIV)

The discovery of the Dead Sea Scrolls, and particularly the Great Isaiah Scroll, proves that there have been virtually no alterations to the Hebrew scriptures over vast periods of time.

About forty miles and nineteen centuries from Nazareth, where Jesus unrolled the Isaiah scroll, three shepherds were supposedly searching for a lost sheep. Their names were Muhammad ed-Dibh, Juma Muhammad and Khalil Musa. It was 1947, and the British Palestine Police Force was struggling to counter the rising level of terrorist violence, both Arab and Jewish, in an area where there had been over four thousand terrorist attacks recorded in the previous four years. In these very turbulent times these three men decided to explore some fairly inaccessible caves in the Jordan valley, and they managed to scramble into the small cave entrance halfway up the steep cliff, when they were surprised to see some big jars. Inside there were rolled up manuscripts. They had dealt in a few antiquities, and knew they might be able to earn some extra money, but they had to be careful. They found a buyer, and it was not long before news got out of some amazing document finds, and the secret of the caves was out. Over the following few years, eleven caves were found with documents hidden inside.

Some nine hundred texts were discovered. They mostly appeared to have been written for a group of Essenes, in the main somewhere around 200-50 BC, and were hidden before 70 AD when the Romans came to besiege Jerusalem a second time. These are known collectively as 'The Dead Sea Scrolls', and show the life and teaching of an apocalyptic Jewish group who were eagerly awaiting the arrival of their Messiah. Most of the texts were visions and commentaries and explanations of things in the scriptures, and there were priestly rules for their community. The breakaway Jewish sect who owned them obviously disapproved strongly of the way the Temple was being run in Jerusalem, just a few miles away.

Among the texts discovered at Qumran was a complete scroll of the book of Isaiah. Now, this scroll was not a copy of Isaiah produced by the scribes who copied the texts for the Temple and the synagogues, but one produced for a zealous breakaway group. However, what was discovered confounded many of the 20th century scholars. They found that this scroll had hardly any significant variations from the version of Isaiah found in the Tanakh (official Hebrew Bible).

Isaiah was a prophet working in the second half of the 8th century BC (i.e. approximately between 750 and 700 BC). By the beginning of the 20th century, many biblical scholars argued that not only had there been copying changes by inattentive copyists, but that there were really three different authors of Isaiah. The first one had probably written his part about 500 BC, and the others over the next 300 or 400 years, between about 200 to 100 BC. Within a few years this idea had become mainstream in American and European universities and seminaries. And as the oldest text of Isaiah available anywhere was only nine hundred years old, from about 1,000 AD, theories could be built on the possibility of extensive changes through seventeen centuries and dozens of generations of inattentive copyists before that time. Any idea of respect for the rigour of the Jewish scribal copying traditions did not count for much against this kind of scholarly argument – until some inquisitive Bedouin men went searching among some caves.

The simple fact was that the Great Isaiah scroll was at least 1,100 years older than the next oldest copy of the book, possibly 1,300 years older. It was more than twice as old as anything previously available, and even more, it dated from barely six hundred years after the death of Isaiah, possibly less than five hundred years. It certainly predates the hypothetical second and third 'Isaiahs'. It is a single work with no indications of gaps or changes even between the hypothetical sections attributed to the 'different authors'. At one stroke, it provided evidence that discredited generations of scholarly opinions.

The copying work in the scroll is not of the standards of the Rabbis, and there are modifications of spelling and grammar which match the Aramaic dialect that the Essenes would have spoken (commentator Fred Miller offers the examples of the differences between 'ye' and 'thee', and 'thou' and 'you'). And yet, the correspondence between the Great Isaiah Scroll and the traditional text is remarkable. You will find far greater variations between modern English translations of Isaiah than between this scroll and the Masoretic text. Jeff Benner offers a comparison between the King James translation of the traditional text, and a translation of the scroll using the same style of English grammar and vocabulary, from Isaiah 53:1-3:

> *King James Version (KJV):*
>
> *(1) Who hath believed our report? and to whom is the arm of the LORD revealed? (2) For he shall grow up before him as a tender plant, and as a root out of a dry ground: he hath no form nor comeliness; and when we shall see him, there is no beauty that we should desire him. (3) He is despised and rejected of men; a man of sorrows, and acquainted with grief: and we hid as it were our faces from him; he was despised, and we esteemed him not.*
>
> *Great Isaiah Scroll (with variations underlined):*
>
> *(1) Who hath believed our report? and to whom is the arm of the LORD revealed? (2) For he shall grow up before him as*

> *a tender plant, and as a root out of dry ground; he hath no form nor he hath comeliness; and when we shall see him, there is no beauty that we should desire ourselves. (3) He is despised and rejected of men and man of sorrows, and he knows grief: and we hid as it were our faces from him and despised him, and we esteemed him not.*

These differences are very minor, not changing the meaning of the text in any significant way.

Comment

A vast edifice of critical scholarship has been built up on the speculative hypothesis of 'three Isaiahs', and the prevailing assumption of massive textual corruptions occurring down the centuries. The repeated historical 'anchors' in the text (such as Isaiah 1:1; 6:1; 7:1) linking the work of the prophet to a series of identifiable monarchs were ignored. In other fields of archaeology those would have been seized on as evidence, and once the existence of those monarchs had been independently established, would have been enough to validate the document. There is no historical evidence of this quality available to validate the history of any nation or monarch in Western Europe for many centuries after the date of Isaiah.

The implication of the Greater Isaiah Scroll (a non-expert copyist's work) is that, were Jesus to arrive in a synagogue today and ask for their book of Isaiah, what he would see is something identical in wording to the one he read from in Nazareth about 27 AD. And that would have been virtually identical (except perhaps for a change in the style of script) to the one written by Isaiah himself just over seven hundred years earlier. And if this is true for the book of Isaiah, then it should be presumed true for the other Hebrew scriptures.

Reference links

Background to Dead Sea Scrolls, Dr James Tabor:
clas-pages.uncc.edu/james-tabor/archaeology-and-the-dead-sea-scrolls

The Emmaus Mystery; Carsten Thiede (2005); p. 138; see:
www.telegraph.co.uk/culture/3639501/Gospel-truth.html

Translation of the Great Isaiah Scroll by Fred Miller (2001):
www.ao.net/~fmoeller/qa-tran.htm

Jeff Benner, Isaiah scroll and the Masoretic Text (2007):
www.ancient-hebrew.org/bible_isaiahscroll.html

CHAPTER TWENTY-SIX

By the Rivers of Babylon

> *By the rivers of Babylon we sat and wept when we remembered Zion. There on the poplars we hung our harps, for there our captors asked us for songs, our tormentors demanded songs of joy; they said, "Sing us one of the songs of Zion!" How can we sing the songs of the LORD while in a foreign land?*
>
> *Psalm 137:1-4 (NIV)*

The book of Daniel, which prophesies in detail events that happened between 530 and 160 BC, has been authenticated by archaeological and palaeographic discoveries.

Deciphering marks chiselled into rock, three hundred feet up a sheer cliff face, was not for the faint-hearted, but Henry Rawlinson was an intrepid twenty-five-year old officer, serving with the army of the East India Company. In 1835, he was assisting in the work of training the army of the Shah of Persia when he became fascinated by the carvings high up on a cliff, in the mountains near Behistun (now Bisutun, in Iran). There are three different texts on the cliff, all in the wedge-shaped cuneiform script, and Rawlinson copied out the first one, which turned out to be written in Old Persian.

Figure 24. Behistun cliff carvings.
Courtesy: Hara1603.

This was fortunate, because he had already learned Persian for his army work. He also had help from Georg Grotefend, a cuneiform expert. The next bonus was that in the first section of the inscription was a list of Persian kings, who lived during the 5th century BC. It turned out that the inscription and carvings had been put there by the Persian king Darius, who ruled the Persian Empire from 521 to 486 BC. And the interesting thing about Darius, for Bible students, is that he is the second of the "three more kings"[54] of Persia mentioned in Daniel 11:2. The inscription records Darius' takeover of power in Persia and his successful wars in the first six years of his reign. Darius had taken care to protect his inscriptions by having the hillside beneath the inscriptions removed, to leave a sheer cliff face.

Rawlinson progressed in the army, and was able to return to Behistun in 1843. This time, he set up planks to cross the gap between

[54] NKJV.

the Old Persian text and the other two cuneiform inscriptions further across the cliff. He copied these, and made casts of them with papier-maché. They turned out to be the same statement in the Elamite and Babylonian languages. Babylonian was a form of the Aramaic language, in use by many nationalities from the Eastern seaboard of the Mediterranean across to Persia. Having the same the inscription in these three languages provided the means to decipher and translate a large range of other texts found in these and similar languages. Hebrew differs from Aramaic in the way that, say, Spanish differs from Italian or Portugese.

In 1854, Rawlinson was serving as a diplomat in Baghdad, when he discovered a clay cylinder with the records of King Nabonidus on it, and a clay tablet with the chronicles of Nabonidus. These provided a record of the history of Babylon from 556 to 539 BC, when it fell to the Persians. It explained the position of Belshazzar (Daniel chapter 5), confirming that he ruled Babylon as co-regent under his father, and that he was every bit as irresponsible and dissolute as Daniel said. This was the first extra-biblical evidence of the existence of Belshazzar, whose name had been lost to history after the 5th century BC.

Daniel is the only book of the Hebrew Bible to be written in two languages, Aramaic and Hebrew. Daniel 1:1 to Daniel 2:4a and Chapters 8 to 12 are all written in Hebrew, while Daniel 2:4a to 7:28 (the passages dealing with the activities of the Babylonian and Persian courts) are written in Aramaic. These facts caused many critics to argue that the use of Aramaic reflected a late date for the writing of the whole book of Daniel.

The developing study of Aramaic has shown that the Aramaic section of the book of Daniel, far from being evidence for a late date, instead proves an early one (before 500 BC). This is because the Aramaic in Daniel was a form used only by the royal courts of the region, known as 'Imperial Aramaic', which went out of use as Persian power grew (and was then replaced by the Greeks). There are also some Persian words used in Daniel; these were also held to be evidence of a late date of writing (assuming that the use of the Persian language became more widespread in the centuries between Cyrus and Alexander the Great). More recent analysis shows that these Persian words belong to Old Persian, which fell out of use before 300 BC.

The use of Imperial Aramaic and Old Persian in the same document is the 'signature' of a writer who must have served in the courts of both the Babylonian and the Persian Empires (and therefore at the precise time of the historical events in Daniel).

It has also been argued that the existence of Greek words in Daniel show a late (post 335 BC) date of writing, reflecting the influence of the Greek-speaking empire of Alexander the Great. In fact, there are only three such words. In Daniel 3:5-7 are references to three musical instruments which have Greek names. The instruments are translated into English in a few different ways (as can be seen by studying different Bible translations), showing that there is uncertainty about what the differences are between them.

Possible translations for these three Greek instruments (sambuke, psalterion, symphonia) include "lyre, harp, pipes" (NIV); "sackbut, psaltery, and dulcimer" (KJV); "harp, psaltery, bagpipe" (NAB); "zither, lute, bagpipe" (CJB).

There are many stone carvings and vase paintings from territories to the west of Babylonia during the first millennium BC showing stringed instruments that are surprisingly similar in use over this wide region, and the numbers of strings vary from four to ten. What has not been achieved is a clear identification of the names of each instrument.

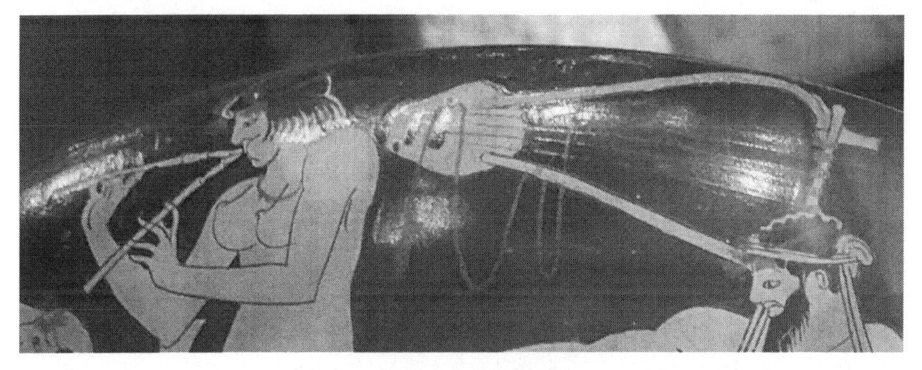

Figure 26. Greek vase. Girl with pipes and 5-string harp. 480 BC
Fitzwilliam museum, Cambridge.
© Martin Johnson.

Figure 27. Greek vases showing musicians with pipes and eight- and seven-string instruments, ca. 470/480 BC. Fitzwilliam museum, Cambridge. © Martin Johnson.

This is not surprising; does everyone today in the Western world know the difference between a violin and a viola? Or a banjo and a mandolin? Or how many strings a guitar should have? There was a horn or trumpet-type instrument, a flute or pipe, three different stringed instruments, which could be described as harp/lyre, zither and dulcimer, and something that was possibly a bagpipe. The last is the most difficult, as the Greek word used for it is similar to the later Greek word 'symphonia', used to describe instruments playing together.

The band that was ordered to play for Nebuchadnezzar that day was probably made up of Greek musicians. It seems that the Jews were not the only ones ordered to get their instruments out and sing for their overlords (as in Psalm 137).

The Dead Sea Scrolls include a few copies of Daniel, made between about 150 BC and 50 BC. These are copies made from different earlier manuscripts, showing that the original text is centuries older than any of these copies. Many of the other Dead Sea Scrolls have extensive citations from, and references to, the book of Daniel, showing that the original was revered as scripture long before then. One book, the *Genesis Apocryphon,* demonstrates that the Hebrew grammar and syntax used in the later chapters of Daniel are a good match for that used in the 6th and 5th centuries BC.

Comment

Daniel is attested by contemporary records, paleo-linguistic studies, archaeology and textual findings from the Dead Sea Scrolls. Its internal language reflects a writer who worked at the level of the imperial court in Babylon and early Persia. The fact that there are only three Greek words in the book (and those for musical instruments) indicates the writing must have been done long before the Greek conquest of Palestine and Babylon (and Persia) under Alexander the Great (336-323 BC).

This would normally be regarded as great and unchallengeable support for the authenticity of an ancient book. Why is this not the case for the book of Daniel? The answer lies in the prophecies he wrote, which indisputably came to pass, suggesting that they had come from a God who knows the future. This is an idea that many historians and Bible scholars are opposed to.

Darius, who had his record carved in stone at Behistun, is only one of many kings whose activities are listed in the book of Daniel before they happened. The prophecy of four successive empires delivered to Nebuchadnezzar was already halfway fulfilled (in number of empires) by the time Daniel died, but the details of the empire of Alexander the Great and the subsequent break-up into four kingdoms under the Ptolemies and their battles between themselves were still to some. Critics of the authenticity of Daniel are usually searching for ways to deny that it is possible for anyone to have recorded such detailed history before it happens. The Bible says:

Remember the former things, those of long ago;
I am God, and there is no other;
I am God, and there is none like me.
I make known the end from the beginning,

from ancient times what is still to come,
I say, 'My purpose will stand, and I will do what I please.'

Isaiah 46:9-10 (NIV)

Reference links

The musical instruments in Nebuchadnezzar's orchestra; T Mitchel, R Joyce (1965); at:
https://biblicalstudies.org.uk/pdf/daniel_mitchell.pdf

Daniel Doings; Kevin Closson & J P Holding; at:
www.tektonics.org/af/danieldefense.html

The Linguistic Argument for the Date of Daniel; W D Jeffcoat; at:
www.apologeticspress.org/rr/reprints/Linguistic-Argument-for-the-Dat.pdf

A review of the arguments for and against a late dating for Daniel:
www.christian-thinktank.com/qwhendan3a.html

Musical instruments in Ancient Greece:
www.metmuseum.org/toah/hd/grmu/hd_grmu.htm

Chapter Twenty-Seven

Landfill Sites and Scriptures

When you come, bring the cloak that I left with Carpus at Troas, and my scrolls, especially the parchments.

2 Timothy 4:13 (NIV)

I have much to write to you, but I do not want to use paper and ink. Instead I hope to visit you and talk with you face to face, so our joy may be complete.

2 John 12 (NIV)

Early papyri prove that the books of the New Testament were being circulated in their present form no later than 100 AD.

Although he was only twenty-nine years old, Bernard Pyne Grenfell had already published three books containing translations of ancient texts during the previous two years. His most recent work, *An Alexandrian Erotic Fragment and other Greek Papyri,* had been co-authored with his new colleague, Arthur Surridge Hunt. They were both former scholars of Queen's College, Oxford, and were destined to become partners in the discovery of the greatest collections of papyrus texts ever found. Even today, over a hundred years later, there are more of the texts they found waiting to be deciphered, translated and published than have so far been done.

In the winter of 1897/1898, on the outskirts of the former Greek-Egyptian town of Oxyrhynchus, two hundred miles South of Cairo,

Grenfell and Hunt looked at some old heaps of city refuse, twenty feet high, covered with sand. At first sight, it looked as if it was only refuse. Then, they realised that there were scraps of papyrus among the refuse, just under the sand. The arid climate meant that, in the previous 1,800 years or more, there had not been enough rainfall or water to rot the ancient paper. In the ten years of excavation that followed, 100,000 pieces of papyrus were unearthed. 90% of these were not literary texts, but financial accounts, legal documents, domestic correspondence – even shopping lists. Among the literary texts there has been found a treasure trove of ancient Greek literature, and examples of a wide variety of early Christian writings, including fragments from the Gospels of Matthew and John. These particular texts have been dated to the early part of the second century AD, that is, between 100 and 150 AD. The papyrus finds were shipped to Oxford University, where they remain.

A few years later, farther south in Egypt, near Tebtunis, on 16 January 1900, Grenfell and Hunt were excavating a site where they were hoping to find some human burials (because of the papyrus texts usually placed with mummies). They had found a cemetery of mummified crocodiles, which were thought to be useless for archaeology, when an angry workman broke a container with a crocodile inside. Everyone was astonished to see that the crocodile was wrapped in papyrus, and also stuffed with it. Of the thousand-plus crocodiles at this site, only thirty-one were found with papyrus stuffing, which were shipped to Berkeley University, California. Most of the twenty-three thousand fragments in this collection have yet to be fully catalogued, let alone deciphered and translated. The Tebtunis papyri came from an Egyptian community centred on a nearby temple, and date from around 200 BC to 50 AD, and evidence the widespread use of written documents in the region. The Oxyrhynchus papyri have proved to have much more literary value, and to be important for the study of the development of the early Christian church and the New Testament documents.

One important papyrus find is the 'Rylands Papyrus P52', a fragment of John's Gospel chapter 18, believed to date from between 100 and 125 AD. Others include the 'Magdalen Papyrus', purchased in Luxor, Egypt in 1901, the 'Barcelona Papyrus', a codex also found in

Egypt, with fragments of Matthew's Gospel, and the 'Bodmer' papyri, a collection of documents with several secular and classical texts, but also a large part of the Gospels of Luke and John (two copies), and the epistles of Jude and 1 and 2 Peter. These have mainly been dated between 150 and 200 AD.

A major controversy erupted in 1994, after the papyrologist Professor Carsten Thiede published the results of tests he had done on the Magdalen papyrus and a fragment of Mark's Gospel 6:52-3 from cave 7 at Qumran (papyrus 7Q5). The Magdalen papyrus (Matthew 26, fragments of ten different verses) had been dated around 200 AD, but comparisons with the finds at Qumran led Thiede to the conclusion that it was of a similar age to them, and particularly to the fragment from cave 7. The point about this is that the caves at Qumran were sealed and abandoned prior to the Roman conquest of Jerusalem in 70 AD. Analysis of the Magdalen and similar papyri had previously rested on the styles of writing, but Thiede focussed on the papyrus used. He was an expert on the Dead Sea Scrolls, and he had tested the Magdalen papyrus with a scanning laser microscope, and coupled this with his undoubted expertise in recognition of writing styles. The laser microscope could detect not only the thickness of the leaves which made up the papyrus, but also the pressure and slant applied to the pen, and the depth of the ink penetration. Thiede argued that this document could date from as early as 50 AD, and that if the document in question were not a passage from Mark's Gospel, his findings (based on papyrology) would be unremarkable.

Cave 7 at Qumran also produced other important papyrus fragments, which the Jesuit scholar Jose O'Callaghan identified as being from 1 Timothy, James, Acts, Romans and 2 Peter. This analysis threatened to overturn much New Testament scholarship, which had been built on the assumptions of late dating of the manuscripts. In *Reference links* are some examples of the range and depth of this controversy. It remains safe to say that if these fragments were of any other ancient book, then they would probably have been accepted long ago. From our perspective, they are reasonable evidence that all these books were in circulation around the Mediterranean world well before Cave 7 was sealed (probably 68 AD).

Figure 28. Magdalen Papyrus (left); Qumran fragment 7Q5 (right).

What do the papyri mean?

Nowadays, in leading universities such as Oxford, Manchester and Berkeley, teams of papyrologists are spending their time sifting through these fragments of two-thousand-year-old papyrus. The work is a combination of jigsaw puzzle and code-breaking. New technologies are helping to display faded marks to show more of the writing and make clearer the letters that are on each page and each fragment.

A LITERATE SOCIETY

What they are studying is the clear proof of a literate society in Egypt, where ordinary people centuries before Jesus were reading and writing, making notes about everyday things, busily jotting down the trivia of their day-to-day lives. The pages that were no longer needed were treated as waste – some even being recycled into stuffing for mummified crocodiles. The evidence of a literate society is important to show that writing and the possession of written documents was no longer the exclusive preserve of priests and government officials.

GOSPEL FRAGMENTS MEAN GRASS-ROOTS CHRISTIANITY

Where someone copied out a play or poem, it was for their private or local use. Similarly, where someone wrote down a collection of sayings of Jesus, or copied an extract of a Gospel or letter of the apostle Paul, it was so they could have it for their own use, or with their friends. The fact that these bits of paper got thrown out with the rubbish shows that these were not treasured documents. There is nothing here of the ancient Jewish veneration for their scriptures, where the vellum scrolls of the scriptures were ceremonially buried when not fit for further use. The fact that the rubbish heaps contained fragments of the New Testament books and Christian writings shows above all that Christianity was a grass-roots movement, thriving among the ordinary people. It was going to be another 1,400 years before the arrival of the printing press, and the flood of books it produced. There was no cheaper or better way for ordinary people of getting written material than copying it out themselves.

EARLY DATES OF THE WRITTEN NEW TESTAMENT

If the local Christians in a town in central Egypt were copying out the New Testament books around 100-125 AD, then editions existed for them to copy from. Ancient tradition assigns the Gospel of Matthew to the apostle of that name, a tax-gatherer. Mark's Gospel is traditionally believed to be the memoirs of Peter, who was executed by about 65 AD. Luke's Gospel is believed to have been written by the companion of Paul, a Syrian doctor, who says at the beginning of his Gospel that he has collected his material from many sources. Luke records no events later than about 61 AD (prior to the murder of James, the brother of Jesus). Paul was executed by emperor Nero at a similar time to Peter. John's Gospel records none of the events after the death of Peter (alluded to in John 21:19), and certainly not the destruction of Jerusalem in 70 AD. Therefore, all the Gospels, the book of Acts, and the epistles of Paul and Peter must have been completed before then.

RAPID SPREAD OF THE WRITTEN DOCUMENTS

The dates of these papyri allow about fifty years for the Christian documents to have been copied and circulated throughout the Christian world before the copies were made which turned up at Oxyrhynchus. The survival of the papyri found by Grenfell, Hunt and those that came after them is by an accident of climate. What was happening in central Egypt is likely to have been repeated all over the Mediterranean region and the Near East. There are traditions that the gospel had reached

India, China and Britain within the lifetimes of the apostles themselves. This is consistent with a grass-roots movement, whose members were obeying the instruction, "...go and make disciples of all nations..."[55]

Further textual evidence

The oldest example of a complete, or near-complete, edition of the New Testament is the Chester Beatty papyrus (200-250 AD), which is supported by thousands of manuscripts in later centuries. When compared to other ancient documents, there are vastly more copies of the New Testament books, and from dates far closer to the original time of writing. One of the most famous ancient books is Homer's Iliad, written about 700 BC, a contemporary of Isaiah. Homer's work with 643 copies known to exist is the ancient book with by far the largest number of manuscript copies after the New Testament, but the oldest (full) manuscripts date from the 10th century AD, with fragments as old as the 3rd century BC.

Julius Caesar wrote his famous work *Gallic Wars* around 50 BC, one hundred years before the Gospels. The oldest surviving manuscript available dates from about 900 AD, making it nearly a thousand years after the date of writing. Only nine or ten good manuscripts survive of this famous work. The New Testament, however, is by far the most widely copied ancient book of all, with around 24,000 manuscripts surviving. Even though many of the copies have letter-level variations, a result of enthusiastic but untrained copyists, the accuracy of the text so preserved can be shown to be around 99.5%. And no variations result in any changes of fact or doctrine in what is recorded.

Comment

It has been claimed that the early Christians were not literate, and committed everything to memory, and that a gap of centuries took place before the New Testament circulated in anything like its present form. It has also been claimed that church leaders adapted the writings for their own purposes, and that the historical Jesus was nothing more

[55] Matthew 28:19 (NIV).

than a charismatic rabbi, who did not perform miracles or get resurrected.

The papyrus evidence shows that the arguments and assumptions behind all these ideas are false. Of all the ancient books ever written, the New Testament books are supported by the strongest evidence of all, and from within a generation of the crucifixion. No other ancient work has manuscript evidence from so close to its time of writing, or in such abundance.

Reference links

Treasure of the Mummy Crocs; Kathleen Scalise (1996); at:
www.berkeley.edu/news/berkeleyan/1996/1211/crocs.html

Bancroft Library, Berkeley University, centre for the Tebtunis Papyri, at:
tebtunis.berkeley.edu/collection/contents.html#mummies

John Rylands Papyrus collection, Manchester University, at:
www.library.manchester.ac.uk/about/support-us/jrri/priority-collections/papyrus-collection

Oxyrhynchus Papyri at Glasgow University, at:
special.lib.gla.ac.uk/teach/papyrus/oxyrhynchus.html

Manuscript evidence for superior New Testament reliability by Matt Slick 2008, at:
www.carm.org/evidence/textualevidence.htm

Homeric papyri, at:
homermultitext.blogspot.co.uk/2010/07/homeric-papyri-and-homer-multitext.html

A rebuttal of Thiede's views on 7Q5, and O'Callaghan's identifications of the Cave 7 fragments can be found at: *bible.org/article/7q5-earliest-nt-papyrus*
Dr Bill Cooper (among others) explains this as a determination to uphold the old critical consensus, and it may be compared with Carsten Thiede's explanation at:
www.forananswer.org/Top_Ath/GreekQumranFrag.htm
A list of 'dissenting' works on this subject is at: *www-relg-studies.scu.edu/facstaff/murphy/courses/sctr027/artifacts/qumran-gospel-frgs.htm*
Bill Cooper covers the controversy in depth in his book, *The Authenticity of the New Testament Pt. 1,* and gives examples of the mendacity of some of the leading critics:
www.amazon.co.uk/Authenticity-New-Testament-Part-Gospels-ebook/dp/B00EZVOSVW

Excellent book on this subject: *Evidence that Demands a Verdict, Vol II;* Josh McDowell; Here's Life, San Bernardino CA (1986); available at:
www.amazon.com/Evidence-That-Demands-Verdict-Vol/dp/0840743793

CHAPTER TWENTY-EIGHT

Friends and Enemies: What the Church Fathers Said

For it has been granted to you on behalf of Christ not only to believe on him, but also to suffer for him.

Philippians 1:29 (NIV)

The fathers of the early church, some of whom were personal friends of the apostles, referenced the twenty-seven books of the New Testament extensively in their writings.

The mob packed the stadium and was screaming in fury. They demanded that the dignified old man standing with the ruler of the city be torn apart by wild beasts. The ruler, Philip the Asiarch, checked with his aides, who said that because the games were over, there were no lions left. When the crowd was told this, they roared, "Burn him alive!" Philip the Asiarch agreed, but told the crowd they would need to bring the wood, and turned back to continue his conversation with the condemned man. In no time at all, men were running to and fro, and a big pile of logs and brushwood was built. The old man calmly stripped to the waist, but struggled with taking off his shoes: as a wealthy landowner, this was something his servants usually did. Then the executioners came with hammer and nails, to fix him to the stake, but he asked politely that they just tie him with rope.

He promised them he would be able to withstand the flames, and his natural dignity and authority was such that they agreed. From his position at the stake, he prayed out loud, thanking and praising God and Jesus Christ. When he had finished, they set fire to the wood and great flames roared up. What they saw next, though, astonished them. The flames went up in a ring and curved over, above the old man, so they did not burn him. The mob was so enraged by this that one of the soldiers in the execution team had to take his short sword and stab the old man to death. Then a section of the mob demanded that the body should not be given to his friends, and they were allowed to take it away and burn it, and only after that were his friends allowed to bury his bones.

The old man, Polycarp, was Bishop of Smyrna, and the execution took place on 22 February 156 AD. He had been challenged and pleaded with many times by the police chief and the rulers of Smyrna to just declare, "Caesar is Lord," and all would be well. He had said he could not, because this would mean renouncing Jesus:

> *"Eighty-six years have I served Him, and He has done me no wrong: how then can I blaspheme my King who saved me?"*[56]

So ended the life of the last man known to have been trained personally by any of the apostles. The apostle John himself had appointed him Bishop of Smyrna. The angriest and most strident section of the mob in Smyrna was that of the Jews of the town, those of whom John had written, "those who say they are Jews and are not, but are a Synagogue of Satan"[57]. This was the group who had insisted that the body of Polycarp not be given to the Christians until they had made sure it could not be preserved in recognisable form. It is believed that these people practised a form of semi-pagan worship with Jewish 'trappings'.

---

[56] *A New Eusebius;* ed. J Stevenson; SPCK, London (1982); p. 21.
[57] Revelation 2:9 (NIV).

More early church fathers

Polycarp was only one of many prominent Christians who were arrested and executed ("martyred") during the first three centuries after the resurrection of Jesus. Christian leaders who were martyred before Polycarp included Ignatius, second Bishop of Antioch (Syria). He was arrested and deported to Rome in 107 AD, to die in the arena; there are seven surviving letters, which he wrote to different churches on his journey to his death in Rome.

Another close acquaintance of the apostle John was Papias, Bishop of Hierapolis (near Laodicea). Writing soon after 100 AD, he explains how carefully he himself checked out the authenticity of the New Testament Gospels and books – he wrote five books himself. He affirms that Mark's Gospel was written down by Mark from the apostle Peter, and says that Matthew's Gospel was originally written in Aramaic (the language of Syria, Galilee and Judea).

Clement, who became Bishop of Rome in 89 AD, is almost certainly the person mentioned by Paul in Philippians 4:3, and he wrote letters to the Corinthian church which still survive.

The importance of the testimony of the fathers of the early church

Again and again, the church fathers give testimony of how believers resisted state persecution even though it meant cruel tortures, and even crueller deaths. The charge of 'atheism' levelled at many of the martyrs was because they would not acknowledge the divinity of Caesar, or the 'Genius' of Rome. These were the followers of a Jesus who had gone to death on the cross – for them. This is how important their belief in Jesus was. And yet, they were not a death-seeking group; they believed it their duty to flee persecution (and Polycarp taught his followers this).

> *And when you are persecuted in one place, flee to another.*
>
> *Matthew 10:23 (NIV)*

However, they stood in opposition to teachings that would have allowed them to compromise with the established systems, and pagan practices, and made persecution unavoidable. This brought them further trouble, and much of the writings of the early fathers is directed at the false arguments brought by those who wanted to 'water down' Christianity.

The importance of the writings of the fathers

The quantity of writings of the church fathers is enormous, and in virtually everything they wrote, they quoted scripture. Polycarp quotes the New Testament about fifty times. There are about 1,200 New Testament references or citations in the surviving works of Irenaeus (2nd century); and 2,500 in the works of Tertullian (also 2nd century). All in all, in the surviving writings of the church fathers prior to 325 AD, 86,000 citations were catalogued by John Burgon, a 19th century Bible scholar[58], while Sir David Dalrymple (18th century Scottish judge) claimed to have identified all but eleven verses of the New Testament from these sources. These people were writing during a period which was hostile to their beliefs, and with determined and skilful opposition. They would not have got away with fabricating scriptures, or claiming that books had apostolic authority when they did not.

It is also clear from the writings of the fathers that all the books which form the New Testament as we know it gained this status during the period when the leaders personally trained by Peter, Paul and John were still alive.

Comment

The story of the martyrdom of Polycarp shows the social conflict felt by the authorities in having to take such action against a prominent and dignified old man. Their custom was to show enormous respect to the elderly, and they even appealed to Polycarp to show respect for his own great age. This contrasts very strongly with the insane hatred of the mob. But Polycarp, at the end, knew he was following a tradition of martyrdom that began with Jesus Christ, and he could do no other. The information we have on this period of history is very considerable, yet

[58] Dean John Burgon not only catalogued these 86,000 citations, by 76 "Church Fathers" writing before 400 AD, he also used them to demonstrate the reliability of the Byzantine text of the New Testament. See: *www.deanburgonsociety.org/DeanBurgon/whowasdb.htm*

some modern writers (e.g. Dan Brown, *The Da Vinci Code*) write as if it is a time about which little can be known.

The Synod of Hyppo in 393 AD listed the twenty-seven books in the present New Testament canon, but in doing this it merely affirmed the authority of the canonical books that had been established for over 250 years by then. The church fathers were also well aware of a range of spurious pseudo-Christian writings. The idea that there are 'lost Gospels' has been surfacing periodically since the 2nd century. Most of these have their roots in Gnosticism, which is an attempt to marry Christianity to Eastern religious ideas, where 'secret knowledge' plays an important part. All of these spurious documents betray the writers' familiarity with the original Gospels, which they then falsify in different ways. This itself proves the early date of the originals!

The church fathers provide independent evidence of a very robust kind for the authenticity of the books of the New Testament, and very many of them paid with their lives so that we would know the truth.

Reference links

S Carlson's translations of Papias, at:
www.hypotyposeis.org/synoptic-problem/2004/10/external-evidence-papias.html

Papias of Hierapolis, at: *www.textexcavation.com/papias.html*

Ignatius of Antioch, at: *justus.anglican.org/resources/bio/270.html*

Biography of Polycarp, at:
www.christianitytoday.com/history/people/martyrs/polycarp.html

Chapter Twenty-Nine

Eyewitness Evidence

That which was from the beginning, which we have heard, which we have seen with our eyes, which we have looked at and our hands have touched – this we proclaim concerning the Word of life.

1 John 1:1 (NIV)

The New Testament has many eyewitness statements which show it was written by people who were present at the events described.

Maybe, they wondered, Yeshua would use the gathering of crowds for the coming Passover to declare that he was Messiah, come to overthrow Roman rule, and bring in a godly reign for Israel. What they saw that day, however, took them completely by surprise. He fed five thousand people with just five loaves and two small fishes. This reminded them of the manna, feeding their forefathers in the wilderness, or the miracles of Elijah. Here was one greater than either Moses or Elijah! The feeding of the five thousand made such an impact on the disciples of Jesus that it is the only miracle recorded in all four Gospels.

What we can see in the words in this story in Mark's Gospel[59] are the clues that Mark wrote this down from the eyewitness account of a native Aramaic speaker (the apostle Peter). This is just one of many possible examples of eyewitness narratives throughout the books of the

---

[59] Mark 6:30-44.

New Testament. Just in two verses, Mark 6:39-40, we have a wealth of information:

> *Then Jesus directed them to have all the people sit down in groups on the green grass. So they sat down in groups of hundreds and fifties.*
>
> *Mark 6:39-40 (NIV)*

The clues are:

- *The time of year – in verse 39 the grass is green.* Matthew (14:19) and John (6:10) mention the grass; only Mark says it is green. This sets a time in the spring of the year: after April, the grass would have turned dry and brown, except immediately adjacent to a stream where it could have stayed green until the beginning of July. The crowd was far too large to have sat on the banks of a stream.
- *The Greek words 'symposia symposia' in verse 39 (translated "in groups"[60]).* These words literally translate as 'picnic party, picnic party'. This reflects the Aramaic and Hebrew way of doubling a word to say "picnic party by picnic party". The underlying Aramaic (similar to Hebrew) word, probably 'haburta', here translated into Greek, was used to describe a group of people eating the Passover meal together. A native Greek speaker would be more likely to have written "kata symposia" to mean sitting down 'in parties', so the Greek text demonstrates that it is translating an evocative Aramaic expression, and that the translator was probably not a native Greek-speaker.
- *In verse 40, the words translated "in groups" are this time 'prasiai prasiai'.* 'Prasiai' literally means 'flower beds' or 'garden beds', and has been found in rabbinic literature in the exact corresponding Hebrew form describing the way students sit before a rabbi, gaining knowledge. It implies also the colourful appearance of the groups of people. This phrasing would only have been used by a Jewish person.

[60] NIV.

These two short verses reveal the mood of the crowd – excited, as if at a party. They also convey their colourful dress and attentive manner, with the implication that the event resembled both a Passover meal and a rabbinic teaching session. In John's Gospel we are told there was a lot of grass, Matthew tells us they sat on grass, Mark tells us the grass was green. These are all indicative of eyewitness testimony, but the depth of evidence in Mark cannot be explained other than by an eyewitness who was an Aramaic-speaking Jew, and written down by someone who used Greek as a second language. This fits the traditional account that Mark wrote down his Gospel from Peter's recollections. The four Gospels harmonise in this story, yet Mark, the shortest Gospel, has the fullest and most colourful description of the event. This passage is also a good example of the difficulties involved in translation from one language and culture into another![61]

Another passage in Mark, one that does not involve trying to penetrate two languages and cultures below the English translation, suggests an eyewitness other than Peter:

> *A young man, wearing nothing but a linen garment, was following Jesus. When they seized him, he fled naked, leaving his garment behind.*
>
> *Mark 14:51-52 (NIV)*

Most commentators down the ages believe that the "young man" in this curious passage is none other than John Mark himself (the writer of this Gospel). The house where the disciples held the Last Supper was possibly the home of John Mark's mother. The linen garment abandoned here is an expensive one. The point about this passage is that it appears only in Mark's Gospel, and it follows the verse which says, "...everyone deserted him and fled." Therefore, the most likely witness to a naked teenage boy escaping in the darkness would be the boy himself.

---

[61] *The Cambridge Greek Testament Commentary: Mark's Gospel;* C E B Cranfield (1955); pp. 216-223, discusses the language shifts found here, while in *Simon Peter, a Study of Discipleship;* Lord Elton; Northumberland Press, Gateshead on Tyne (1965); pp. 80-82, Elton notes Turner's commentary that, "No English rendering can reproduce Peter's visualisation of the scene."

The Gospels are full of narrative statements that indicate eyewitness reporting, with dialogue and events unlikely to have been dreamed up long afterwards by people who were not there.

The New Testament says, *we were there!*

> *We did not follow cleverly invented stories when we told you about the power and coming of our Lord Jesus Christ, but we were eye-witnesses of his majesty. For he received honour and glory from God the Father when the voice came to him from the Majestic Glory, saying "This is my Son, whom I love; with him I am well pleased." We ourselves heard this voice that came from heaven when we were with him on the sacred mountain.*
>
> *2 Peter 1:16-18 (NIV)*

Comment

The many eyewitness statements in the Gospels and other New Testament books distinguish them from the fictitious and literary works being circulated during that period. The Gospels of Matthew, Mark and John have always been held to be the direct accounts by the apostles of their time with Jesus. Luke has always been presented as a work of compilation, but validated by the authority of Paul.

The testimony of these people is that Jesus lived, worked miracles, raised the dead and was put to death on a cross. Then, he was resurrected from the dead, and seen by these people and many that knew him. The Gospels are accurate history testified to by people that were there. It took over a hundred years before people appeared who wanted to deny these things had happened: that Jesus was really only a man who was not resurrected, or alternatively that he was a kind of visible spirit who was never truly human.

Reference links

J Warner Wallace provides good summaries in: *coldcasechristianity.com/2016/rapid-response-i-dont-believe-the-gospels-were-written-by-eyewitnesses*
coldcasechristianity.com/2016/the-apostles-wrote-the-gospels-as-eyewitness-accounts

A good review of Carsten Thiede's work published in *Eyewitness to Jesus;* Doubleday, New York (1996). See: *www.preteristarchive.com/Books/1996_thiede_eyewitness.html*

CHAPTER THIRTY

The View from Outside the Church

It seemed good to the Holy Spirit and to us not to burden you with anything beyond the following requirements: you are to abstain from food sacrificed to idols, from blood, from the meat of strangled animals and from sexual immorality. You will do well to avoid these things.

Acts 15:28-29 (NIV)

Christianity, and therefore the New Testament books, had spread widely by the end of the 1st century AD.

The emperor Trajan agreed with the senate in Rome that the situation in Bithynia had gone too far. The province (along the north coast of present-day Turkey) was a shambles. Five consecutive governors had been sent out there who had failed. The local landowners had cooked up accusations against them – which all had to be dealt with in protracted court cases back in Rome. There was extensive mismanagement and corruption in the towns and districts. The tax revenues had collapsed, and the town leaders kept dreaming up expensive prestige building projects they couldn't afford. And the local leaders let their Roman rulers know they were socially and culturally superior to them with their Greek heritage. The place was trouble, but as long as they didn't rise up in rebellion, the emperor couldn't send the army in to knock heads together and teach them proper respect.

So, they made a plan. There was a man in Rome, a senator of consul rank who had a reputation as a brilliant finance manager and a very sharp lawyer. His own wealth, breeding and cultural accomplishments would make him more than a match for the snobbery of the locals. His last major task had been to sort out the problems with the sewers of Rome. But (as his contemporaries would have said) he could bore for Italy. Who could forget the court case about eight years earlier, when he had delivered a speech lasting five whole hours! Had he not understood the emperor's polite hint about brevity? Mind you, his book praising the emperor had been well done and popular, and so had his poems; and then there was the book he published of love letters he had written to his new wife, the lovely Calpurnia. They had married seven years earlier when he was forty and she was fourteen – unusual for an elderly widower to land such an eligible young bride!

One of his inscriptions began, "Pliny the Younger, Curator of the Beds and Banks of the Tiber and the Sewers of Rome, Prefect of the Treasury of Saturn, Prefect of the Military Treasury, Praetor, Tribune of the people, Quaestor of the Emperor, Commissioner of the Roman Knights…" He was just the trouble-shooter they needed for Bithynia!

He took on the task in 109 AD at the age of forty-seven, a good ten or twelve years older than normal governors. And he got the province sorted out: stopped the nonsense, improved a number of the amenities, and (most important) in just a year he was able to report that a financial surplus had been created.

Apart from being a good auditor, and taking steps to recover overdue debts, he sorted out a few building projects causing problems. When confronted with a tricky situation, he used a technique of referring questions to the emperor for advice. This stalled a few situations and gave time to resolve problems without having to act harshly. But, there was one problem that did surprise him: what to do about the Christians?

Pliny wrote to Trajan in about 112 AD seeking advice. He explained that he really did not know whether there were special factors that should be taken into account when people were accused of Christianity:

> *Meantime, this is the course I have taken with those who were accused before me as Christians. I asked them whether*

> *they were Christians, and if they confessed, I asked them a second and third time with threats of punishment. If they kept to it, I ordered them for execution; for I held no question that whatever it was that they admitted, in any case obstinacy and unbending perversity deserved to be punished...*
>
> *As for those who said they neither were nor ever had been Christians, I thought it right to let them go, since they recited a prayer to the gods at my dictation, made supplication with incense and wine to your statue, which I had ordered to be brought into court for the purpose together with the images of the gods, and moreover cursed Christ – things which (so it is said) those who are really Christians cannot be made to do.*[62]

He reported finding people who had given up being Christians as much as twenty years earlier. His real surprise, though, was discovering that all the ex-Christians said they did was to meet before daylight on one day a week and worship, and bind themselves not to commit theft or robbery or adultery. And because Pliny had banned 'clubs', they had complied with his law. Cannibalism and incest were, astonishingly, not taking place! He describes how he had two "maid servants" who were deaconesses (servants of the church) put to torture, just to make sure of this information. Any who came before him and refused to abandon Christ were put to death – to let everyone know that Roman rule would be upheld. His view was that anyone who was failing to honour Caesar was acting defiantly, and deserved to be executed.

The reports of innocuous and moral behaviour might have led Pliny to think the Christians were not a problem, but he was not concerned with morality (remember, this man was an accountant!) There was a major problem with temples that had fallen into disuse all over the area and become deserted. That meant that the trade of supplying animals for sacrifice, and fodder for the animals for sacrifice and so on, had all fallen away. Christianity was upsetting the economy of the region! He

62 *A New Eusebius;* Ed. J Stevenson; SPCK, London (1982); pp. 13-16.

concluded that he felt the measures he had put into effect should reverse this decline in temple worship!

His reply from Trajan[63] has also survived, and it confirmed the correctness of Pliny's actions in investigating the problem and suppressing "defiant" Christians. The letters also dealt with the problem of receiving anonymous accusations – which were to be ignored. This was an important bonus for the Christians, because under Roman law, if someone made a false accusation of a crime against someone else, they themselves were liable to be given the punishment that the false accusation could have caused. This meant that accusations alleging people to be Christians dropped off dramatically (it could have been a way of working off grudges or getting rid of business competitors).

Pliny was a contemporary of the Roman historians Tacitus and Suetonius, who both confirm widespread Christianity by the end of the 1st century AD, and also of Josephus, the Jewish historian. Josephus writes in some detail about Jesus, and recounts the murder of James, the brother of Jesus, at the hands of the corrupt chief priest in Jerusalem (62 AD).

Comment

All over the Roman Empire at end of the 1st century AD, Christianity was a political crime that merited the death penalty. Worshipping the emperor as god was a test of political loyalty, much as it would be in North Korea 1,900 years later. Pliny, a conscientious administrator, had no qualms about having people executed for their faith; he only wanted to make sure he followed correct procedure. His writings demonstrate that Christianity was widespread in Bithynia no later than 90 AD.

The story of Pliny also demonstrates the existence of a literate society, with popular books that included several of his works. As a Roman aristocrat, in the service of a few emperors, he knew that Christians were a problem, but not one he had given any thought to until he went to Bithynia.

---

[63] Ibid.

Bithynia was about as far north of Jerusalem as central Egypt was south. Both areas clearly had many Christians within sixty to seventy years of the time of Jesus, and at least four contemporary non-Christian historians confirm that Christianity was a major force among the ordinary people.

The vulnerability of Christians to informers is clear, and this relates both to the history of persecutions which had taken place in many places already, and to the implications of more to come, as in the letters to the seven churches of Revelation.

The spread of stable and consistent Christian beliefs as evidenced by historians such as Pliny presupposes a widespread circulation of Christian literature, especially the New Testament documents. Considering the penalty for being a Christian, the continued prevalence of Christianity in Bithynia around 110 AD is astonishing.

Reference links

Pliny the Younger, at: *www.livius.org/pi-pm/pliny/pliny_y.htm*

The Antiquities of the Jews; Josephus (translated by William Whiston, 1867); at: *sacred-texts.com/jud/josephus*

CHAPTER THIRTY-ONE

Despair and Destruction: The Holocaust in Prophecy

You will live in constant suspense, filled with dread both night and day, never sure of your life.

Deuteronomy 28:66 (NIV)

More than 2,700 years ago, a nation named Israel was destroyed and its surviving population was deported and resettled in other territories of the Assyrian Empire. These comprised about 60% of the descendants of the Hebrew people who settled in the area known originally as Canaan and in present times as Palestine under the leadership of Joshua. They have vanished from the historical record, and the whereabouts of most of their descendants is not known. The remainder of this group, the inhabitants of the territory known as Judah (and later Judea) became known as Jews. Their nation was finally destroyed in 70 AD, and the residual population deported. Below is a summary of their systematic and continual persecution, slaughter and forced migration.

Date	Event
722 BC	Conquest of Israel and Samaria by Sennacherib of Assyria: population deported and scattered. The end of the nation named Israel.

Date	Event
586 BC	Conquest of Judah and Jerusalem by Nebuchadnezzar: population deported to Babylonia and Persia. Destruction of Solomon's Temple.
70 AD	Conquest of Judea and Jerusalem by Titus, 500,000 Jews slaughtered: survivors enslaved, deported to Alexandria and elsewhere in Roman Empire. Destruction of 2nd Temple. End of nation/territory named Judah/Judea.
131 AD	Destruction of Jerusalem by Hadrian. City renamed Aelia Capitolina. Expulsion of remaining Jews.
415 AD	Jews expelled from Alexandria by Bishop Cyril.
561 AD	Jews expelled from Diocese of Uzes, France.
1096 AD	First Crusade: 12,000 Jews murdered in Rhine Valley area.
1099 AD	All Jews in Jerusalem forced into synagogue and burned alive during the Crusade.
1121 AD	Jews expelled from Flanders.
1180 AD	Jews expelled from France by King Philip.
1290 AD	Jews expelled from England by King John.
1298 AD	Persecution of Jews in Austria, Bavaria, Franconia: 100,000 murdered in 6 months.
1306 AD	100,000 Jews expelled from France.
1321 AD	5,000 Jews burned at stake in Guennes, France
1394 AD	Jews expelled from France.
1492 AD	300,000 Jews expelled from Spain; those remaining were forced to convert to Christianity.
1497 AD	20,000 Jews expelled from Portugal; these had left Spain in 1492.
1540 AD	Jews expelled from Naples.
1550 AD	Jews expelled from Genoa and Venice.
1582 AD	Jews expelled from Netherlands.
1648/9 AD	Ukrainian war of independence from Poland; Ukrainians murdered 200,000 Jews.
1915 AD	Forced internal migration of 600,000 Jews in Russia; 100,000 Jews died.
1917 AD	Russian civil war: Jews targeted, 200,000 killed.

Date	Event
1933-45 AD	Holocaust in Germany: official policy to destroy all Jews within Germany and occupied territories. 6,000,000 Jews killed.

Figure 28. Summary of major expulsions and killings of the Jewish people, 722 BC - 1945 AD.

This list does not include the hundreds of massacres of smaller numbers of Jews in Europe during the period shown, or the scores of laws that were passed institutionalising persecution of Jews in virtually every European country. For example, during the three years of the Black Death (1347-49), at least 350 different massacres of Jews are recorded. While there were many instances during the first two hundred years of the Christian Church when Jewish groups persecuted Christians, almost as soon as Christianity became the faith of the Roman Empire the situation reversed.

The historical record shows that problems for the Jewish people began long before the foundation of the church, and the book of Esther is an account of a failed attempt to exterminate all Jews in the Persian Empire around 470 BC. After a very brief time of peace and prosperity under kings David and Solomon, the fate of the Israeli and Jewish people has been to confront extreme hostility throughout the ages in different places. The latest and worst event was the Holocaust under Hitler's Third Reich. At this time, the country of Poland had been a place that for a few centuries had been very supportive of Jews, so the Jewish population there had reached around three-and-a-half million, of whom three million were killed between 1941 and 1945. Is there a biblical perspective on this dreadful history?

The beginning of the prophecies

> *Yet in spite of this, when they are in the land of their enemies, I will not reject them or abhor them so as to destroy them completely, breaking my covenant with them. I am the LORD their God.*
>
> *Leviticus 26:44 (NIV)*

In this passage, God plainly says that, despite all, the Jewish people will survive. This is the aspect of the Holocaust prophecies which is most astounding at the beginning of the 21st century. There are many passages which speak of the long-term persecution and oppression of the Jewish people, but also there are others which emphasise their ultimate survival. While there have been many peoples who have endured horrific oppression and persecution during the past two thousand years or more, there are none who have a set of prophecies foretelling both their oppression and also their survival, written long before any of it came to pass. What happened to them (according to the Bible) could have been avoided – if only they had been obedient to the Lord.

Figure 31. Auschwitz-Birkenau: The road to the gas chambers.
(The last road walked by more than one million people.)
© Martin Johnson.

Leviticus 26 – the five cycles of discipline

This chapter begins with a promise of peace and prosperity for the people of Israel, subject only to their abhorring idols and keeping the Sabbath law. Then it sets out five cycles of national discipline, becoming progressively more severe. These begin with the warning:

But if you will not listen to me and carry out [my] commands...

verse 14, similarly verses 18,21,23,27 (NIV)

It appears that, each time, there is the opportunity for the nation to reverse the situation by returning to obedience. The link to the Sabbath law is important. The rabbinic teaching is that the seventy-year exile in Babylon followed from the failure of the nation to have observed the Sabbath (seventh) year command to leave the land fallow during the previous 490 years. On this simple understanding, the Babylonian exile (dated from destruction of the temple in 586 BC to its reinstatement in 516 BC) was a matter of 'catching up' on the missing years. Below is a list of what was prophesied if the nation refused to repent and return to obedience. Traditionally, this is believed to have been written by Moses prior to 1,400 BC.

V.	Promise	Event	Date
29	...you will eat the flesh of your sons and your daughters...	Cannibalism recorded in sieges of Jerusalem.	586 BC 70 AD
30	I will destroy your high places, cut down your incense altars, and pile your dead bodies on ... your idols.	Destruction of Israel, by Sargon II.	722 BC
31	I will turn your cities into ruins and lay waste your sanctuaries.	Repeatedly, but finally complete following Roman wars.	70/73 AD 132 AD
32	I will lay waste the land.	Until time of resettlement began: many travellers through the Holy Land during the 19th century reported how desolate it was.	1920 AD
33	I will scatter you among the nations and will draw out the sword and pursue you.	First under Assyrians, then under Babylonians, then under Romans.	722 BC 586 BC 70 AD

V.	Promise	Event	Date
36	As for those of you who are left, I will make their hearts so fearful in the land of their enemies that the sound of a wind-blown leaf will put them to flight...	From the end of the Roman Empire, there are no records of successful Jewish armies until 1948.	350 AD to 1948 AD
37	...you will not be able to stand before your enemies.	See table in figure 28.	168 AD to 1948 AD
38	You will perish among the nations; the land of your enemies will devour you.	See table in figure 28.	70 AD onwards.
39	Those of you who are left will waste away in the land of your enemies.	See table in figure 28.	As above.

Figure 29. Prophecy and fulfilment. Leviticus 26:29-39 (NIV).

Supporting scriptures

These curses are spelled out even more fully in Deuteronomy 28-29. There is much additional detail there, including:

> *The LORD will send you back in ships to Egypt on a journey I said you should never make again. There you will offer yourselves for sale to your enemies as male and female slaves, but no-one will buy you.*
>
> *Deuteronomy 28:68*

This latter event took place following Titus' defeat of Jerusalem in 70 AD, when captured Jews were shipped to Alexandria, and caused a glut in the market for slaves. The prophecies listed above have all been fulfilled, some on more than one occasion, and apply both to the people and to the territory they used to inhabit.

Comparisons

Firstly, it must be said that the troubles which have afflicted the Jewish people including the Holocaust are not a unique set of experiences. Mass murder and genocide have been a regular feature of human history. What sets the Jewish people apart is their survival against incredible odds. The table below gives a short list of some of the more prominent events of the 20th century.

Year	Event	Others affected
1915-17	1,000,000+ Armenians killed by Ottoman Turks.	Assyrians, Greeks
1932-39	Stalinist reign of terror, 17-23 million Russians died, most starved to death, though executions accounted for possibly 1,000,000+.	
1933-1945	Nazi Germany, 12 million civilians killed, half of whom were Jews.	Poles, Romanies, people with disabilities, communists, homosexuals
1945-96	Yugoslavia, 750,000 killed.	
1948-49	Indian partition, 1,000,000+ killed, Hindu, Moslem, Sikh.	
1958-61	Chinese cultural revolution, between 30 and 50+ million Chinese killed.	
1965-66	Indonesia government-run massacre of 'Communists', 500,000+ killed.	Ethnic Chinese, Christians
1966-98	East Timor, West Papua, 800,000 killed.	
1967-70	Biafra, 1,000,000 killed.	
1971	East Pakistan/Bangladesh 2 million+ (mainly Hindu) killed.	
1975-79	Cambodia, Pol Pot 1,700,000 - 2 million killed.	
1979-1982	Afghanistan, 900,000 killed by Russians.	
1994	Rwanda, 800,000+ killed.	

Figure 30. Major mass murders of 20th century.

In addition to the above list, there were at least twenty-five other genocides or campaigns of mass murder during the 20th century that resulted in the deaths of between 20,000 and 500,000 civilians other than during the two World Wars. We should not overlook the earlier enormous mass murders which followed the Spanish conquest of Central America in the 16th century, or the systematic destruction of native North Americans between about 1600 and 1900, both of which resulted in death tolls of millions. The continuing oppression of Tibet by the Chinese has lasted some fifty years and resulted in large scale loss of life and determined attempts to suppress the native religion. Several of the worst events during the 20th century appear to be based on religious differences which also demarcate ethnic groups (e.g. Hindu and Moslem in the Indian sub-continent).

How does the history of the Jews differ?

Although the Nazi attempt to destroy the Jews in the territory they controlled was not the most murderous event in the 20th century (in total numbers) it stands out for the cold-blooded mechanical efficiency deployed. To stand at Auschwitz Birkenau is to see a place where the fires of hell have literally raged and gone cold, but also where the visitor will be amazed at the sheer scale of the enterprise. This is a place where the people for the most part went meekly to their deaths, many not believing what was about to happen. Proportionately, the Nazis killed approximately one third of all Jewish people alive on earth at the time, but that is similar to the proportion of Cambodians killed by Pol Pot. What seems to separate out the history of the Jewish people from all the other victims of genocide mass murder and religious persecution is the time they have been enduring it and the fact that they have survived as an identifiable people. There is no other group of people who have been persecuted so viciously, for so long, and in almost every country of the earth.

Comment

It would be easy to try and interpret the warnings of Leviticus 26 and Deuteronomy and similar passages as legalistic warnings from a heartless and cruel God. These passages should first be set into their full context, which is in fact a set of instructions on how to live and prosper and avoid all such difficulties. It is as if the Bible sets out teachings which are linked to the non-material cause and effect principles of the universe, and says, "Look, behave this way and all will be well," and then goes on to spell out what will happen if the positive instructions are ignored.

The problem for people is the gap of experience and time between a causative action and its effect. The Bible typically speaks of effects that may take generations to work through from the root cause, to people, unfortunately, who tend to react based on what may be happening day by day or week by week. The evidence of persistent appalling atrocities being inflicted on people in all continents and throughout history would suggest that the whole world is 'running' on the curses listed in Leviticus, but that only the Bible is offering a way to bring such things to an end.

The Bible contains clear prophecies about the fate of the Jewish people which have been fulfilled again and again, with the Holocaust only the latest and most terrible event in a long list. The other aspect of the prophecies, the desolation of the territory, has also been completely fulfilled. This is one area where the fate of the Jewish people differs markedly from most other persecuted peoples.

Reference links

Gerald Sloyan, Templeton University, on Christian persecution of Jews:
https://www.ushmm.org/m/pdfs/20070119-persecution.pdf
and a link to the US Holocaust Memorial Museum:
www.ushmm.org/research/center/church/persecution

CHAPTER THIRTY-TWO

Psalm 22 – The Crucifixion Experience

About the ninth hour Jesus cried out in a loud voice, "Eloi, Eloi, lama sabacthani?" – which means, "My God, my God, why have you forsaken me?"

Matthew 27:46 (NIV)

At about 9.00 a.m., as we reckon time nowadays, Jesus was crucified. Six hours later, he cried out the opening words of Psalm 22, a Psalm written by King David one thousand years earlier. That Jesus did this, no-one doubts. That he was able to do this is astonishing. By the time a man had spent six full hours of the day hanging on a cross, undergoing one of the most extremely painful methods of execution ever devised, he should not be able to speak in more than a croak or a whisper. A few minutes later, he cried out again in a loud voice, "Father, into your hands I commit my spirit,"[64] and died. This, too, is extraordinary – it could take a man a couple of agonizing days before he finally suffocated to death as his lungs filled up with fluid.

The punishment of crucifixion had been invented about five or six hundred years earlier, either by the Assyrians or the Babylonians. The Assyrians were exceptional in devising extremely cruel tortures and using them on their captives. Four or five hundred years before anyone invented crucifixion, however, David wrote the psalm that Jesus

[64] Luke 23:46 (NIV).

declared the opening words of. And this psalm describes precisely what it feels like to be crucified as Jesus was.

> *But I am a worm and not a man, scorned by men and despised by the people.*
>
> *Psalm 22:6 (NIV)*

The condemned man was stripped naked and exposed in public, in a culture where public nudity was regarded as very shameful. This humiliation was the first part of the punishment.

> *All who see me mock me, they hurl insults, shaking their heads.*
>
> *Psalm 22:7 (NIV)*

The executions were always public. David even describes some of the specific insults:

> *He trusts in the LORD ... let the LORD rescue him. Let him deliver him, since he delights in him.*
>
> *Psalm 22:8 (NIV)*

The Gospel writers tell about the mocking and insults Jesus endured – Matthew 27:39-44; Mark 15:29-32; Luke 23:35-37.

> *"He trusts in God, let God rescue him now..."*
>
> *Matthew 27:43 (NIV)*

There are also references to how the crucifixion would have felt physically:

> *Roaring lions tearing their prey open their mouths wide against me.*
>
> *Psalm 22:13 (NIV)*

> *...they have pierced my hands and feet.*
>
> *Psalm 22:16 (NIV)*

> *...rescue me from the mouth of the lions.*
>
> *Psalm 22:21 (NIV)*

The nails, about six to seven inches long, were driven through the wrists and ankles, sometimes right through the ankle bones (they tried to avoid this, as it made the nails harder to re-use). The weight of the body was then either hanging down from nails through the wrists, or being born on the nail(s) through the ankles. Much like having a lion's fangs biting you.

> *I am poured out like water, and all my bones are out of joint...*
>
> *Psalm 22:14 (NIV)*

> *I can count all my bones.*
>
> *Psalm 22:17 (NIV)*

The victim's arms are stretched out and nailed onto the cross bar, and he is then lifted up. What happens as the weight of the body falls onto the stretched-out arms is that the shoulder and elbow joints dislocate. This, too, is extremely painful.

> *My heart has turned to wax, it has melted away within me. My strength is dried up like a potsherd, and my tongue sticks to the roof of my mouth; you lay me in the dust of death.*
>
> *Psalm 22:14-15 (NIV)*

Because of the forced posture of the victim, their ability to breathe becomes restricted to small movements of the diaphragm (the layer of muscle at the base of the chest cavity). The normal ability to expand the ribcage has been prevented. It is very hard to exhale in this situation, and the only way it can be done is by pushing the body up with the legs (from the nailed ankles). Jesus had spent the previous night and early morning either being walked through Jerusalem under guard, being beaten or being tortured (metal and bone-tipped flail, crown of thorns). By midday (the "sixth hour"), he would have been very dehydrated.

> *They divide my garments among them and cast lots for my clothing...*
>
> *Psalm 22:18 (NIV)*

The unusual feature here is 'casting lots', as it would be more normal to break the garments along the seams and share out the cloth. This was not possible with Jesus' tunic, however. The apostle John tells us why:

> *When the soldiers crucified Jesus, they took his clothes, dividing them into four shares, one for each of them, with the undergarment remaining. This garment was seamless, woven in one piece from top to bottom. "Let's not tear it," they said to one another. "Let's decide by lot who will get it."*
>
> *John 19:23-24 (NIV)*

Other details in the psalm include the reference to "dogs" (verse 21), which by the first century AD was slang for Gentiles (people who were not Jews), while "bulls" and "bulls of Bashan" could refer to the wealthy chief priests and elders (Matthew 27:41). Note that the implication of "chief priests" in the plural indicates both Caiaphas and Annas (his father-in-law) were present. There should only ever have been one chief priest at any time, but Annas continued to act in authority long after his term of office had ended, thereby ignoring the law.

The detail in John's Gospel about what happened after Jesus died is also very revealing:

> *Instead, one of the soldiers pierced Jesus' side, with a spear, bringing a sudden flow of blood and water.*
>
> *John 19:34 (NIV)*

Some commentators have observed that in a normal crucifixion the water would have appeared first. It is suggested that this implies that Jesus died when his heart ruptured, filling his chest cavity with blood – he died, quite literally, from a 'broken heart'.

Comment

Zechariah 12:10 says:

> *They will look on me, the one they have pierced, and they will mourn for him as for an only child, and grieve bitterly for him as one grieves for a firstborn son.*[65]

---

[65] NIV.

Isaiah 53:5 says:

> *But he was pierced for our transgressions, he was crushed for our iniquities; the punishment that brought us peace was upon him, and by his wounds we are healed.*[66]

There is no way to evade the horrific death endured by Jesus; and the fact that he entered into it of his own free will is central to the Christian faith. The glorious fact is that he was then resurrected. The suffering he went through was real, and the prophetic testimony of Psalm 22 brings this home.

Reference links

The Science of Crucifixion; Cahleen Shriner (2002), at: *www.apu.edu/articles/15657*

---

[66] NIV.

CHAPTER THIRTY-THREE

A City Becomes a Ploughed Field

The word of the LORD given to Micah of Moresheth during the reigns of Jotham, Ahaz, and Hezekiah, kings of Judah – the vision he saw concerning Samaria and Jerusalem. Hear, O peoples, all of you, listen, O earth and all who are in it, that the sovereign LORD may witness against you, the Lord from his holy temple.

Micah 1:1-2 (NIV)

The opening verses of Micah's prophecy tell us who he is, where he comes from and when he lived. Moresheth was a town in southern Judah, not a place of any great consequence. King Jotham reigned from 758 to 742 BC, and he was followed by Ahaz who reigned from 742 to 726 BC. Hezekiah succeeded Ahaz, and reigned from 726 BC to 697 BC. We can therefore say that Micah's visions date from between about 750 BC and 700 BC.

The first part of Micah prophesies destruction to Samaria, the capital of the northern kingdom of Israel, and this happened in 721 BC when the Assyrian Empire under Sargon II destroyed Israel and deported the population. The Assyrians (under Sennacherib) later invaded Judah in the time of Hezekiah, but failed to capture Jerusalem.

Micah's theme throughout is the godlessness, evil and corruption of the rulers of his country, which he prophesies will bring about its downfall just as it will for Israel and Samaria. This theme is really a fresh statement of the principles in Leviticus 26 and Deuteronomy 28 (see chapter 31), about what happens to any country that behaves in this way. Micah also says that his message is for all the people of earth, not just his immediate countrymen. It is as if to say, "See what happens here, and learn the lesson about what happens to countries who behave this way." The story of the period is told in 2 Chronicles 28-32. King Ahaz became a vassal (under-ruler) of the Assyrians, and paid them off. This brought poverty and further defeat on his country.

His son Hezekiah reformed the country (possibly because of the prophecies of Micah and Isaiah), and led a successful resistance against the Assyrians when they invaded in 713 BC and again in 709 BC. The 530-metre-long water tunnel he constructed to help prepare for a siege by the Assyrians[67] was rediscovered in 1838, and has been described as "one of the great water-engineering projects of the pre-classical period"[68].

Because of the scepticism about biblical prophecy accurately foretelling the future, and the argument that much of Micah (such as the fall of Samaria) could actually have been written after the event, we will examine some statements about the future of Jerusalem. These will show that Micah prophesied accurately what happened there in 135 AD, about 850 years after the date of the prophecy. This is also centuries later than the earliest copies available of the book.[69]

> *Hear this, you leaders of the house of Jacob, you rulers of the house of Israel, who despise justice and distort all that is right; who build Zion with bloodshed, and Jerusalem with wickedness. Her leaders judge for a bribe, her priests teach for a price, and her prophets tell fortunes for money. Yes, they look for the LORD's support and say, "Is not the LORD among us? No disaster will come upon us."*

---

[67] See 2 Chronicles 32:30.

[68] *www.bibleplaces.com/heztunnel*

[69] A copy of Micah has been found among the Dead Sea Scrolls incorporated in a collection of the "Minor Prophets" in Greek translation. This scroll has been dated between 50 and 1 BC, indicating it was copied from much earlier copies of the individual prophets.
See: *www.deadseascrolls.org.il/featured-scrolls*

> *Therefore, because of you, Zion will be ploughed like a field, Jerusalem will become a heap of rubble, the temple hill a mound overgrown with thickets.*
>
> *Micah 3:9-12 (NIV)*

The reign of Hezekiah included massive improvements to the fortifications of the part of Jerusalem known as the City of David, and Zion. This was the ancient Jebusite city captured by King David, and where his palace was built. Immediately north of it was the temple mount. You can see this area today on Google Earth. The Dome of the Rock and the Al-Aksa Mosque stand on the Temple Mount, which has been built up over the years to create a large level platform, while the City of David is the small nondescript promontory immediately to the south. The steep valley that once lay on the west side of the City of David is now largely filled in with three millennia's worth of refuse.

At the time of this prophecy (and indeed for eight hundred years after it was given) it would have seemed very improbable that the old original fortified city would become a ploughed field, or that the Temple Mount would be overgrown with bushes.

Figure 31. Coin of Hadrian, commemorating the ploughing of Jerusalem.

What happened?

The Jewish wars of 66-70 AD resulted in the complete destruction of the main city and Temple, under the army of Titus. However, over the following years it was re-established, and became a centre of rebellion again. This began with guerrilla-style attacks against the Romans in 123 AD, until in 132 AD it became a full-scale rebellion under the leadership of Simon Bar-Kokhba. The main rebellion had been sparked by the decision of Hadrian to build a temple to Jupiter, and to rename the city Aelia Capitolina in honour of the god. The ceremony of preparing the site for the new temple began with the ground being cleared and a yoke of oxen ploughing the ground. This desecration ignited the large-scale revolt.

Hadrian moved twelve legions into the region. By 135 AD the Romans had destroyed all fifty Jewish fortresses and 985 villages. The Roman record says 580,000 Jews were killed (though Jewish sources put the figure much higher). The Roman forces had suffered very heavy casualties, and it had been a bitterly fought war. At least one legion (XXII Deiotariana) is believed to have been completely destroyed. Jerusalem and its Temple Mount were then cleared, levelled and ploughed. Jerusalem was renamed Aelia Capitolina, and Judea was renamed Syria-Palaestina, commemorating the Philistines, ancient enemies of the Jews. Jews were forbidden to live in the old area of Jerusalem, and were only permitted to enter on the 9th of Ab each year, to honour their dead. Hadrian attempted to eradicate all traces of Judaism because of his belief that it was the religion itself which caused such regular and bitter wars.

Micah makes it plain that Jerusalem and the Jewish people will survive the degradation of this prophecy, and we can see that Hadrian's very determined attempts to obliterate the Jews, Judaism, Jerusalem and the name of Judah have all proved fruitless even while he fulfilled the prophecy of Micah 3:12.

Comment

This short prophecy is one that would have sounded over the top and most improbable until it actually happened. The 850-year gap between the time of the prophecy and its exact fulfilment is of interest, because the next prophecy in Micah, chapter 4:1-5 cannot be said to have happened yet. It starts by saying, "In the last days..." which implies that those days are still to come. The subsequent prophecy, 4:6-8, might be argued to have been partially fulfilled during the period of the Maccabees (168-37 BC), and also in the present age since 1948. The passage immediately following this (4:9-10) refers specifically to the exile in Babylon, which would also have seemed very improbable in the period 740-690, as Babylon was a small subject state of the Assyrian Empire.

Micah is also famous for the prophecy in 5:2:

> *But you, Bethlehem Ephrathah, though you are little among the thousands of Judah, yet out of you shall come to me the One to be ruler in Israel, whose goings forth are from of old from everlasting.*[70]

The first part of this prophecy was fulfilled about seven hundred years later with the birth of Jesus, while the second part has yet to happen (the Messiah ruling in Israel). Micah shows a number of good examples of the long time span that may be involved between a prophecy and subsequent fulfilment.

Reference links

Hezekiah's Tunnel, at: *www.bibleplaces.com/heztunnel.htm*

The Bar-Kokhba revolt 132-135 AD, at:
www.jewishvirtuallibrary.org/jsource/Judaism/revolt1.html
and also in Wikipedia, where there is a picture of Hadrian's coin showing the ploughing of Jerusalem: *en.wikipedia.org/wiki/Bar_Kokhba_revolt*

---

[70] NKJV.

CHAPTER THIRTY-FOUR

Nahum – The Fall of Nineveh

Woe to the bloody city! It is all full of lies and robbery. Its victim never departs. The noise of a whip and the noise of rattling wheels, of galloping horses, of clattering chariots!

Nahum 3:1-2 (NKJV)

Although the prophet Nahum does not cite the king reigning during the time he received his vision, it is easy to work out when he lived. He was also a resident of the kingdom of Judah. At the time he was writing, Assyria was the dominant nation in the region and at the height of its power. Assyria was overthrown by the combined forces of Media under Cyarxes, and Nabopalassar, the founder of the Babylonian Empire, in 612 BC. The final years of the Assyrian Empire were characterised by weak and divided rule. Nahum also says (3:8-10) that the fate of Nineveh, their capital city, will be like that of No-Amon (Thebes, in Egypt). This city fell in 663 BC to the Assyrians under Assurbanipal.

The Assyrian Empire had stood for some 1,400 years by the time of Nahum, and was formidable in warfare. They had invented the process of mining under city walls to create breaches, and they had also invented the military pontoon bridge for crossing rivers. To their credit is also the invention of plumbing, flush toilets, electric batteries and guitars, among other things. The time of Nahum was at the end of a century of almost continuous expansion of this empire under successful rulers. A civil war broke out in 652 BC, between Assurbanipal and his brother Shamash-shum-ukin who until then had been co-regent in Babylon. Assurbanipal defeated his brother, but by then the empire had been weakened. After his death in 626 BC, many of the vassal territories began rebelling. Nahum must, therefore, have written this vision between 663 BC and 626 BC.

The comparison with Thebes is interesting. Thebes had the Nile running through it, and Nineveh had the Tigris running along one side, while another substantial river, the Khosr, ran through it. The circumference of Thebes has been measured at twenty-seven miles, and its reputation was as a great wealthy and ancient city. Nineveh was even greater than Thebes. The total circumference was sixty miles, and within this was a citadel with seven miles of walls one hundred feet high and wide enough at the top for three chariots abreast. It seemed impregnable because of its fortifications, its formidable army and its great wealth. Yet Assyria was also a byword for cruelty. One recorded way of treating prisoners was to put bronze hooks through their lower jaw, coming out in their mouth, and to lead them about by these hooks (like fish). One method of execution (and they had also introduced crucifixion) was by skinning people alive. This extremely painful and cruel punishment was reserved for the more important captives, whose skins would then be hung on the walls. Many monuments and inscriptions show their pride in their cruel and inhuman treatment of their victims.[71]

Nahum said:

Nineveh would fall quickly

> *All your fortresses are like fig trees with their first ripe fruit; when they are shaken the figs fall into the mouth of the eater.*
>
> *Nahum 3:12 (NIV)*

---

[71] An article on Assyrian torture by Erika Belibtreu (2002) supplies many of their carvings showing these practices: *faculty.uml.edu/ethan_Spanier/Teaching/documents/ CP6.0AssyrianTorture.pdf*

The final siege of Nineveh lasted only three months. Lesser cities would normally have withstood siege for years (the siege of Ashdod lasted twenty-nine years). Nineveh had ample water supplies and a stockpile of twenty years' supply of essential foods. The walls were immense, and surrounded by a moat 150 feet wide. The combined army of Medes and Chaldeans were prepared for a long battle.

THE DEFENDERS WOULD BE DRUNK

> *You too will become drunk; you will go into hiding and seek refuge from the enemy.*
>
> *Nahum 3:11 (NIV)*

The Assyrian king, Sin-shar-ishkun, had his army established outside the fortress, ready to engage the Medes and Chaldeans in battle, when he decided the situation was safe enough for him to organise a feast for his troops. They roasted livestock and brought out supplies of drink, and the army partied hard. Word of this got out to the leader of the Medes and Chaldeans, and he launched a surprise attack, which routed the Assyrians. The king withdrew inside the fortress, and prepared for a siege.

THE RIVER WOULD CAUSE COLLAPSE

> *He summons his picked troops, yet they stumble on their way. They dash to the city wall, the protective shield is put in place. The river gates are thrown open and the palace collapses... Nineveh is like a pool and its water is draining away.*
>
> *Nahum 2:5-6,8a (NIV)*

These verses show the panic retreat of drunken men. Once the city gates were shut, they thought themselves safe. However, their assailants broke a dam either on the Tigris or the Khosr, which were both in flood because of heavy rains. The flow of water resulted in the collapse of the walls for "twenty stadia"[72] (2.5 miles) according to the Greek historian

---

[72] From report of Greek historian Diodorus Siculus.
See: *www.jstor.org/stable/4436159*

Didorus Siculus. He reports also that a prophecy was known in Assyria which said that no enemy would ever take Nineveh by storm unless the river shall first become the city's enemy. The statement "Nineveh is like a pool" describes the condition of the city in the flood that caused its collapse. King Sin-shar-ishkun ordered his possessions and concubines into the palace, where he had it set on fire with himself and his family inside. They were all burned to death. His brother escaped and attempted a resistance against the invaders which ultimately failed.

THE CITY WOULD NOT BE RESTORED

> *The LORD has given a command concerning you, you will have no descendants to bear your name. I will destroy the carved images and cast idols that are in the temple of your gods. I will prepare your grave, for you are vile.*
>
> *Nahum 1:14 (NIV)*

> *Nothing can heal your wound; your injury is fatal. Everyone who hears the news about you claps his hands at your fall, for who has not felt your endless cruelty?*
>
> *Nahum 3:19 (NIV)*

Unusually for such a prominent city, after its fall it was completely abandoned, and within two or three hundred years, knowledge of its location was lost. In the 1820s, a British diplomat based in Baghdad, Mr Rich, noticed the mounds and learned that some carvings had been found there, but it was Austen Henry Layard who began excavating the site in 1845 and discovered that he had found the site of Nineveh.

ISRAEL WOULD BE RESTORED (IN CONTRAST TO NINEVEH)

> *The LORD will restore the splendour of Jacob like the splendour of Israel, though destroyers have laid them waste and have ruined their vines.*
>
> *Nahum 2:2 (NIV)*

This prophecy is arguably being fulfilled in the present age following the restoration of the nation named Israel in 1948. The nation of Judah remained in existence (under changing government) for another seven hundred years after Nahum's time, but this reference is to a nation named Israel which had been destroyed in 722 BC.

Figure 33. Nineveh, eastern city wall from outer rampart to the east. Source: Wikimedia. Courtesy: user: Fredarch.

Zephaniah

Zephaniah prophesied in Judah during the reign of Josiah, shortly after Nahum. He also gave a prophecy for Assyria and Nineveh, in which he wrote:

> *He will stretch out his hand against the north and destroy Assyria, leaving Nineveh utterly desolate and dry as the desert. Flocks and herds will lie down there, creatures of every kind...*
>
> *Zephaniah 2:12-13a (NKJV)*

This prophecy looks to the distant future for Nineveh, and aptly describes how it has been for most of the last 2,500 years – and still is today, as the photograph above shows. The greatest city on earth in its day, now a place where sheep and cattle graze.

Comment

There are many more details which could be identified in Nahum concerning the manner of the destruction of Nineveh and the reasons given for it in the book. Some may attempt to argue that the book could have been written after the destruction of Nineveh, but then its language would be strange, as it would be describing the seeming invincibility of a city that was already defeated.

The story of Nineveh and Assyria is really a normal life cycle of nations and empires, and the prophet's message is that we should not be fooled by appearances. This resembles the very rapid collapse of the British Empire in the 20th century (most of it gone between 1947 and 1958) which had ruled a vast area of the world. Even after World War 2 in 1945 it was the biggest empire the world had ever seen. Similarly, the break-up of the Soviet Union and Warsaw Pact countries between 1989 and 1991 was not foreseen even ten years earlier. The compelling aspects of this prophecy are the permanent desolation of Nineveh (which would have been thought very unlikely at the time), and the restoration of the nation Israel, which the Assyrians had destroyed even to the extent of deporting most of the population.

Reference links

An Introduction to Nahum; Al Maxey; at: *www.zianet.com/maxey/Proph10.htm*

A Brief History of the Assyrians; Peter Betbasoo (2013); at: *www.aina.org/brief.html*

The end of Nineveh: *www.varchive.org/tac/end.htm*

A good review of ancient sources is at: *www.jhsonline.org/cocoon/JHS/a058.html*

CHAPTER THIRTY-FIVE

The Fall of Babylon

After these things I saw another angel coming down from heaven. He had great authority, and the earth was illuminated by his splendour. With a mighty voice he shouted: "Fallen! Fallen is Babylon the Great! She has become a home for demons and a haunt for every evil spirit, a haunt for every unclean and detestable bird. For all the nations have drunk the maddening wine of her adulteries. The kings of the earth committed adultery with her, and the merchants of the earth grew rich from her excessive luxuries."

Revelation 18:1-3 (NIV)

The fall of Babylon is proclaimed by Isaiah (21:9) and Jeremiah (51:8) in very similar words to the passage in Revelation 18:2 (also proclaimed in Revelation 14:8), and these verses all echo the declaration by Nebuchadnezzar in Daniel 4:30:

...he said, "Is not this the great Babylon I have built as the royal residence, by my mighty power and for the glory of my majesty?"[73]

[73] NIV.

Figure 33. Babylon's Ishtar Gate,
Pergamon Museum Berlin.
© Martin Johnson.

Babylon has significance both as an historic reality and as a symbol of worldly depravity. It is referred to in the Bible nearly three hundred times, in fifteen books of the Old Testament and four books of the New Testament. At the time of the New Testament writers it might have been supposed that most of the specific prophecies in Isaiah, Jeremiah, Ezekiel, Daniel, Micah and Zechariah would be regarded as fulfilled, but, evidently, the apostle John in writing Revelation did not think so.

Babylon was captured by the army of Medes and Persians under Cyrus on the night of 12 October 539 BC without a fight. This was because Cyrus' generals learned of ancient waterworks including a great lake which had been built generations earlier to drain the river Euphrates through Babylon in order to line the riverbed with brick and control its flow. The river entrances to the city were protected by great two-leaved bronze lattice gates through which the river ran. The pressure of the river kept the gates firmly shut, but when the Persian army re-dug the old waterways and began draining the Euphrates into the old lake bed, the water in the river dropped. As night fell, the water was shallow enough for the army to enter the riverbed (which was lined with brick, making movement easy for the men), and approach the great gates.

The river gates could now be opened, and the army went in, guided by Babylonian deserters, and seized the palace where Belshazzar, co-regent of Babylonia, was carousing with his court. This is the party described in Daniel chapter 5, where Belshazzar sees the 'writing on the wall'. This event so frightened Belshazzar that "his knees knocked together and his legs gave way"[74]. (Actually, the Hebrew implies he had a bout of bowel incontinence!) Belshazzar was captured and later executed. On that night, the greatness of Babylon ended after a period of supremacy of only seventy years.

Jewish tradition states that the Jewish leaders met Cyrus and showed him the following passage from the book of Isaiah:

> *Thus says the LORD to His anointed, to Cyrus, whose right hand I have held – to subdue nations before him and loose the armour of kings, to open before him the double doors, so that the gates will not be shut: I will go before you and make the crooked places straight; I will break in pieces the gates of bronze and cut the bars of iron.*
>
> *Isaiah 45:1-3 (NKJV)*

Cyrus' treatment of the Jews was kind and good, and he restored their Temple treasures to them and commanded the reconstruction of the Temple in Jerusalem. From his time onwards, Babylon deteriorated, eventually becoming abandoned within three hundred years. The references in the verses above appear to include the great river gates and

[74] Daniel 5:6 (NIV).

the many bronze gates in the city wall for which Babylon was famous. This is another city considered impregnable until the moment it fell. The walls were enormous (though possibly not the three hundred feet high recorded by the Greek historian Herodotus) and the defences extensive. Alexander the Great captured the city in 331 BC, and planned to restore it for his own capital, but unfortunately he died. Building activity continued there for about another fifty years after Alexander, but the condition of the existing buildings was very poor, and the Seleucid rulers of Babylonia moved their capital to Seleucia.

Many of the prophesies of Isaiah (ca. 740-680 BC) and Jeremiah (626-586 BC) concerning Babylon were fulfilled in the fall of Babylon to Cyrus in 539 BC. This has had the effect of commentators claiming they must therefore have been written after the events described, so this study will look at two aspects of these prophecies that happened later than the 2nd century BC (date of the Great Isaiah Scroll).

BABYLON WILL BE UNINHABITED FOR MANY GENERATIONS

> *It will never be inhabited, nor will it be settled from generation to generation; nor will the Arabian pitch tents there, nor will the shepherds make their sheepfolds there.*
>
> *Isaiah 13:20 (NKJV)*

> *Babylon shall become a heap, a dwelling place for dragons, an astonishment and a hissing without an inhabitant.*
>
> *Jeremiah 51:37 (KJV/NKJV)*

The first report of Babylon being just ruins is from the Roman emperor Trajan, who invaded Babylonia in 116/117 AD. He was most disappointed that there was nothing there but mounds. By the beginning of the 19th century AD, Babylon was regarded as semi-legendary. The German archaeologist Robert Koldewey identified the site in a series of digs over thirteen years from 1900. The quantity of cuneiform tablets discovered is so great that even a hundred years later, many have not yet been transcribed and interpreted. The nature of the ground has been such that no grazing crops grow there, therefore no sheepfolds or shepherds are there. There had been a few previous archaeologists working on the site, including Layard in the 1850s and

Rassam in the 1880s. The development of cuneiform studies is the main tool that assisted Koldewey in the confirmation that the site was Babylon. A number of archaeologists and travellers in the 19th and early 20th centuries confirm the desolation of the area, and that the local Arabs avoided it and would not stay there overnight. Google Earth provides good satellite coverage of the area, showing the current state of ruins in the desert.

Figure 34. Babylon today.
Courtesy: U.S. Navy no. 030529-N-5362A-001.

THE FOUNDATION STONES WILL NOT BE REMOVED

> *They shall not take from you a stone for a corner nor a stone for a foundation, but you shall be desolate forever.*
>
> *Jeremiah 51:26 (NKJV)*

Babylon was mainly constructed of bricks, nearly all of which show the stamp of Nebuchadnezzar. It has been established that the only stone-built structures recorded were the foundations of a big ziggurat, and the north wall of the Northern Citadel. Both these structures have been identified, and the stone is still there. This is remarkable because stone was a very sought-after building material, and ancient sites everywhere get used as quarries for later building works. The bricks from Babylon have been found re-used over a wide area beyond Babylon. The survival of the stones is due to the collapse of the structures above and around them.

Comment

The challenge for the Bible student is not that Babylon is an ancient city of the Middle East, whose destruction was foretold by the prophets and which disappeared from sight for many centuries. It is rather that its fate is spoken of as if in the future in the book of Revelation. By comparison, Damascus is a city that has survived continuously since before 2000 BC, but it only has 20% of the number of references in the Bible that Babylon has. Nineveh has only half the number of references of Damascus, but was prominent in the affairs of Israel for roughly twice the length of time that Babylon was.

The answer probably lies in the origins of Babylon in the story of Babel in Genesis 11. This is the place where the spirit of rebellion against God first manifested after Noah's flood, and this appears to lie behind the prophecies concerning Babylon in Revelation. The original city of Babylon may have been a ruin for most of the past two thousand years, but something about it is still very present in the affairs of mankind. This implies that many of the prophecies about Babylon may be liable to some kind of repeat fulfilment.

Starting in 1982, Saddam Hussein, the ruler of Iraq, ordered that one of the three great palaces of Babylon be rebuilt. This was done without much serious attention to what the original may have looked like, but one principle was copied from Nebuchadnezzar: Saddam Hussein's name was stamped on bricks used in the project. The project was still underway when the war of 2003 toppled him from power. In a way, this is similar to the story of several rulers beginning with Alexander the Great who planned to restore Babylon and identify themselves with its illustrious history, but ultimately failed. It is clear that the idea of Babylon and what it represents still exercises a powerful grip on people's imagination (in a way that, say, Nineveh or Thebes never have, even though they were great and glorious cities in their day).

Reference links

Nebuchadnezzar, at: *www.christiananswers.net/dictionary/nebuchadnezzar.html*

A report on the Cyrus Cylinder, at: *www.livius.org/ct-cz/cyrus_I/babylon05.html*

Satellite photograph of Babylon, on Google Earth:
maps.google.com/?ie=UTF8&om=1&z=15&ll=32.539542,44.425836&spn=0.020586, 0.034676&t=k

Saddam Hussein's restoration project;
query.nytimes.com/gst/fullpage.html?res=9E05E1D81030F93AA2575BC0A9659C8B63

CHAPTER THIRTY-SIX

Four Empires

Then Daniel praised the God of heaven and said: "Praise be to the name of God for ever and ever; wisdom and power are his. He changes times and season; he sets up kings and deposes them. He gives wisdom to the wise and knowledge to the discerning. He reveals deep and secret things; he knows what lies in darkness, and light dwells with him."

Daniel 2:19b-22 (NIV)

Daniel had two visions of a sequence of four world empires. The first was a dream that Nebuchadnezzar had in 603 BC, which troubled him so much he threatened to have all his 'counsellors' executed if they couldn't explain it to him. The difficulty he gave them was that he would not tell them what he had dreamed, and this is the first occasion Daniel came into prominence. Daniel was the son of a prominent citizen of Judah, taken by the Babylonians in 605 BC with a number of other youths to serve as hostages to ensure the good behaviour by their families in Judea, which was now subject to Babylonian rule. The account of the dream is in Daniel chapters 2 and 3.

This vision was of an awesome statue of a man. The head was of fine gold, the chest and arms were of silver, the belly and thighs were of bronze, the legs of iron, and the feet partly iron and partly clay. The explanation given was that the different metals were successive kingdoms, each of inferior quality. At the end of the dream a stone came which destroyed the statue so that all traces of it would be blown away. In the time of the final kingdom, "the God of heaven" would establish a kingdom which would never be destroyed.

The second vision, in Daniel 7, received by Daniel in 553 BC, was of a sequence of great beasts. The first beast was like a winged lion, the second was like a lopsided bear, the third was like a leopard with four wings and four heads, and the fourth was a great devouring monster with huge iron teeth and ten horns. Out of one of the horns of the fourth beast came a figure like a man, which spoke in a very pompous and arrogant manner, and also made war with "the saints"[75]. The explanation again was that the beasts each represented successive kingdoms, and the final beast would be overcome by the power of God.

Daniel had a third vision (chapter 8), in 550 BC, of two more creatures, a ram and a goat. These referred successively to the kingdom of Media and Persia (the ram with unequal horns), and the kingdom of Greece (the goat).

Daniel is told that the head of gold in the first vision is the Babylonian Empire under Nebuchadnezzar, which would be replaced by the silver empire, meaning the Medes and the Persians. The Medes and Persians were an unequal alliance, and silver was the precious metal of choice used by them. Daniel served under the Medo-Persian rulers for some years after Babylon fell to them. The first beast represented Babylon, and the symbol of the winged lion has been seen in many statues and carvings found there. The lopsided bear stands for the Medes and Persians, who maintained an alliance over a long period, with first one side more powerful and then the other. The three ribs that bear is devouring are believed to represent Lydia, Babylonia and Egypt, all of whom fell to this alliance. The same activity is represented by the ram in the third vision.

The activities of the first two empires took place during Daniel's lifetime, and the Medo-Persian Empire continued for another two centuries. It is the third and fourth empires that demonstrate the power and accuracy of these interlinked prophecies.

---

[75] Daniel 7:21.

THE THIRD EMPIRE – ALEXANDER THE GREAT

Alexander the Great was king of Macedonia, a minor country in Greece. His father, Philip II, had unified many of the small Greek city-states under his rule, but he was assassinated when Alexander was only twenty years old. Alexander became king in 336 BC, and immediately began his military campaigns. He is regarded as one of the most successful military commanders of all time, and by the time he died of illness shortly before his 33rd birthday, he had conquered all of the Persian Empire, including Egypt, and also Afghanistan and an area of northern India. Several cities were named Alexandria after him, including the Alexandria in Egypt and Kandahar in Afghanistan. The Greek armies used a lot of bronze for their armour and weapons (corresponding to the statue of Daniel's vision), and were extremely rapid in their conquests (hence the winged leopard as an appropriate symbol).

The Jewish historian Josephus records that when Alexander's army approached Jerusalem, the priests and ruler of the city were very nervous, but Alexander told them he had had a vision before he set out to conquer the Persians in which he saw the high priest who came out from Jerusalem to meet him. He worshipped at the Temple in Jerusalem, and was shown the book of Daniel the prophet, which he believed spoke about him. As a result, he allowed their request that they be allowed to follow the Jewish faith, and not have to pay tribute every seventh year (the Year of Jubilee).

Daniel 8:8 says that the horn identified as Alexander would be cut off in its prime, and replaced by four others. This also aligns with the leopard-beast which had four heads. What happened after Alexander died was a vicious struggle for succession, which ended two years later with Alexander's four chief generals each controlling a part of the conquered territories. This is also referred to in a later vision, in Daniel 11:1-4.

The Ptolemy dynasty ruled Egypt, the Seleucids Mesopotamia, the Antigonids Greece and Macedonia, and the Attalids Asia Minor. They became rivals, and many wars were fought between them. The consequence of Alexander's empire and its aftermath was the spread of Hellenistic civilisation through the area, and the use of Greek as the international language for trade and commerce. Many interpreters identify the prophecies in Daniel 11 with the subsequent wars of the successor kingdoms of Alexander, at least into the mid-2nd century BC. At some point in the narrative, however, possibly Daniel 11:40, the prophecy seems to move to a date in the far future.

The fourth empire – Rome

During the 2nd century BC, the Roman Empire gradually spread out along the coast of the Western Mediterranean. This process accelerated in the following hundred years, until by 44 BC they controlled most of western Europe, the northern coast of Libya and Egypt, Greece, Asia Minor and Syria (which included northern Palestine). The Roman army had developed very robust infantry tactics, and the use of cavalry (as opposed to chariots). Their armour and weapons were predominantly of iron. At its full extent, it covered Mesopotamia, the whole of the Mediterranean coastal territories, the island of Britain as far as central Scotland, and western and northern Europe as far as the Rhine.

After many turbulent years, Constantine the Great progressively seized control of the whole empire (which had been ruled as four parts). In 324 AD, he announced the move of his capital from Rome to a new city he built for the purpose, Constantinople, on the Bosphorus. After his death, the empire split into western and eastern parts, ruled from Rome and Constantinople respectively. Rome was attacked several times, buts its final fall was in 476 AD, after which it ceased to be a centre of power. The eastern empire continued for another thousand years, until Constantinople fell to the Ottoman Turks in 1453 and became part of the Islamic world. The eastern empire is generally known as the Byzantine empire, but the inhabitants described themselves as Romans to the end, and their country as Romania, a name still preserved by one country in that region.

The concept of the Roman Empire in the West was revived by Charlemagne in 800 AD. The Christian church had regarded Rome as its centre throughout the intervening period, and even though there was no unified political rule, the tendency to regard the Pope (usually) in Rome as a spiritual authority had continued to develop. The empire of

Charlemagne became known as the Holy Roman Empire. This continued until it was dissolved by its last emperor, Francis II in 1806.

The Christian church continued to grow and flourish after the fall of Rome, and it was not until 1054 that the differences between the churches in the east and those in the west resulted in a split, known as the 'Great Schism'. From this time on, the eastern church based on Constantinople was known as Eastern Orthodox, while the western church based on Rome was known as Roman Catholic.

In the present age, there are three distinct parts of the world influenced by this history. The largest territory covered by the Eastern Orthodox church was Russia, where they developed the theology that the Russian church was the persecuted woman of Revelation 12, who preserves the true faith in the wilderness for the ultimate salvation of the world. This concept was inherited to a substantial degree by the Russian communists in their vision of the destiny of Soviet Russia (which collapsed in 1991).[76]

The second part is in the history of Western Europe. When Hitler declared a Third Reich (Reich = Empire), he was claiming to be the successor to the Holy Roman Empire. There was a lot of occult mysticism in the Nazi beliefs, including their belief in 'Christian' relics, which they tried to obtain, such as the 'Spear of Longinus', which was reputed to have pierced Jesus on the Cross. The idea of a united Christian Europe is at the basis of the treaty of Rome, which has led to the present European Union. It is very significant that this movement is based on the concept of Rome, and it should be recalled that the original idea of Rome was based on democracy (which did not survive).

The third part of the world is that under the commercial or political dominance of the United States. This is a country explicitly founded on the idea of Rome, and the only one of the three areas where the senior elected representatives are called 'senators' just as in ancient Rome. Their principal government buildings at both state and federal level are

---

[76] See, for example: *Modern Russian Theology: Orthodox Theology In A New Key;* Paul Valliere; Bloomsbury, London (2000); pp. 93-94.
How this was transposed into soviet communist ideology has been set out by Martin Scharlemann in *The Theology of Communism* (1969) at: *www.ctsfw.net/media/pdfs/ScharlemannTheologyCommunism.pdf*

called 'capitols' commemorating the meeting place of the Roman Senate. The Roman symbolism is explicit in the layout of Washington DC, the capital city. This is the only major democratic nation where the head of state is also Commander in Chief of the country's armed forces, just as the Caesars were in ancient Rome.

Comment

Many students of Daniel are unaware how long the Roman Empire continued in explicit political forms, or how far the concept of Rome underpins so many of the governmental systems of the world today. Also, that it operated as two parallel church and governance systems for more than a thousand years. At the same time, however, it is important to consider how the first vision showed that during the time of the fourth empire, identified as Rome, the Christian church (by implication) would spread out over the entire world.

The history of the empires alluded to in Daniel is very complex, but the overview provided by these prophecies supplies a way of understanding them. These prophecies have been fulfilled very thoroughly, though we clearly have not reached the end of them yet. It is also obvious that it would be very hard to use them to predict the future with any degree of accuracy. The fulfilment is easy to recognise when it happens, but hard to see beforehand.

Reference links

History of Alexander the Great, in Wikipedia:
en.wikipedia.org/wiki/Alexander_the_Great

A History of the Holy Roman Empire: *www.heraldica.org/topics/national/hre.htm*

CHAPTER THIRTY-SEVEN

Hebrew and Israel – A Language and a Nation Reborn

This is what the Sovereign LORD says: On the day I cleanse you from all your sins, I will resettle your towns, and the ruins will be rebuilt. The desolate land will be cultivated instead of lying desolate in the sight of all who pass through it. They will say, "This land that was laid waste has become like the garden of Eden; the cities that were lying in ruins, desolate and destroyed, are now fortified and inhabited." Then the nations around you that remain will know that I the LORD have rebuilt what was destroyed and have replanted what was desolate. I the LORD have spoken and will do it.

Ezekiel 36:33-36 (NIV)

On 14 May 1948, an amazing thing happened. A Jewish state named Israel was declared on the ancient territory that had last borne that name 2,600 years earlier. The first person in modern times to think it a realistic possibility that Israel could be reborn as a nation was a man named Theodore Herzl, who had grown up in Budapest and Vienna (then in Austro-Hungary). In the 1880s, he had recognised the prevalence of anti-Semitism in Europe, and following the Dreyfuss affair (France, 1894) he had concluded it was a problem which would never go away. He was not a religious man, but the only feasible solution he saw to deal with anti-Semitism was the creation of a Jewish nation. He convened the first of a series of Zionist congresses in 1897 at Basle in Switzerland. He believed then he had initiated the founding of the Jewish state, though he felt it could take fifty years before people would realise it. He began a number of diplomatic initiatives to build support for the vision. He died in 1904.

On 2 November 1917, at the height of the First World War, and amid widespread worries about the spread of revolution following the Russian Bolshevik revolution the previous month, the British Foreign Secretary Arthur Balfour made a public declaration that Britain would favour the creation of a Jewish state in Palestine. On 9 December that year, British forces under General Allenby captured Jerusalem from the Turks, and the conclusion of World War 1 saw the end of the Ottoman Empire and control of Palestine given to Britain. The aftermath of the Holocaust, and the sense of guilt felt in several major countries that could have helped to save German Jews but failed to, influenced the decisions of the new United Nations when it was formed in 1946.

The other amazing event on 14 May 1948 was that the new nation of Israel announced that its official language would be Hebrew. This was the first time in the history of the world that a language that had fallen out of daily use had been restored. Even fifty years before, Hebrew was a language only used for religious purposes, rather like Latin or Sanskrit. Hebrew ceased being the everyday language of the Jewish people during the exile in Babylon about 2,500 years earlier, when they changed to Aramaic.

> *Half of their children spoke the language of Ashdod or the language of one of the other peoples, and did not know how to speak the language of Judah.*
>
> *Nehemiah 13:24 (NIV)*

By the time of the New Testament, the main languages of Palestine were Aramaic and Greek.

The 20th century saw several language preservation movements, such as Welsh and Basque, which aimed to arrest the decline of a language, but the revival of Hebrew was down to the work of just one man. Eliezer Perlman, who later changed his name to Eliezer Ben Yehuda (the Hebrew translation of his father's name) had a vision in 1879 that Israel should be reborn on its native soil. He believed that for this to happen it would be essential that the new nation should have its own language, and that language should be Hebrew. He migrated to Palestine in 1881, and with his wife Deborah they set up the first Hebrew-speaking home. He published a newspaper, and spent his life developing words to fit the modern world using Hebrew and its related languages. In 1917, he saw General Allenby's proclamation of martial law, the first official document to be printed in modern Hebrew (this was a welcome proclamation, because it signalled the end of Turkish rule). He died in 1922, but the language he championed grew and blossomed, so that it now serves for all aspects of modern life in Israel.

The prophecies

Ezekiel 36 (extract above) is one of many passages that says there will be a time, after the Jewish people have been scattered over all the earth, and the land and cities of Israel have been desolate, that they will be restored to their land, and the nation will be revived. This theme is developed first in Deuteronomy 30:

> *He will bring you back to the land that belonged to your fathers, and you will take possession of it.*
>
> *Deuteronomy 30:5 (NIV)*

This prophecy is given before the children of Israel have entered the land for a first time.

Jeremiah 50:4-5 says:

> *"In those days, at that time," declares the LORD, "the people of Israel and the people of Judah together will go in tears to seek the LORD their God. They will ask the way to Zion and turn their faces towards it."*[77]

In this prophecy, the point is made that it will be a united group of people, no longer the divided Hebrew nations. There have been three main exiles of the Hebrew nations: from Israel in 721 BC, and Judah in 586 BC and 70 AD. The only return was a small group of exiles of

---

[77] NIV.

Judah, after 538 BC. Until the 20th century, there had been no major combined return of Jewish people.[78]

From the perspective of the 8th century BC, nations were established over long periods of time. But, Isaiah 66:7 says:

> *Who has ever heard of such a thing? Who has ever seen such things? Can a country be born in a day or a nation brought forth in a moment? Yet no sooner is Zion in labour than she gives birth to her children.*[79]

Only in the 20th century, with the first supra-national bodies such as the League of Nations, and its successor the United Nations, were nations created in such a way. And the day Isaiah foresaw for Zion was 14 May 1948, and the moment was midnight, Tel Aviv time.

Jeremiah 31:23 says:

> *Thus says the LORD of hosts, the God of Israel: "They shall again use this speech in the land of Judah and its cities, when I bring back their captivity: 'The LORD bless you, O home of justice, and mountain of holiness!'"*[80]

---

[78] While the great majority of Jews migrating to Israel during the 20th and 21st centuries have been descendants of the Judean people (essentially, the tribes of Judah and Benjamin) it has been accepted that three groups of migrants are from tribes of the northern kingdom (Israel). These are the Beta Israel (House of Israel), originally known as the Falashas, from Ethiopia, the Bnei Menashe (Sons of Manasseh) from the region of eastern India, Bangladesh, and Burma, and the Bukharan Jews from Central Asia. The Beta Israel have a tradition that they are from the tribe of Dan. The Bukharan Jews believe that they are descendants of the tribes of Issachar and Napthali. Research is currently being conducted to find out if the Pashtuns (Pathans) of Afghanistan and Pakistan are of Israelite origin, as has been believed by many, with their traditions pointing to them being a tribe of Joseph (Ephraim and Manasseh). There are many other groups around the world claiming to originate from the "lost tribes of Israel", but with varying degrees of probability. A web search on "The Lost Tribes of Israel" will reveal the extent of this issue. The essential point, however, is that there is now one undivided Hebrew nation, named Israel, combining, in intention at least, all of the descendants of Jacob.

[79] NIV.

[80] NKJV.

While the Hebrew word "speech" refers in this verse primarily to what was said, it also implies the language used. And the 'pure speech' of this land was Hebrew. This prophecy promises a return to the land and abundant blessings when this happens. The passage actually means that when Israel is restored, the people will praise God in the Hebrew speech.

Zechariah 10:6,9,10 says:

> *I will strengthen the house of Judah and save the house of Joseph. I will restore them because I have compassion on them. They will be as though I had not rejected them, for I am the LORD their God and I will answer them. ... Though I scatter them among the peoples, yet in distant time they will remember me: They and their children will survive, and they will return. I will bring them back from Egypt and gather them from Assyria. I will bring them to Gilead and Lebanon, and there will not be room enough for them.*[81]

This passage refers to the first and third exiles (Assyria 721 BC, Egypt 70 AD), from which there was no return (unlike the exile to Babylon). It also says there will not be enough space for all of them, which speaks of the current situation in Israel should all known Jewish people decide to return.

Comment

Very many passages in the Old Testament speak of the restoration of the nation Israel and its repopulation by the united descendants of its ancient people. This has only happened during the 20th century. The rebirth of the nation Israel is one of the clearest evidences of biblical prophecy being fulfilled that could be imagined.

The process of fulfilment has sometimes resulted from visionary individuals (such as the restoration of the Hebrew language into an everyday modern tongue) and sometimes through widespread political movements, such as Zionism. At the time of the Balfour declaration,

---

[81] NIV.

most senior people in the British government imagined it would only lead to a small migration.

On 14 May 1948, Israel was declared a nation. On 15 May, the combined armies of Egypt, Transjordan, Syria, Lebanon and Iraq launched an invasion across all the land frontiers of the new nation. Vastly outnumbered and outgunned, the new nation survived the first of many onslaughts aimed at its total destruction. Its survival through the following fifty years is also miraculous.

Reference links

The History of Theodore Herzl, at:
www.jewishvirtuallibrary.org/jsource/biography/Herzl.html

On the 'Israel Lobby': Imperialism, Zionism and the Middle East, at:
www.bolshevik.org/1917/no29/Israellobby.html

CHAPTER THIRTY-EIGHT

The Regathering of the Jews

How good it is to sing praises to our God, how pleasant and fitting to praise him. The LORD builds up Jerusalem, he gathers the exiles of Israel.

Psalm 147:1-2 (NIV)

In that day the Lord will reach out his hand a second time to reclaim the remnant that is left of his people from Assyria, from Lower Egypt, from Upper Egypt, from Cush, from Elam, from Babylonia, from Hamath and from the islands of the sea. He will raise a banner for the nations and gather the exiles of Israel; he will assemble the scattered people of Judah from the four quarters of the earth.

Isaiah 11:11-12 (NIV)

In 1991, Saddam Hussein, ruler of Iraq and spiritual heir to Nebuchadnezzar, launched a total of thirty-nine Scud missiles with high explosive warheads at the main cities of Israel during the First Gulf War. Israel was not a belligerent in this war, but Hussein hoped that by attacking Israel he would separate many of the Arab nations from the coalition attacking him following his invasion of Kuwait. This did not happen, but even more amazingly, only two people were killed directly by the missiles, four died from suffocation in their gas masks, and a further sixty-eight died of heart attacks during the raids, which destroyed a very large number of buildings. Most missiles fell on densely populated areas. The far more primitive and inaccurate V2 rockets fired at London in 1944 and 1945 inflicted a far higher death toll on a population far more experienced in warfare.

While this was happening, a man named Gustav Scheller living in England believed God was telling him to help in the work of bringing the Jewish people home to Israel. He founded the Ebenezer Emergency Fund, and they started mercy flights and then (because passengers could carry very little luggage with them on these flights) a series of sailings from Odessa in the Black Sea to Haifa. By the end of 2006, the Ebenezer Fund had helped around 120,000 Jewish people from the lands of the former Soviet Union to resettle in Israel. People have travelled the length and breadth of countries such as Kazakhstan, Uzbekistan, Kyrgyzstan, Turkmenistan, Tajikistan, Moldova, Belarus, Armenia, the Ukraine, Georgia, Atchara and Russian territories such as Siberia as far as Kamchatka searching for Jewish communities. Often, they found them where people said there were no Jews, and the work of helping them emigrate has involved dealing with every kind of bureaucratic obstruction and corruption imaginable. The emigrants have faced many dangers on their journeys, and many have lost all their possessions and some even their lives en route to Israel.

The 'Operation Exodus' project of the Ebenezer Fund is only one of many such projects during the 20th century aimed at bringing Jewish people to Israel. In 1900 the Jewish population of Palestine was 50,000. By 1948, with the massive migration following the end of World War 2, involving mainly Holocaust survivors, it reached 650,000. By 1991, at the time of the First Gulf War, it had risen to 4 million. In 2017, the total population of Israel stood at 8.7 million, of whom 6.5 million were Jewish.

There have been many unusual events. In 1949, the entire Jewish population of Yemen declared the desire to migrate, and their government agreed they could leave. The move was carried out mainly by Dakota aircraft of Royal Air Force Transport Command with US military transport aircraft as well, and in a secret operation involving 380 flights, all 49,000 Yemeni Jews went to Israel.[82] What is curious is

[82] This operation was popularly known as 'Operation Magic Carpet'. It has been criticised for poor management and a high loss of life; circumstances were very difficult. See: *www.israeled.org/operation-magic-carpet*

that they had had a prophet many centuries earlier who predicted that at the end of the times, before the coming of Messiah, they would all be transported back to the promised land on the wings of a great silver bird. A similar airlift organised by the Israeli government in 1951 moved 113,000 Iraqi Jews to Israel.[83] Many of the passengers on these flights had never even seen an aircraft and took a lot of persuasion to get on board.

Figure 38. Royal Air Force Douglas Dakota transport aircraft. Reproduced by kind permission, www.raf-in-combat.com.

Some groups of people in Ethiopia, the Falashas, were identified as Jews, and there have been several airlifts since the late 1970s. These groups are believed to be descended from Jewish people who migrated to southern Egypt and Ethiopia at the time of Jeremiah (ca. 590 BC) or even earlier. Some groups claim their residence in the area dates back to the time of King Solomon (ca. 950 BC).

The largest single grouping of Jews outside Israel by 1990 was of those in the Soviet Union. The Soviet Union had practised a very

[83] Operations 'Ezra' and 'Nehemiah', details in Wikipedia: *en.wikipedia.org/wiki/Operation_Ezra_and_Nehemiah*

restrictive emigration policy, and Jews applying to emigrate to Israel found they suffered official bureaucratic persecution. Following the break-up of the Soviet Union, around 700,000 emigrated. The Jewish people call this migration 'Aliyah', and the migrants 'Olim'. During the past fifty years, Olim have made Aliyah from China, the far east of Siberia, Argentina and just about every land in between. For the first time in history it can truly be said that Jewish people have returned to Israel from the most distant lands of the earth.

Bible prophecies

> *In that day the Lord will reach out his hand a second time to reclaim the remnant that is left of his people from Assyria, from Lower Egypt, from Upper Egypt, from Cush, from Elam, from Babylonia, from Hamath and from the islands of the sea. He will raise a banner for the nations and gather the exiles of Israel; he will assemble the scattered people of Judah from the four quarters of the earth.*
>
> *Isaiah 11:11-12 (NIV)*

This prophecy says there will be a second regathering (the first was the return from Babylon). Every specific country mentioned has been involved in the Aliyah of the 20th century (Babylonia is now Iraq, Elam is the main part of Iran).

> *I will bring your children from the east and gather you from the west. I will say to the north 'Give them up!' and to the south, 'Do not hold them back'. Bring my sons from afar and my daughters from the ends of the earth.*
>
> *Isaiah 43:5-6 (NIV)*

This again shows the geographical extent of the Jewish people to be recovered. It also appears to refer to the behaviour of the Soviet government in 'holding back' Jews, and the negotiations for release of Jews from Ethiopia and some Arabic countries to the south of Israel.

> *Who are these that fly along like clouds, like doves to their nests? Surely, the islands look to me; in the lead are the ships of Tarshish, bringing your sons from afar, with their silver*

> *and their gold, to the honour of the LORD your God, the Holy One of Israel, for he has endowed you with splendour.*
>
> *Isaiah 60:8-9 (NIV)*

This is one of a few passages suggesting that some of the returning Jews will fly – as has happened in very many cases. It also says that the first migrations will involve "ships of Tarshish". Tarshish is used to refer to lands at the western end of the Mediterranean Sea and beyond. This is one of many hints that the return of the Jews will be actively assisted by Gentiles, as has certainly happened.

There are literally dozens of prophecies like these from Isaiah. Biblical prophets speaking of the regathering of the Jews, as God's people, include Moses, King David (in the Psalms), Isaiah, Jeremiah, Ezekiel, Hosea, Joel, Amos, Micah, Zephaniah and Zechariah. As a prophetic theme, it is one of the most extensive in the Bible, and is also referred to in the New Testament including the Gospels, Romans and Revelation.

Comment

The Aliyah is a work in progress. A considerable number of Jewish people have migrated to Israel, but many have found they could not cope – with the hardships in the earlier years, and more recently with the ever-present threats of war and terrorism. There are still probably far more Jewish people living outside Israel than are in Israel at present. The prophecies seem to say that many more will yet go to Israel, possibly most of the Jewish people on earth. The return of the Jewish people in the past century, however, is another powerful fulfilment of so many of these ancient prophecies.

Reference links

A history of the First Gulf War, from the Israeli perspective, at:
www.jewishvirtuallibrary.org/jsource/History/Gulf_War.html

Details of Operation Exodus available at: *www.operation-exodus.org*

A history of the Aliyah, in Wikipedia: *en.wikipedia.org/wiki/Aliyah*

The changing Jewish population of Israel and as a proportion of Jews worldwide:
www.jewishvirtuallibrary.org/jsource/History/jewpop2.html

CHAPTER THIRTY-NINE

The Iranian Revolution

In my vision I saw myself in the citadel of Susa in the province of Elam; in the vision I was by the Ulai Canal.

Daniel 8:2 (NIV)

Not long before the fall of Babylonia to the Persians, Daniel the prophet had a vision where he saw himself in Susa, the capital of the Achaemenid King Cyrus, to be known to history as 'Cyrus the Great'. Cyrus founded the Persian Empire, which survived two hundred years until the time of Alexander. Daniel and Isaiah both prophesied the rise of Cyrus and his empire, and Daniel also prophesied its later fall. 2,500 years after Daniel, a ruler named Mohammed Reza Pahlavi held fantastically lavish celebrations at the ruined site of Persepolis, a later Persian capital, in honour of the 2,500th anniversary of the founding of the Persian Empire by Cyrus. He held the title 'Shah', which is linked etymologically to 'Caesar', 'Kaiser' and 'Tsar'.

The Pahlavi Shah had usurped the throne from his father in 1940, with the help of British and Russian forces. In the 1950s, he held onto it with the help of the Americans. His father had renamed Persia 'Iran' in 1935. Both father and son treated their people badly, and in 1979, a revolution broke out which resulted in the Shah fleeing into exile, and a revolutionary government taking over supported by the Mullahs of the Islamic Shia movement, in the name of the Ayatollah Khomeini.

Iran turned into a state ruled by Islamic law, and with a mission to support and promote their brand of (Shi'ite) Islam. This they did, even at times by supporting various Islamic terrorist organisations. The Iranians fought a bitter and bloody war with Iraq from 1980-1988 during which hundreds of thousands of Iranians lost their lives, during the repeated attempts by Iraq to invade and destroy Iran. The Iraqis were strongly supported by Western governments during this time. After the fall of Saddam Hussein in 2003, the Iranian government adopted a strong anti-Western stance, and also declared their aim to destroy Israel.

Bible prophecy

> *This is the word of the LORD that came to Jeremiah the prophet concerning Elam, early in the reign of Zedekiah king of Judah: This is what the LORD Almighty says, 'See, I will break the bow of Elam, the mainstay of their might. I will bring against Elam the four winds from the four quarters of the heavens; I will scatter them to the four winds, and there will not be a nation to which Elam's exiles do not go. I will shatter Elam before their foes, before those who seek their lives; I will bring disaster upon them, even my fierce anger,' declares the LORD. 'I will pursue them with the sword until I have made an end of them. I will set my throne in Elam and destroy her king and princes (alt. tr. officials),' declares the LORD. 'Yet I will restore the fortunes of Elam in days to come,' declares the LORD.*
>
> *Jeremiah 49:34-39 (NIV)*

Elam was an empire and nation whose first king was Elam, son of Shem (Genesis 10:22). One of its early rulers was Chedorlaomer, part of the alliance that sacked Sodom and Gomorrah, who in turn were routed by Abraham (Genesis 14). The Elamite empire survived until the arrival of Cyrus the Great, when the capital of Elam was Susa. Although Cyrus introduced the new name 'Persia', he himself adopted Elamite titles and symbols. Elam was to Persia its core territory, almost what Persia is to Iran. It is a country with a continuous history of between four and five thousand years. The system of government has been a monarchy all that time until 1979. At times it has been an independent nation, at times the heart of an empire, and at times a subordinate state of empires such as Babylonia, Greece and Parthia. The first time in history that there was no longer a king ruling there was 1979 AD. This is a specific fulfilment of Jeremiah 49:38b. The statement in verse 38a that the Lord will "set [his] throne in Elam" looks as if it has yet to be fulfilled.

The changes in the country were drastic. A party of Iranian Air Force trainee pilots had been undergoing flying training in America. Immediately following the revolution, they were recalled to Iran. On arrival, they disembarked, were taken behind a shed, and shot. There were many such events. The consequence of this was that many Iranians fled their country and went anywhere they could find support. By 2006 over five million had left. This was the first time in history that people from Iran (Persia, Elam) had ever emigrated in such numbers. This is a fulfilment of verse 36:

> *I will scatter them to the four winds, and there will not be a nation where Elam's exiles do not go.*

Iranian Christians look with hope at verse 39, but cannot help also noting that verses 35 and 37 suggest that times will be bad before better things come. Probably, the Iran-Iraq war is a partial fulfilment of these verses. Iran and its predecessor nations have not experienced such a horrific war as took place then. They were reduced to sending children to fight, often with very little in the way of protection and equipment. The Iraqis used poison gas including the nerve gas Tabun, giving the Iranians the unhappy distinction of being the first nation to be subject to attack by internationally-banned nerve agents.

Comment

Two specific parts of this prophecy had never been fulfilled before 1979 AD and have been fulfilled since. The sequence of events in the prophecy suggests that the exodus of the people takes place before the removal of the king, when it actually happened the other way round. There are parts of this prophecy that are possibly fulfilled by the Iran-Iraq War, and some that have not yet happened.

It may be that the setting of God's throne in Elam could be linked to the return of Jesus as Messiah, or possibly that the religious leadership of the country will turn to follow “the LORD Almighty”. The promise is that the country has a future, and the future will bring blessing. What is certain is that prophetic words written down nearly 2,600 years ago have only been fulfilled in the late 20th century.

Reference links

A concise history of the Iranian revolution is at:
libcom.org/history/1978-1979-the-iranian-revolution

A report of the Iranian diaspora, by Shirin Hakezadeh (2006):
www.migrationpolicy.org/article/iran-vast-diaspora-abroad-and-millions-refugees-home

A short history of the Iran-Iraq war 1980-88:
www.iranicaonline.org/articles/iraq-vii-iran-iraq-war

CHAPTER FORTY

The Philistine War of 1982

All the days of Saul there was bitter war with the Philistines, and whenever Saul saw a mighty or brave man, he took him in his service.

1 Samuel 14:52 (NIV)

In 1948, the Arab nations preparing to invade Israel sent out a warning to all Arab people living in the territory promised to Israel by the United Nations. "Move out," they said, "we'll look after you, and in a little while when we've wiped out the Jews, you can all go home." Except it didn't work out like that, and those who took up this offer never did get to 'go home', but were resettled into refugee camps, where they became known as Palestinian refugees. The subsequent wars in 1956, 1967 and 1973 all failed to destroy Israel, and instead consolidated the territory controlled by Israel and increased it. Many of the refugees had moved to Jordan, and the Palestinian Liberation Organisation (PLO) became active there. In 1970, they supported an attempt to overthrow King Hussein of Jordan, and pitched battles were fought in and around Amman. 2-3,000 PLO fighters were killed, and the event became known as 'Black September', a name adopted by one of the PLO terrorist groups. Black September was the group who massacred Israeli athletes at the 1972 Munich Olympics. The activist groups were thrown out of Jordan and made their bases in Lebanon.

By the summer of 1982, Lebanon was ruled by a number of military factions, some supported by Syria and Iran, some by Israel, some with no obvious foreign support. PLO groups had mounted several terrorist attacks on Israel and Jewish people around the world, including on 3 June 1982 – an attempted assassination of the Israeli Ambassador in London. There had been many attacks launched against northern Israel ('Galilee') from Lebanon by PLO groups, who had become very well organised and equipped. They had around 20,000 Palestinian troops, with 100 tanks and 100-200 artillery pieces, which were used for shelling Israeli towns and villages in northern Israel. There were around 300,000 Palestinians living in Lebanon at that time.

On 6 June 1982, the Israeli Defence Force (IDF) launched a full-scale invasion of Southern Lebanon. They were met with a strong defence by both the Palestinians and the Syrian armed forces. Eighty-six Syrian Air Force jets were shot down by the Israelis, who also had to contend with modern surface-to-air missile defences. They swept through to Beirut, capturing the cities of Tyre and Sidon on their way. One Lebanese group, the Phalangist militia, achieved notoriety by attacking two of the old Palestinian camps, at Sabra and Chatila, where they massacred hundreds of the residents. It is widely believed that the Israeli army could have prevented these massacres but chose not to.

The news of the massacres overshadowed a far more surprising series of discoveries in Lebanon. Menachem Begin, the Israeli Prime Minister, reported that the Israeli Defence Forces found deep underground tunnels and cellars containing vast quantities of up-to-date Russian weaponry. This amounted to sufficient ammunition, armoured vehicles and tanks, small arms, artillery, communications and special forces equipment to equip five or six army divisions (fifty to eighty thousand soldiers). This equipment was far superior to that used by the PLO, and was apparently pre-positioned for a full-scale invasion of Israel and neighbouring countries. A few Soviet army and air force officers serving at the time have said they knew of plans to carry out such an operation. The most startling aspect of these discoveries was that the tunnels had been dug and the weapons brought in with such complete secrecy that the Israeli intelligence agencies had no idea it had been done.[84]

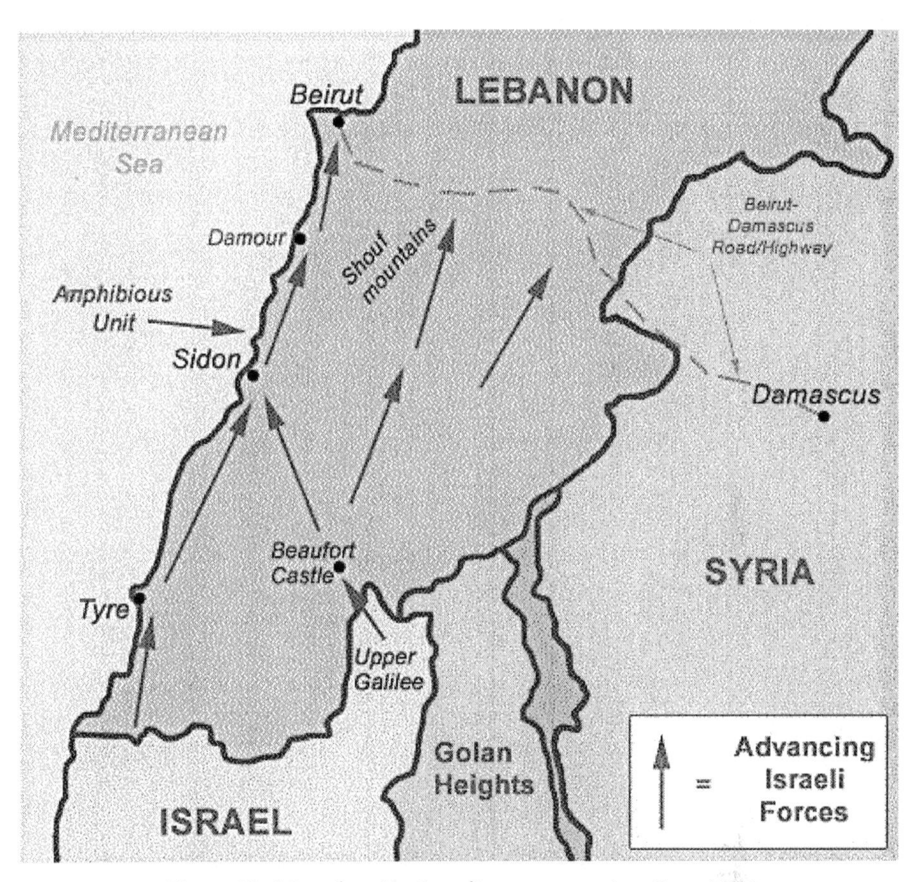

Figure 39. Map showing Israeli army campaign, June 1982. Courtesy: Procon.org.

The Israelis remained in Lebanon until they withdrew to South Lebanon in 1983, having destroyed the PLO infrastructure and fighting capability in the region, though the capacity for terrorism and guerrilla activity remained. Fourteen thousand PLO fighters were captured by the Israelis. A prisoner exchange was agreed after the fighting was over,

---

[84] One of the reports that was published by the New York Times at the time: *www.nytimes.com/1982/10/12/world/israel-puts-captured-arms-on-display.html*

and twelve Israeli troops who had been captured by the Palestinians were exchanged for the fourteen thousand. These were then shipped away, initially to Tunisia, Sudan and Iraq. In Tunisia they attempted to mount a coup to overthrow the king, and in Sudan they caused a lot of upset among the local population. These groups (and others) were transferred to Yemen, where they remained for some time.

Bible prophecy

> *"In those days and at that time, when I restore the fortunes of Judah and Jerusalem, I will gather all the nations and bring them down to the Valley of Jehoshaphat. There I will enter into judgment against them concerning my inheritance, my people Israel, for they scattered my people among the nations and divided up my land. They cast lots for my people and traded boys for prostitutes; they sold girls for wine that they might drink. Now what have you against me, O Tyre and Sidon and all you regions of Philistia? Are you repaying me for something I have done? If you are paying me back, I will swiftly and speedily return on your heads what you have done. For you took my silver and my gold and carried off my finest treasures to your temples. You sold the people of Judah and Jerusalem to the Greeks, that you might send them far from their homeland. See, I am going to raise them out of the places to which you sold them, and I will return on your heads what you have done. I will sell your sons and your daughters to the people of Judah, and they will sell them to the Sabeans, a nation far away." The LORD has spoken.*
>
> *Joel 3:1-8 (NIV)*

The traditional date of the book of Joel is about 800 BC, though liberal scholarship tries to place it as much as four hundred years later. The first point to note is that verses 3-6 describe events that only took place following the sack of Judea and Jerusalem by the army of Titus in 70 AD. This was the time when so many Jewish people were captured and taken into slavery that the price of slaves fell practically to nothing. Josephus reports exactly the transactions prophesied here, and the main bulk of slaves were shipped to Alexandria, a Greek city, by the Romans (who were classed as Greeks in those days).

Verse 4 accuses Tyre and Sidon and the people of Philistia of their involvement. There are no historical records available at present to show this, but the probability is that they would at least have been involved in supplying shipping from the coast of Palestine to Alexandria, and it was also the Roman army's normal practice to raise local 'levies' to augment their troops when necessary. Most troops in the armies of Rome were not Italians, but natives of the various countries where the armies were based.

Verses 1 and 7 say that the Jewish people will be brought back, and recompense will be exacted on Tyre, Sidon, and the Philistine people of the area. This event, therefore, must follow the restoration of the Jewish people after the events of 70 AD, which did not happen until the 20th century. It is a fact that no army or king of Israel or Judah ever conquered Tyre and Sidon. And, although the location of Tyre has moved a short distance from its location in 800 BC, these are both cities (like Jerusalem) that have remained cities continuously for over three thousand years and kept their original names throughout. The first time an Israeli army has ever conquered and occupied these cities was in 1982. And that was in the context of a war against the Palestinians – Philistines, to use the original form of the word. The present-day Palestinians may not be the actual descendants of the Philistines, but they bear the same name and they live in the same territory. The area known today as the 'Gaza strip' is part of ancient Philistia from three to four thousand years ago, and bears the name of an ancient Philistine city.

The final part of the prophecy concerns the selling of the Philistines to the Sabeans for a derisory price, comparable to a session with a prostitute or a cup of wine. This is where the prisoner exchange, valuing one Israeli to a thousand Palestinians, represents a possible fulfilment. The strange thing, though, was how most of them ended up in Yemen – which is the ancient territory of Sheba, or Saba (the Sabeans). The part of this prophecy that does not seem to have been fulfilled is the full judgement of the nations in verse 2. Perhaps that will be soon...

Comment

The timeline of this prophecy is interesting: possibly nine hundred years from the writing of the prophecy to the event that God promises to address (the sack of Jerusalem in 70 AD), and then a further 1,912 years to the precise fulfilment in 1982. The lesson of this is that we cannot use prophecy to predict the timing of events. You could have used this as one of the prophecies promising that the Jewish people would one day be restored to their land – because that is its start point. But the time these things start happening, as they clearly have in the 20th century, means that we should be prepared for more and more of the end-time prophecies to happen around us.

The specific prophecies which foretell an invasion of Israel by a great army led by Russia are in Ezekiel 38 and 39. The IDF discoveries in Lebanon indicate that the time when these prophecies will be fulfilled could be soon.

Reference links

A brief history of the PLO, at: *www.infoplease.com/ce6/history/A0837351.html*

A history of the 1982 war, in Wikipedia: *en.wikipedia.org/wiki/1982_Lebanon_War*

Epicenter: why the current rumblings in the Middle East will change your future; Joel C Rosenberg; Tyndale House, USA (2006)

Index